Asian Responses to the Global Financial Crisis

Asian Responses to the Global Financial Crisis

The Impact of Regionalism and the Role of the G20

Edited by

Jehoon Park

University of Incheon, South Korea

T.J. Pempel

University of California, Berkeley, USA

Geng Xiao

Fung Global Institute, Hong Kong

Edward Elgar

Cheltenham, UK • Northampton, MA, USA

Published by
Edward Elgar Publishing Limited
The Lypiatts
15 Lansdown Road
Cheltenham
Glos GL50 2JA
UK

Edward Elgar Publishing, Inc.
William Pratt House
9 Dewey Court
Northampton
Massachusetts 01060
USA

Reprinted 2014

A catalogue record for this book
is available from the British Library

Library of Congress Control Number: 2012935324

FSC www.fsc.org MIX Paper from responsible sources FSC® C013056

ISBN 978 1 78100 390 9

Typeset by Servis Filmsetting Ltd, Stockport, Cheshire
Printed and bound in Great Britain by T.J. International Ltd, Padstow

Contents

Contributors

Edward K.Y. Chen is Distinguished Fellow of Centre of Asian Studies at University of Hong Kong.

Richard Higgott is Vice Chancellor, Murdoch University, Western Australia, Australia.

David Hundt is Senior Lecturer in International Relations at Deakin University, Australia.

Gil Kim is Professor of Economics at California State University, USA.

Pilhyun Kim is Research Fellow of Korea Economic Research Institute.

Taeyoon Kim is Associate Research Fellow of Center for Emerging Economies Research/Southeast Asia at Korea Institute for International Economic Policy.

Yoonbai Kim is Professor of Economics at University of Kentucky, USA.

Jing Ma is Associate Professor of Economics at Teda College, Nankai University, China.

Woosik Moon is Professor of Graduate School of International Studies at Seoul National University, Korea.

Tomoyoshi Nakajima is Senior Research Fellow of Economic Research Institute for Northeast Asia, Japan.

Wei Pan is Professor of School of International Studies at Peking University, China.

Jehoon Park is Secretary General of Asia Economic Community Forum and Professor of School of Northeast Asian Studies at the University of Incheon, South Korea.

T.J. Pempel is Professor of Political Science at the University of California, Berkeley, USA.

Sean Quirk is Research Fellow at Columbia University's Global Center | East Asia, China.

Lihui Tian is Professor of Finance and Acting Dean of the Institute of Finance and Development at Nankai University, China.

Immanuel Wallerstein is Senior Research Scholar of Yale University, USA.

Geng Xiao is Director of Research and Senior Fellow of Fung Global Institute, Hong Kong.

Jing Yang is Graduate Student of HSBC School of Business at Peking University, China.

Liu Yongtao is Professor of International Relations at Fudan University, China.

Deok Ryong Yoon is Senior Research Fellow of International Macroeconomics at Korea Institute for International Economic Policy.

Preface

This book is the product of the second conference of the Asia Economic Community Forum which was held on 7–9 November 2010 at Songdo Convensia in Incheon, South Korea. The Asia Economic Community Foundation (AECF) was established in 2008 with the goal of eventually establishing an Asia Economic Community. The main activity of the foundation to date has been organizing the annual Asia Economic Community Forum (AEC Forum) with the eventual goal of transforming that forum into 'Asia's Davos Forum'. One of the co-editors of this volume, Professor Jehoon Park, is Secretary General of the AEC Forum.

Even though the AEC Forum is benchmarking the Davos Forum as its model, the conference was initiated by academics with the participation of business and political leaders. The theme of the forum is 'Creating One Asia Together'. In 2010, the theme of the second conference was 'Post Crisis New World Order: Asia and G20' considering the fact that the G20 Summit was to be held in Korea on 11–12 November right after the forum. In that sense we could say that the second AEC Forum became a pre-G20 forum.

There were three plenary sessions: 'Grand Debate About the 21st Century Capitalism', 'Grand Compromise among the US, China and the EU' and 'Grand Dialogue between Asia and the West'. More than 1300 official participants actively shared their interests and views concerning the future of Asia and the roles of the G20. There were 25 sessions where more than 80 papers were presented. This book collects the 14 best papers from among those 80. The three co-editors of this volume are all core members of the AEC Forum.

This book deals with various issued related to Asian responses to the global financial crisis. It focuses on two aspects. One is regionalism in Asia. The other is the G20. Many Asian countries actively participate in the G20 as member countries. So the G20 is becoming a global institution showing the increasing powers and roles of Asian countries in global issues. While interest in regional integration and regionalism in East and Northeast Asia has been increasing recently, most publications have been written in national languages and hence are limited in their inclusion and in their audiences. Some are written in English, but mainly by Western scholars. This book includes contributions by Asian scholars as well as Western writers. The book also has a unique feature in that contributions are made from an interdisciplinary approach covering economics and political science. The book deals with various issues such as the World System analysis, the debate over the Washington Consensus versus the Beijing Consensus, the roles of the G20, the roles of middle powers like Korea and Australia, and applications of European experiences to Asia as well as perspectives of each country from the region and perspectives from outside the region (the United States).

Jehoon Park, T.J. Pempel and Geng Xiao 2012

1. Northeast Asia in the multipolar world-system

Immanuel Wallerstein[1]

1.1 INTRODUCTION

The period of United States hegemony in the world-system is now definitively at an end. The slow decline since the 1970s was transformed into a precipitate decline brought about by the self-defeating tactics of the presidency of George W. Bush (Wallerstein, 2007a).

We are now living in a world-system in which there are emerging eight to ten centers of relative geopolitical autonomy. The word 'relative' should be underlined. The four strongest such centers are located in what is sometimes called the global North. The first three are in my opinion the United States (which continues of course to be an extremely strong power center, if far less powerful than previously), Western Europe (based on the critical France–Germany tandem) and Russia. The fourth such center is Northeast Asia, by which I mean China, Korea and Japan, the group meeting here as the Asian Economic Community.

The strength of these four centers can be measured by the overall combination each one has assembled of military strength, economic strength, and political and ideological strength. The proportion of each of these factors is of course different for each of the four, but each combination adds up to considerable strength. The relatively autonomous centers in the global South are no doubt less strong overall than these four. Nonetheless, the geopolitical power of each is not negligible. And together, even without any collective organization, they are likely to play an increasingly important geopolitical role.

A world of eight to ten relatively autonomous geopolitical centers is, almost by definition, chaotic. In such a situation, no one center can thrive in isolation or in arrogant disregard of the others. Each therefore is forced to seek to maintain and improve its relations with other centers. The question for each is, with which other centers?

We are at the stage where all the centers are seeking to maintain relatively good relations with all the other centers. This is of course impossible in any medium term, but this is a fair description of the current policies of the multiple eight to ten centers. In addition, none of these centers is internally unified in a very stable fashion. All are torn by conflicts, not only about their internal structures but also, perhaps especially, over what they believe ought to be their global strategy.

In this kind of situation, what we are witnessing is a constant zigzagging of these centers, both internally and in their relations with other centers. Indeed, the zigzagging is so intense that those who seek to analyze what is going on are in very little agreement. We are regularly being offered quite opposite and often fast-changing appreciations of the world situation – by the governments, by the media and by public opinion in general. This is why what is going on merits the label of a chaotic situation.

No one likes a chaotic situation. It breeds intense anxiety and therefore often a quite unreasonable degree of anger and lashing out at scapegoats. How may we expect those in positions of state power to handle this kind of chaotic situation?

Their first consideration will clearly be to look for ways to strengthen their own hand vis-à-vis other centers. This means trying simultaneously to deal with internal divisions and to find the particular paths that will augment their comparative standing in the world-system. This is not at all an easy task for governments. And the missteps of the governments quite frequently lead to strong reactions from their own public opinion, which expresses itself in different forms in the various centers of geopolitical power. In none of them is it easy to be an incumbent in power because public opinion rapidly blames the incumbents, even for matters beyond the power of the incumbents to control. Worldwide, there is a low level of public tolerance for their own governments.

I propose to discuss the five arenas in which this chaotic turbulence will play itself out in the short run, by which I mean the period up to 2020: (1) internal strains within each geopolitical center; (2) economic prospects of each center – growth, employment and polarization of distribution; (3) currencies; (4) the military sphere: wars, nuclear proliferation and extranational military bases; and (5) choice of primary geopolitical alliances. I shall here discuss these arenas not from the perspective of each of the centers but primarily as seen from the perspective of Northeast Asia.

1.2 INTERNAL STRAINS WITHIN NORTHEAST ASIA

I have previously written on this matter in an article I published in a Korean journal in 2007 (Wallerstein, 2007b). I will therefore only briefly summarize my position. Of all the four principal geopolitical centers, the situation is most complicated in Northeast Asia. That is because we are dealing with three countries that have as yet no formal common structure, not even a confederal structure like the European Union. Of the three countries, both China and Korea are still trying to achieve national unification. And the degree of unresolved historical anger and grievances among the three countries continues to weigh heavily over the region.

Despite all of this, I am convinced that there exists great structural pressure for far closer relations among the three countries in the period to 2020. This is because the medium-run prospects for each separately are heavily dependent on their ability to reach viable political compromises among the three. I think it is fairly clear that, without such political compromises, each of the three will find itself weaker on the world scene and therefore find itself hampered in its ability to achieve better conditions for its citizens and a more stable base for the future.

Nonetheless, achieving a degree of political integration among the three will be no easy task. While relations between the authorities in Taiwan and the People's Republic of China (PRC) are much better than previously, a full political accord (perhaps mirroring somewhat the accord that was achieved between Hong Kong and the PRC) does not yet seem imminent. The joining together of the two Koreas seems even more difficult. Both sides want unification – and do not want it, fearing its consequences. Finally, the bilateral relations of China and Japan, and of Korea and Japan – again while better than previously – remain subject to considerable abrupt ups and downs, which escalate unexpectedly and sometimes with great passion.

What then do I mean by structural pressure to integrate further? There is first of all a strong economic logic to further integration. I believe that, for each of the three, the most advantageous trade and investment partners are each other, and that this is borne out by the economic trends of the first decade of the 21st century. Secondly, nationalism is a potent force that impels opinion within divided China and divided Korea, especially as the ideological differences of the Cold War fade considerably. Thirdly, overcoming the historic anger between China and Japan and between Korea and Japan will become easier as time goes by, with the fading of active memories as a result of generational change.

Perhaps I paint too rosy a picture. Perhaps none of these structural pressures will be sufficient to transform the situation by 2020. But if they do not, the geopolitical prospects of Northeast Asia will be less than if they do.

1.3 ECONOMIC PROSPECTS

I have suggested three different variables to consider: growth, employment and polarization of distribution. We all know the summary picture of recent economic growth. Japan seemed to be doing phenomenally well in the 1970s and 1980s, and then suddenly slowed down. China, by world comparative standards, has done remarkably well since the 1980s, and particularly in the first decade of the 21st century. Korea never quite matched either of the other two at their height, but on the other hand it has consistently done reasonably well throughout the whole period, having weathered the storm of 2007–10 better than many countries.

So, for the pundits, there was a time when everyone was predicting that Japan would come to dominate the world economically, and now many of these same pundits are saying the same thing about China. I have no doubt that by comparison with, say, the period 1945–1970 all of Northeast Asia has improved its overall economic strength considerably. The consequences are visible in the construction of infrastructure and buildings, in the stores, and in the standard of living of a large segment of the population – that segment usually referred to as the 'middle class' (or classes).

Permit me nonetheless to be a bit skeptical of the permanence of the growth rates. Large spurts in growth rates have been a frequent occurrence in the 500-year-long history of the modern world-system. There have always been some countries that profited more than others from the economic expansions and contractions of the world-economy. Still, no country has ever maintained a very high growth rate indefinitely. And many countries that experienced high growth rates during one period came to have serious reversals in these rates in later periods.

Maintaining the high growth rates of the past decade in the next decade is, in my view, dependent on the overall state of the world-economy. Producers need customers. And I do not think that the number of customers (the worldwide effective demand) looks promising at the moment. I think myself, and have regularly argued, that the so-called 'Great Recession' is really a world 'depression' out of which we are not going to emerge quickly (Wallerstein, 2010).

In any case, I think it is a mistake to measure economic health by gross national product (GNP) or gross domestic product (GDP) or growth rates. Economic health is first and foremost a function of rates of full-time employment at levels of remuneration above so-called poverty lines.

What we need are figures that most governments and analysts do not collect. The numbers of persons who are chronically unemployed are almost always underestimated because we usually count only those who are actively seeking work. Those who are totally discouraged because of chronic lack of success in finding work tend not to be counted. These are to be found in two main categories: young, relatively unskilled persons for whom no work is in fact available; and skilled persons over 40 years who have lost their employment and cannot find new employment because of their age, or who can at best find employment at much lower levels of skill and remuneration.

Then there are the people who are underemployed. And then there are the people who must work 70 hours a week or more in one job or more in order to obtain a minimum level of income. And finally there are the fake employed, who perform little or no work and are in fact thereby receiving financial transfers without contributing to the collective welfare of the community.

All of this is well known. But what it adds up to is the fact that the remarkably high worldwide unemployment rates of the moment, which will probably increase by 2020, are a vast underestimate of the real numbers of unemployed. Quite aside from the social and political consequences of this worldwide high rate of unemployment, the direct economic consequence reinforces the problem of insufficient effective demand to which I already referred.

Finally, there is the issue of the polarization of distribution. Whether we use Gini coefficients or other measures, it is clear that the polarization has increased considerably since the 1970s, and is increasing still. This is particularly true of those parts of the world-system that have been showing high growth rates, such as Northeast Asia. Of course, this has not only affected Northeast Asia. Even in those parts of the world-system that for political reasons have had relatively low polarization, such as Western Europe, the pressures on state revenue that have resulted from the depression in which we have found ourselves have led to attempts to curtail the so-called welfare state, and thereby increase the internal polarization of distribution.

Once again, quite aside from the social and political consequences of increased polarization, the economic result is to increase still further the problem of effective demand. In any medium term, less polarization is not only morally desirable but also economically efficient. The world has not been moving in that direction, either as a world-system or within the various states.

1.4 CURRENCIES

Currencies are a very particular economic problem, for currencies are the one true win–lose relationship. Whatever the merits of revaluing or devaluing a particular currency, these merits only are wins if others are losers. Everyone cannot devalue simultaneously. It is logically impossible and therefore politically meaningless.

Once again, the world situation is well known. We have been living in a world in which the dollar has been the reserve currency. This of course has given the United States a privilege that no other country has. It can print its currency at will, whenever it thinks that doing so solves some immediate economic problem. No other country can do this; or rather no other country can do this without penalty as long as the dollar remains the accepted reserve currency.

It is also well known that the dollar has been losing its value in relation to other currencies for some time now. Despite the continuing fluctuations, the curve has been downward for perhaps 30 years at least.

The countries of Northeast Asia have pursued currency policies that other countries have criticized. Indeed this is the subject of constant media attention. However, to be fair, it is by no means easy to establish the wisest policy at the moment, even from the selfish perspective of each country. For example, a special 2010 issue of *International Relations of the Asia-Pacific* (**10**(3)) has the title is 'A Post-American East Asia? Networks of Currency and Alliance in a Changing Regional Context'. The authors do not at all agree about either the prognosis or the policy recommendations.

I consider the underlying issue to be simpler than the convoluted explanations of most policy analysts. I start with a few assumptions. The status of the dollar as the reserve currency of the world-system is the last major advantage that the United States has in the world-system today. It is therefore understandable that the United States will do what it can to maintain this advantage. In order to do so, it requires the willingness of other countries (including notably those of Northeast Asia) to use the dollar not only as a mode of calculating transfers, but also as something in which to invest their surpluses (particularly in US treasury bonds).

However, the exchange rate of the dollar has been steadily slipping. This means that surpluses invested in US treasury bonds are worth less as time goes by. There comes a point at which the advantages of such investment (the principal advantage being that it sustains the ability of US enterprises and individual consumers to pay for imports) will eventually be less than the loss of real value of the investments in the treasury bonds. The two curves move in opposite directions.

The problem is that which is posed in any market situation. If the value of a stock is falling, owners will want to divest before it becomes too low. But rapid divestment by a large stockholder can impel a rush to divest by others, thus causing even greater losses. The game is always to find the elusive moment to divest that is neither too late nor too soon, or not too slow but not too fast. This requires perfect timing, and the search for perfect timing is the kind of judgment that quite frequently goes awry.

I see this as the basic picture of what is happening and will happen with the US dollar. It cannot continue to maintain the degree of world confidence that it once enjoyed. Sooner or later, economic reality will catch up with it. This may happen in a five-minute shock or in a much slower process. But when it does, the key question is, what happens then?

There is no other currency today poised to replace the dollar as a reserve currency. In that case, when the dollar falls, there will be no reserve currency. We shall be in a multipolar currency world. And a multipolar currency world is a very chaotic world, in which no one feels comfortable because the constant swift shifts of exchange rates make minimally rational short-term economic predictions very precarious.

The former managing director of the International Monetary Fund, Dominique Strauss-Kahn, publicly stated in 2010 that the world was plunging into currency wars, whose outcome 'would have a negative and very damaging longer-run impact'.[2] One real possibility is that the world may revert (it seems to me, is already reverting) to de facto barter arrangements – a situation that is not really compatible with the effective functioning of a capitalist world-economy.

1.5 THE MILITARY SPHERE

My picture of short-term currency chaos is, if anything, less uncertain than the short-term world military picture. Let me start by saying that I see no country as being interested in deliberately starting a major military conflagration. But local and regional wars can be very draining, especially if they are basically unwinnable, like the United States and North Atlantic Treaty Organization (US–NATO) war against the Taliban in Afghanistan.

What the first decade of the 21st century has demonstrated beyond doubt is that the United States military machine is at one and the same time fantastically and overwhelmingly strong, and essentially useless for serious military victories. The basic problem for the United States is simple. It can bomb anything anywhere all it wants, but really winning wars is done on the ground with human troops. And there is no way that the United States can politically assemble the necessary number of trained troops to win such wars, even if it has the collaboration – the uncertain collaboration – of allies.

Since withdrawing troops, once engaged, has severe negative consequences both internally and geopolitically, the wars once launched drag on and on. The costs for the United States are enormous economically, and sooner or later in this world depression will seem too great to US voters and their politicians. Just as currency wars lead to protectionism, so unwinnable, expensive wars lead in the direction of isolationism. There is no obvious way for the United States to resolve its dilemmas without a serious further loss of geopolitical clout.

One major consequence of this decline in US geopolitical power is the undermining of the entire antiproliferation process. When the Nuclear Non-Proliferation Treaty (NPT) was signed in 1968, it was intended that possession of nuclear weapons be limited to the five permanent members of the Security Council. Three countries immediately refused to sign the treaty – Israel, India and Pakistan – and promptly in the succeeding years all three countries became nuclear powers.

It is true that for a while following the signing of the NPT, a number of countries that had previously launched programs did dismantle them. But once the so-called Cold War between the United States and the Soviet Union came to an end, many of these countries began to reconsider their decision. As of today, we know that North Korea has nuclear weapons, and Iran seems clearly en route to obtaining them.

Is this all? I do not believe so. The genie is out of the bottle, and the race is on – first of all here in Northeast Asia. Despite all the public denials, and internal disputes on the issue in each presently non-nuclear state, I believe that South Korea, Japan and Taiwan are all going to start such programs, and may indeed have achieved them by 2020. Furthermore, there are other countries around the globe that will do the same. My guess is that by 2020 or 2025, there may be perhaps 20 nuclear powers.

I am neither advocating this nor denouncing it. I am merely predicting it. Indeed, I personally am in favor of total nuclear disarmament, but I see no reason to believe that this is a politically realizable scenario in the short term or even the middle term.

There is a mild but persistent hysteria about the terrible consequences of such proliferation. I believe the hysteria is much exaggerated. One can make a good case that the mutual deterrence of the United States and the Soviet Union was a stabilizing pillar of the world-system for 40 years. I think one can make the same case for the consequences of India and Pakistan both being nuclear powers.

There are of course dangers in proliferation. The one most frequently evoked is that non-state actors might purchase, steal or otherwise acquire such weapons, and proceed to use them. Perhaps. But even without any further proliferation, this danger exists, and I am not sure that it becomes greater with further proliferation.

The second danger is that a rogue military figure might launch an attack despite specific orders to the contrary. I do not discount this either.

However, I do believe that this danger too already exists, and once again I am not sure that it increases with further proliferation.

We are, I am afraid, destined to live with this proliferation. It does however change the geopolitical scene. It does unquestionably reduce the ability of the United States to pursue wars as it thinks fit. It does the same for other powerful military forces in the world. The link between multipolarity and a chaotic geopolitical scene is displayed in this emerging reality.

Finally, there is the issue of military bases outside one's own borders. The United States is of course by far the leader in the number and ubiquity of its bases. But it is not the only country to have foreign bases. One can predict that there will be increasing pressure for all countries to pull troops back from these bases, even dismantle them entirely. The pressure will derive from many different factors. One is the sheer economic cost of these bases, a forceful consideration when the revenue of governments has become significantly reduced. A second is increased nationalist strength within countries where such bases are located. And a third is a reassessment by the military leadership of the actual strategic value (as opposed to the political value) of such bases.

How much dismantling of foreign bases will actually occur by 2020 or 2025 is a very murky question. What I feel confident about predicting is that there will be a serious rise in public debate about bases. Foreign bases will come to seem increasingly illegitimate to world public opinion.

Will, however, the result of withdrawal from foreign bases be a reduction in chaos? Or will it mean that internal civil wars can more easily flourish around the globe? This is another very open question at this point.

1.6 PRIMARY ALLIANCES

We now come to what I consider to be the most interesting question about the period to 2020, and the most crucial one for Northeast Asia. I have argued already that a multipolar world with 8–10 centers of relatively autonomous power is unsustainable. Each of the centers, in its maneuvering for relative advantage, will be forced to consider the question of primary alliances. No center can be equally friendly to all the other centers. It does not pay off in the middle run. Centers therefore tend to decide where their primary interests push them.

So let me, somewhat audaciously, outline the choices for Northeast Asia, on the presumption that a Northeast Asian entity is coming into existence via increased coordination of the states and perhaps new interstate institutional structures. Such an entity would have to weigh the advantages for it of closer ties to Russia, to Western Europe and to the United States.

Let me start with the least likely: Western Europe. The two regions are distant geographically, historically and culturally. Even more importantly, it could be argued that in the drive to advance their economic interests in developing new leading industries, they are direct competitors. If there is (if there were to be) a race to become the next hegemonic power in the world-system in the next 50–75 years, the race would be between Northeast Asia and Western Europe. Never mind the fact that I do not believe such a race will ever reach its culminating point. Both of these entities will assume it might. So, politenesses aside, these two centers of geopolitical power are rivals.

What about Russia? In a sense, a Russia–Northeast Asia link-up would be perceived as, and in fact be, an anti-US alliance. It would inevitably reawaken the now weakening alliance between the United States and Western Europe. What would it gain Northeast Asia? Access to Russian energy and minerals? The possibility of profitable investments in Russia? Cooperation in relation to various secessionist threats, particularly in Central Asia? Would this be enough for Northeast Asia against what it might lose, geopolitically?

Just to list the advantages for Northeast Asia is to underline the disadvantages for Russia. Russia, above all things, does not want to be cast in the long-term role of a semiperipheral exporter of energy and minerals, which a Northeast Asian–Russian alliance might create or reinforce. Russia wants to promote advanced productive technology inside its borders, while augmenting its military strength. It can make better deals for these two objectives elsewhere, primarily a deal with Western Europe.

That leaves the United States. The world of analysts – in governments, in academia and in the media – insists on the great US–China split. I see virtually no real evidence of this. On the contrary. I see both countries as having pulled back constantly at every possible moment of real conflict in the last 30 years – under all the successive governments in both countries.

Why should this be? Looked at from the point of view of the United States, what are the real alternatives? The long-standing alliance with Western Europe is wearing thin, largely because of the sense in Western Europe that it is desirable, indeed crucial, for it to re-establish its autonomy, especially in a post-Cold War world.

Western Europeans never inwardly accepted culturally the dominance of the United States, their cultural offshoot. They accepted United States hegemony only because they were deeply weakened geopolitically after the Second World War and believed that they needed to rely on the American shield. But geopolitical realities have changed, and so therefore have their own attitudes. If in addition they can collectively make arrangements with Russia, they will want to do so. For one thing, Russia's military in alliance with those of Western Europe adds up to something the world would take seriously.

Now look at it from Northeast Asia's point of view. China and the United States have increasingly had much to offer each other in the economic sphere. This will be all the more true as the bubble of the growth of so-called emerging nations meets the limits of effective demand throughout the world-system.

In addition, the world climate crisis can only be effectively treated if these two countries come to terms with each other in ways that will meet both their interests. The internal pressures on each to do something serious about global warming and the negatives of carbon as a major energy source will only increase. And a quid pro quo seems to me not all that difficult to work out.

Finally, if, as I have argued, there is to be an effective collaboration between China, Korea and Japan by 2020, Japan and South Korea will be relieved by the prospect of a closer collective alliance with the United States. It would mean that arrangements with China would not force a geopolitical break with the United States. And China will probably find that this serves China's interests as well by reinforcing the Northeast Asian community in formation, especially as China's military strength increases.

So, despite all the constant brouhaha in the world media about the deep conflicts between the United States and China, I believe that structurally the two countries will move closer, and more overtly so, by 2020.

1.7 CONCLUSION

I should conclude these remarks, which perhaps seem to you somewhat going against the stream of current geopolitical analyses, by emphasizing two points. Firstly, my own analyses derive from what I consider to be structural pressures. They are not policy recommendations but policy predictions.

Secondly, these are analyses of what might happen by 2020. Nonetheless, what I see as the geopolitical rearrangements by 2020 do not augur a new global stability. There is much that I have not discussed above, including what I believe are the long-run structural crises of the capitalist world-economy as a historical system. I have written previously, and in a number of places, of why I do not think that our existing historical system will be able to persist for much longer.[3]

I consider that the chaotic fluctuations we see today will grow stronger, not weaker, by 2020. I believe that our historical system has entered into a bifurcation that will culminate in a new world-system (or perhaps multiple world-systems) that will be different from that in which we are presently living.

However, as I have also repeatedly said, we cannot know, in this bifurcation, which of two possible alternate paths the world shall take in the end, and we cannot be sure that what will emerge will be morally and politically better or worse. It may be, at the end of this period, as a new historical system takes form, that the existing states will take on entirely new forms and roles in which all this talk of geopolitical alliances will seem much less important.

In 2020, the political leadership of the Northeast Asian countries – and indeed of the rest of the world – will almost certainly be different. I do not know if they will be wiser but they will be different. So will be the expectations of the populations. We are living amidst the greatest possible global uncertainty, and we must tread our paths cautiously, but hopefully intelligently.

NOTES

1. This is the Keynote Address at the 2nd Asian Economic Community Forum, Incheon, Korea, 7–9 November 2010.
2. Interview with Alan Beattle in the *Financial Times*, 5 October 2010.
3. See one major statement in Wallerstein (1998).

REFERENCES

Wallerstein, I. (1998), *Utopistics, or Historical Choices of the Twenty-first Century*, New York: New Press.

Wallerstein, I. (2007a), 'Precipitate Decline: The Advent of Multipolarity', *Harvard International Review*, Spring, 54–9.

Wallerstein, I. (2007b), 'Northeast Asia and the World-System', *Korean Journal of Defense Analysis*, **19**(3), 7–25.

Wallerstein, I. (2010), 'Structural Crises', *New Left Review*, **62**, 133–142.

2. The other 80 percent: understanding economic drivers of global transformation

Geng Xiao, Sean Quirk and Jing Yang

2.1 INTRODUCTION

In 2007, globalization's rising tide began to recede quickly. As boats were lowered, the collapse of major US financial institutions triggered the tsunami of the global financial crisis, knocking many into the water. We have been struggling to find the surface in the years since, and just as we are climbing back into our boats, the water seems to be receding again. The question remains: are we going to brace for another economic tsunami? Or are we going to see the industrialization, urbanization and globalization achieved over the last few centuries for the 20 percent of the world's population in advanced economies spread over the next few decades to the other 80 percent of humanity? These are two divergent depictions of our global economy at the crossroads.

Developed countries of the Organisation for Economic Co-operation and Development (OECD) still dominate the world economy in terms of income, consumption and wealth. As shown in Figure 2.1, advanced economies today only account for 18 percent of the world's population, yet they contribute 68 percent of global gross domestic product (GDP). These countries are currently leaders in the global economic system. Their multinational corporations, such as Airbus, Apple, Wal-Mart, and so on, still dictate how supply chains are organized around the world to generate employment, products, incomes and wealth.

The optimists like ourselves note that with today's technical knowledge and economic development, the 21st century will likely see the 80 percent in emerging markets experience extensive industrialization and urbanization. Figure 2.2 shows the steady growth of developing countries, particularly in East Asia and the Pacific region. Economies such as those of Brazil, Russia, India, China and South Africa (BRICS) will be at the forefront of this transformation. Indeed, even in the midst of the so-called

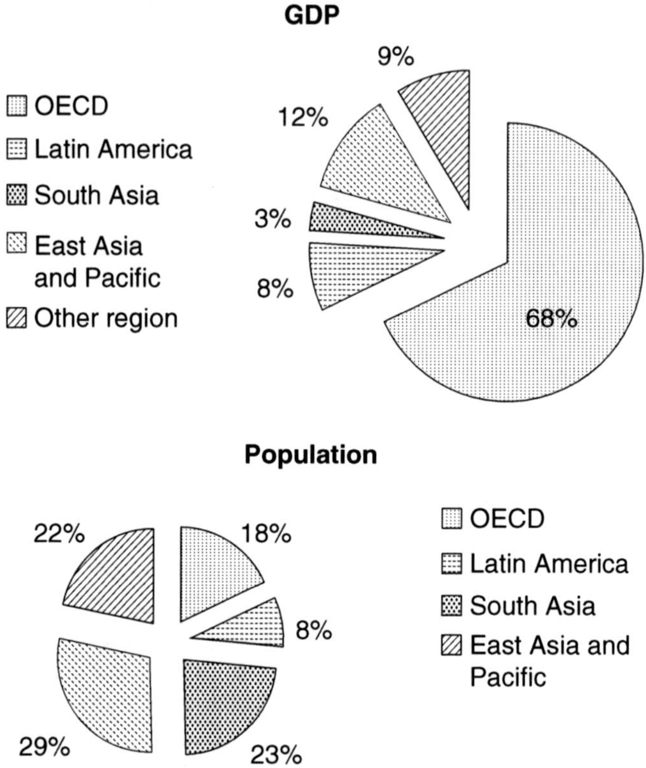

Source: World Bank Database (the statistics for Latin America, East Asia and Pacific, and South Asia are developing countries only).

Figure 2.1 GDP and population by region in 2009

Great Recession since 2008, humanity has never witnessed such a plethora of economic opportunities, either in advanced or in developing countries. Adam Smith said that industrialization's workman, 'even of the lowest and poorest order, if he is frugal and industrious, may enjoy a greater share of the necessaries and conveniencies of life than it is possible for any savage to acquire' (Smith, 1776). Once remote corners of the world are now entering a period of rapid industrialization, which is likely to spread as far and wide as the agricultural revolution we once experienced.

On the other hand, past stewardship from the developed world is fading fast. After nearly 50 years of growth, developing countries have increasingly prominent roles on the world's stage. Their economies still only account for 30 percent of world GDP, but emerging economies' growth

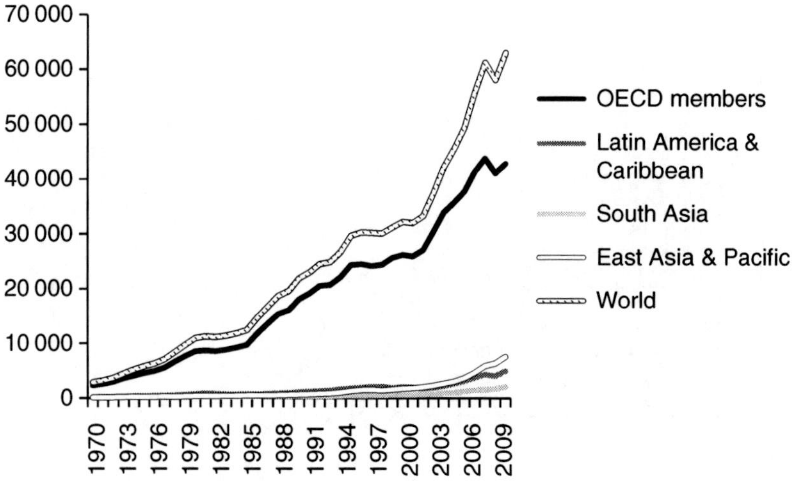

Source: World Bank Database (the statistics for Latin America, East Asia and Pacific, and South Asia are developing countries only).

Figure 2.2 World and regional GDP in current billions of USD

rates markedly exceed those of advanced economies. Developing countries are thus catching up, fueled by 80 percent of the world's population. The data in Figure 2.3 depict how the world once followed growth patterns of the rich; however, recent years have seen developing – primarily Asian – countries serving as engines of growth.

Recent growth rates illustrate the increasing resilience of the developing Asian markets in particular. Turbulence in the global economy continues to reverberate around the world. In the recent financial crisis, however, Asia's real economy experienced milder economic trauma. Whereas growth rates dropped over 200 percent for OECD members, decreases were around 45 percent and 55 percent for emerging economies of the East Asia-Pacific and South Asia regions, respectively. It should be noted that growth rates in Latin America and the Caribbean suffered greatly. Yet, all in all, developing economies fared far better than their advanced counterparts.

Investors and consumers, especially those in the West, have reason to hold pessimistic views toward globalization following the financial crisis of the late 2000s. Again and again, the economic malaise seems to expose new problems far faster than statesmen can forge solutions, even though average living standards weighted by the world population are keeping a decent long-term growth trend. Moreover, positive and negative

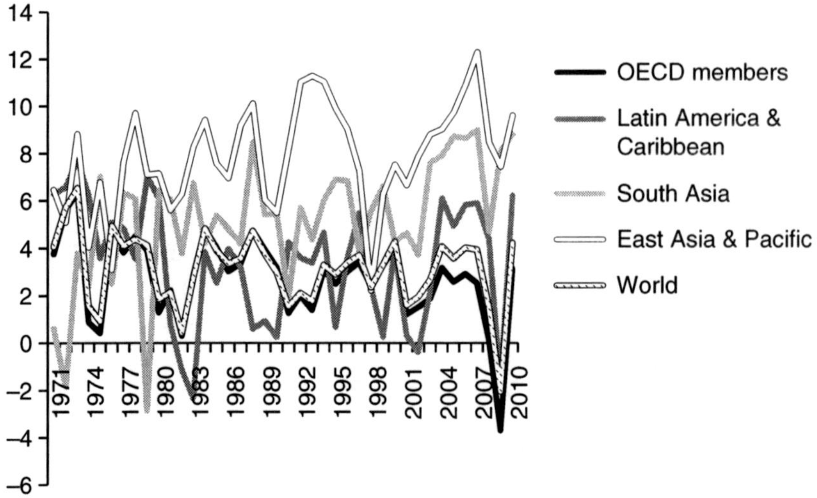

Source: World Bank Database (the statistics for Latin America, East Asia and Pacific, and South Asia are developing countries only).

Figure 2.3 World and regional growth rate percentages

developments in one country can no longer be contained within national borders. The essence of the short-term financial crisis happening around the world is the implosion of accumulated problems in outdated economic and financial systems, or outdated growth models. Developed and developing countries put forth economic stimulus packages that temporarily buttressed their economies, but larger structural issues remain as pressing as ever. Those most skeptical of international cooperation in the crisis predict that a global economic downturn could persist over a decade. Our new media easily support this pessimistic view with their tendency to report all bad news and neglect long-term, positive trends.

The short-term crisis in the West has thrown significant weight behind convergence theory – the notion that emerging economies will develop faster than advanced countries as technology and knowledge diffuses throughout the developing world. Wages, infrastructure and technology are to converge through globalization, bringing better living standards to the 4 billion in the developing world. The so-called 'catch-up effect' was in essence accelerated in the last few years as advanced nations stalled, while developing nations narrowed the GDP gap. Albeit the divide is still significant, the crisis has hinted of the structural growing pains to come – pains that will be localized in advanced economies.

However, we need to remember that convergence is a result of successful catching up by the developing economies and is good for our global economy going forward. The upside is unlimited for the continuation and deepening of globalization, industrialization and urbanization. The risks and localized losses are quite limited and can be handled if we work beyond the short term as defined by our election cycles. Thus, we need to take a serious look at the long-term economic drivers for our current global transformation and try to incorporate them into our short-term policymaking processes.[1]

2.2 THREE ECONOMIC DRIVERS OF GLOBAL TRANSFORMATION

If the catching-up and convergence to modern industrialization and urbanization goes smoothly, three fundamental changes in the global economy will emerge over the next few decades:

- increased productivity and non-tradable value growth, such as rising property prices, along with rising wages;
- a higher return on capital and rising prices for capital, that is, through the real interest rate, due to rapid industrialization and urbanization; and
- rising costs of carbon emission and natural resources.

These drivers of transformation will come from emerging economies but impact markets around the world, creating both massive gains and opportunities as well as risks and localized losses – especially in the relatively stagnant advanced economies.

2.2.1 The Rapid Growth in Productivity will Push up Wages and Prices of Non-Tradables in the Emerging Markets, Generating Structural Inflation and Structural Currency Appreciation There

Non-tradables are central to convergence theory and the future of the global economy. These sectors include the goods and services that are created and consumed domestically in any given country – hence, not traded internationally – such as unskilled labor and commercial or residential property. The prices of non-tradables are determined by the local markets for non-tradables. However, the local markets for non-tradables are linked to the international markets for tradables through the production factors markets that provide labor, office buildings and other inputs.

Many developing economies have now become major manufacturers, resource extractors and service providers for advanced nations through their exports and the advanced economies' sourcing processes. This modern system of supply chains is improving manufacturing productivity rapidly around the world, particularly in China and East Asia.

Productivity gains in the modern manufacturing sectors will raise wages for unskilled labor and non-tradable prices, such as property values, in the emerging markets, generating healthy domestic structural inflation in these countries. The minimum wage in China has been rising about 20 percent per year since 2005, while property prices in China have been growing more than 10 percent per year since 1990. Such structural inflation contrasts sharply with the deflationary pressures in the advanced economies caused by the balance sheet adjustment after the recent global financial crisis.

Take China as an example. According to the Balassa–Samuelson theory, rising productivity in China's tradable sector (for example, manufacturing) should raise the wages of Chinese engineers. This development should entice workers from the non-tradable sector (for instance in a hair salon) to shift to the manufacturing sector. If there is no surplus labor in the economy, rising wages for manufacturing workers will cause wages for hairstylists to rise as well, due to the decreasing supply of labor. This wage increase will occur despite little productivity gains in the haircutting business. The effect on property prices is the same. The same building in Shanghai, with no change in its structure and functions, will be worth much more today than ten years ago, due to the productivity growth in the companies and people housed inside it.

Increases in wages and prices for all sectors brought about by the productivity growth are good, but will lead either to inflation or necessitate local currency appreciation.[2] Inflation in China and renminbi (RMB) appreciation will both contribute to the convergence of China's wages and costs towards those in the advanced economies. In the process of convergence, China will lose its export competitiveness due to rising costs, while the advanced economies like the United States will regain competitiveness and will see the reshoring of some of their manufacturing activities previously 'outsourced' to China.

Therefore, productivity growth in the tradable goods sector in China and India brought about by the 'outsourcing' from the advanced economies like the United States and the European Union (EU) is the ultimate driver for structural inflation and currency appreciation in the emerging markets. With inflation running above 5 percent and RMB appreciation continuing at 5 percent a year in China, while the United

States and EU are facing deflation and weakening currency, the convergence of incomes and costs among economies is rapidly occurring in front of us right now.

Before structural inflation and currency appreciation can take off significantly, however, an economy first needs to reach a state of full employment. This state was achieved soon after industrialization began in countries like Japan, Korea and Hong Kong. This process will take much longer for China and other large emerging economies. But after 30 years of reform and high growth, China is approaching this full-employment turning point, called the 'Lewis Turning Point' to honor the Nobel Prize winning British economist Arthur Lewis who developed a theory to explain the industrialization of the United Kingdom a few hundred years ago.

Unfortunately, modern macroeconomics in the last few decades has focused almost exclusively on the advanced economies where processes of structural inflation and structural currency appreciation were completed a long time ago. Macroeconomic policymakers and business leaders in China and other emerging markets need to take into account the long-term trend of structural inflation and structural currency appreciation when they are making policy and business decisions to deal with short-term cyclical issues.

2.2.2 Rising Price of Real Capital over the Mid and Long Term Against the Low Nominal Interest Rate Environment in the Global Financial Markets in the Short Term

The rising demand for infrastructure work required for industrialization and urbanization will lead to an increasing scarcity of real capital in the developing economies. Figure 2.4 illustrates the world's rapid industrialization, with Latin America and Caribbean urbanization rates surpassing those of OECD members, and East Asia catching up with dramatic speed. Real capital scarcity lies in opposition with the surplus of financial capital now in the advanced economies, and even in some developing economies like China. Thus, a capital-tight world will exert pressure for the real interest rate – that is, the price of real capital – to rise over the mid and long term.

Unfortunately, our global financial markets have not yet developed the necessary institutions to ensure that the financial sector serves the needs of the real sector on a global scale. The global financial crisis since 2008 has left a large debt burden, high unemployment and fiscal deficits for the United States and some European economies. Their local conditions have necessitated a low-interest-rate policy environment for the

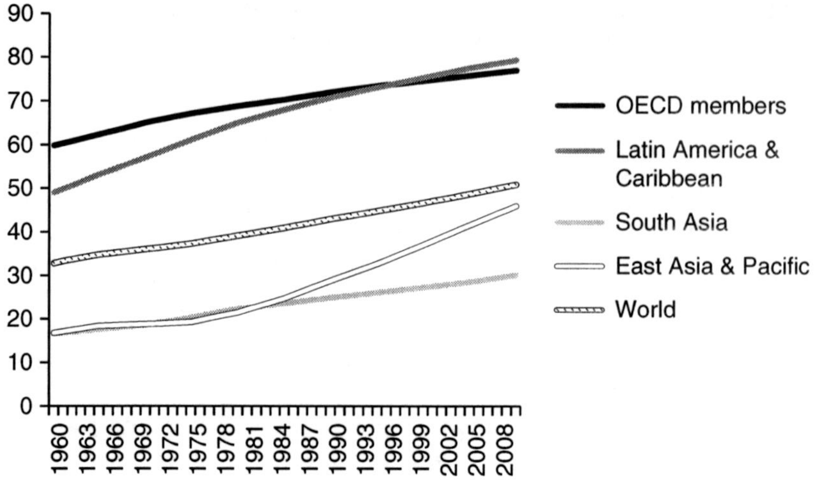

Source: World Bank Database (the statistics for Latin America, East Asia and Pacific, and South Asia are developing countries only).

Figure 2.4 World and regional urbanization percentages

advanced economies since 2008, and this reality may persist until 2014–15, or perhaps even longer if we use Japan as a precedent. The trouble is that the global macro, monetary and financial policies are still dominated by the advanced economies where the size of financial transaction volumes is 10–100 times the trading volume for the real goods and services. This means that the emerging markets where the real economy is still growing rapidly with high returns on real investment have to deal with artificially low interest rates that are largely set or influenced by the policies in the advanced economies.

A worldwide coordination framework is needed to meet the challenges of tremendous demand for real capital by the 80 percent of the world's population, and the large volume of liquidity and financial capital created artificially by the monetary authorities in the advanced economies since the 2000s and leading up to the financial crisis.

2.2.3 Rising Costs of Emissions and Natural Resources

Lastly, increasing recognition of the harmful effects of carbon emissions and the rising demand for natural resources will raise costs. Such a reality will revolutionize the inefficient energy and natural-resource use that we now see in many developing – and even some developed – countries.

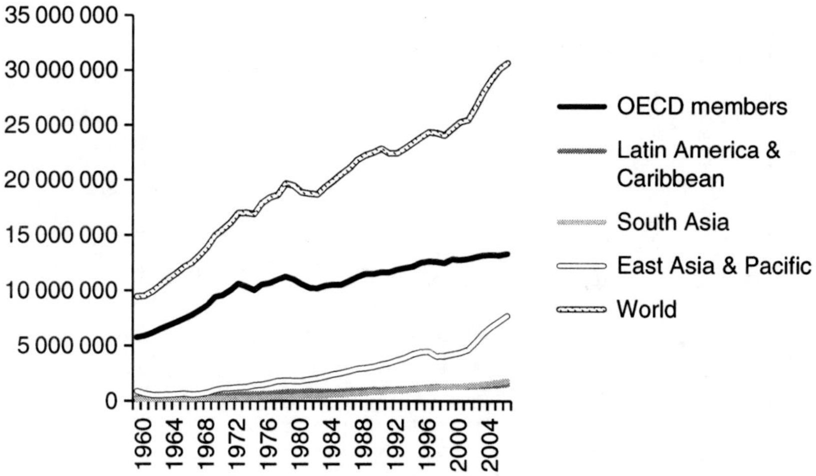

Source: World Bank Database (the statistics for Latin America, East Asia and Pacific, and South Asia are developing countries only).

Figure 2.5 World and regional CO_2 emissions (kilotonnes)

Convergence theory at least seems to be holding remarkably true for pollution. Major emerging economies such as India, Indonesia and China remain underdeveloped but are already first-rate polluters (see Figure 2.5). China long surpassed the United States as the world's largest producer of carbon dioxide emissions, producing a massive 7.7 million tonnes annually, over 2 million tonnes more than the United States and almost twice that of Europe (EIA, 2011). Carbon emissions are also on the rise in Asia, Africa and the Middle East. Yet, per capita emissions in China, India and other developing countries remain only a small fraction of those in the advanced economies (see Figure 2.6).

In the short run, the advanced economies are pressing China to reduce savings and increase consumption to facilitate global economic recovery. However, if China, India and other developing economies are converging toward the lifestyle and consumption patterns developed in the advanced economies, the world will run out of natural resources, given today's technology.

As the scarcity of natural resources become more and more serious, costs of energy, raw materials, transportation and material consumption will rise. These escalating costs will then stimulate changes in the structure and distribution of global supply chains, shifting jobs, income and wealth across borders over time.

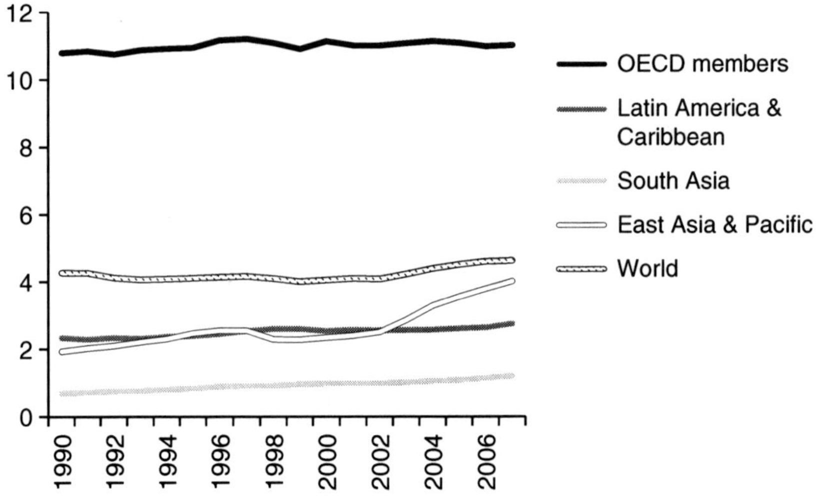

Source: World Bank Database (the statistics for Latin America, East Asia and Pacific, and South Asia are developing countries only).

Figure 2.6 World and regional CO_2 emissions (metric tons per capita)

2.3 GOOD AND BAD NEWS ABOUT MAJOR ECONOMIC TRENDS

Large emerging economies are thus the drivers of economic global transformation – changes that are exposing structural deficiencies in advanced and developing economies. The above three economic development trends are largely positive corollaries derived from the West's success with industrialization and urbanization. Structural changes are coinciding with many optimistic trends: the rapid spread and improving quality of modern education is accelerating the speed and scale of technological innovation. Invention of modern information and transportation technology is in turn dramatically decreasing the costs of global interaction. The law of large numbers means that the emerging markets will contribute more and more in patents, business-practice innovations, and even innovations in policymaking and implementation. The most competitive global companies are thriving in this new global economy with ever expanding markets beyond borders. As shown so clearly by fashionable consumer products like the iPad and iPhone, a good product or company can serve the global 7 billion person consumer market.

But, in a world of dramatic structural changes, we face two pre-eminent challenges: of global coordination and international wealth inequality. Firstly, global coordination capacity lags well behind the demand for global coordination because national policies for short-term objectives futilely address global, longer-term issues. Secondly, gains and losses amidst current global structural changes remain distributed unevenly across nations. This international inequality causes serious trade protectionism and undermines beneficial economic policies in many countries.

In a world lacking true global governance and sturdy institutions, we need to emphasize worldwide, system-wide and multidisciplinary policy research to tackle the world's short-term challenges while keeping in mind the long-term driving forces and constraints. We must cooperate with global-level policymakers, academics, and business professionals to actualize data-driven policy recommendations. Only then can we work toward the world's long-term sustainable transformation into a modern and industrialized global society.

NOTES

1. For a recent and comprehensive discussion on this topic, please see Michael Spence's book *Next Convergence: The Future of Economic Growth in a Multispeed World* (2011).
2. For an in-depth discussion on China's inflation and RMB appreciation, please see Xiao (n.d.).

REFERENCES

Smith, Adam (1776), *An Inquiry into the Nature and Causes of the Wealth of Nations*, Dublin: Printed for Messrs Whitestone et al.

Spence, Michael (2011), *Next Convergence: The Future of Economic Growth in a Multispeed World*, New York: FSG.

United States Energy Information Administration (EIA) (2011), 'International Energy Statistics', 20 October, available at http://www.eia.gov/cfapps/ipdbproject/IEDIndex3.cfm?tid=90&pid=44&aid=8.

World Bank (2001), 'Data Catalog', 26 September, available at http://data.worldbank.org/data-catalog.

Xiao, Geng (n.d.), 'China's Structural Inflation: Impact on Growth Model', available at http://www.fungglobalinstitute.org/publications/articles/chinas-structural-inflation-impact-on-growth-model-54.html.

3. Asian capitalism: Beijing Consensus as an economic development model for the 21st century

Edward K.Y. Chen[1]

3.1 INTRODUCTION: VARIETIES OF CAPITALISM

Capitalism is characterized by the private ownership of the means of production, the production of commodities for sale, and the use of the market mechanism for allocating resources. Some (Weinberg, 2002) assert that the development of capitalism also depends on conditions such as: (1) institutional arrangements to ensure a dependable supply of labor; (2) a degree of social productivity sufficient to permit sustained investment; (3) commercial organization of the market whose scope is adequate to the productivity of the community; (4) a political process whereby economic power can become translated into government policy; and (5) a legal structure which is sufficient to protect private property. There is no pure capitalism in the real world; the type of capitalism depends of course on the degree of state ownership and the degree of state intervention in resources allocation. Furthermore, capitalism can be classified in accordance with the factors governing the behavior and strategy of firms. While earlier studies were on firm-based governance mechanisms to minimize transaction costs in shaping firm strategy (Williamson, 1985), the more recent literature puts emphasis on the importance of the institutional arrangements (such as capital and labor markets, environment, social welfare policies, industrial relations, interfirm relationships, state–business relationships) and the complementarities of these institutions in affecting firm strategy (Hall and Soskice, 2001).[2] Different types of capitalism (varieties of capitalism) would then produce different 'emblematic' firms which adapt to the particular institutional environment. Thus the variety of capitalism is not only differentiated by the degree of private ownership and the extent of government invention in the market but also by the organizational characteristics of the firm.

Specifically, we can classify capitalism systems into American (United States) capitalism, European capitalism and Asian capitalism. American capitalism, unlike European capitalism, is not a transformation from feudalism. Industrialization started early and democratization was largely attained before the emergence of a fully fledged capitalistic economy in the early 20th century.[3] Also, American capitalism was developed at a time of a small public sector – less than 10 percent of gross domestic product (GDP) – and weak government intervention in the economy, making a favorable environment for successful private businesses from the beginning and its development less confrontational. American capitalism was also developed mostly organically without significant foreign influence and Marxian opposition, very much unlike the development of capitalism in Europe and Asia.[4]

American capitalism can be characterized by the following:[5]

1. The economic sector is predominated by private enterprises with little or no presence of state-owned enterprises.
2. Its market economy is free and open domestically and also with regard to foreign countries.
3. It can be described as entrepreneurial capitalism in which fair competition, free entry and equal opportunities predominate. The overall orientation is pro-market rather than pro-business. 'Even before the internet boom created many young billionaires, in 1996 one in four billionaires in the US can be described as "self-made" – compared to just one out of ten in Germany' (Zingales, 2009). Also, most of these billionaires made their money in competitive businesses rather than in government-protected or regulated sectors.
4. Policymaking is through a democratic process, allowing different interest groups to participate in the discussion and exert their influences. As a result, the American capitalist system has been perceived as fair and gained public support.

European capitalism has the following characteristics:[6]

1. The economic sector is dominated by private ownership but with state enterprise still in considerable existence.
2. The market economy is coordinated with considerable government intervention.
3. The open competition is intermingled with collaboration within and among economic actors (including the state).
4. The political system is democratic but there is an uneven influence on economic policy formulation by different interest groups.

Asian capitalism is difficult to generalize. It was recognized that there are varieties of capitalism among Asian countries. Generally, East (or Northeast) Asian capitalism is regarded as somewhat different from Southeast Asian capitalism.[7] The discussions on Asian capitalism are also subject to a wide range of interpretations:

1. from microeconomic theory of the firm to macroeconomic development strategies and models;
2. from the role of the state to state–business relationships;
3. from political systems to institutional arrangements in general; and
4. from sociological and cultural determinants to distinctive organizational arrangements and management practices.

In general, Asian capitalism of the various types can be broadly described as follows:

1. The state has significant control over economic actors and there is a significant presence of state enterprises.
2. The market economy is coordinated with significant government intervention in the market.
3. The economy is open to foreign trade and foreign investment, but very often in selected sectors and industries only. Liberalization is usually applied only to the trade account but not the capital account until a much later stage of economic development.
4. In economic activities, open competition is limited. There are close alliances between state and business; called private–public partnership (PPP) when successful, called cronyism when not so successful. Chinese (or Asian or Italian) business practices such as interfirm networking in sourcing and marketing, predominance of clans and business groups, and contract enforcement based on trust rather than the law, are largely followed.
5. Politically, the countries are in the early stages of democratization. Only selected groups are allowed to participate in economic policy formulation. Economic success largely depends on state strength and government strategic intervention in the market.

For Southeast Asian countries, the state is generally less strong than East Asian economies and in consequence there is less direct intervention in the market at the micro and macro levels.[8] At the firm level, in both Southeast Asia and East Asia the Chinese business practices described above are followed quite closely.

3.2 ASIAN CAPITALISM: THE RISE, FALL AND RESURGENCE

Since the early 20th century, capitalism in general and American capitalism in particular has been glorified as the gold standard for economic success.[9] Economic growth in the socialist economies of the USSR and China in the 1950s was regarded as temporary and transitory because of their dependence on the intensive use of capital and labor and not on innovation and creativity.[10] A prolific literature on Asian capitalism or an Asian model of economic development emerged after the great economic success achieved by East and then Southeast Asian economies in the 1970s and 1980s.[11]

In many ways, Asian capitalism is different from American capitalism as explained above in this chapter, though there are some similarities between Asian capitalism and capitalism in some European countries.[12] The East Asian economic development model based on state intervention in the market which is nonetheless open to foreign trade and investment, non-democratic political systems (development-oriented hard states) and Chinese culture-oriented business practices became an alternative to the World Bank model of unilateral liberalization and getting the prices right. Indeed, most developing countries would use the East Asian experience as the basis for formulating their development strategies. The case in point is the ASEAN-4 (Malaysia, Thailand, the Philippines and Indonesia), which followed in the steps of the Four Little Dragons (Hong Kong, Singapore, Taiwan and South Korea) and achieved rapid growth and structural change after the early 1980s. At the same time, China has emerged as a superstar in economic development and growth since the early 1990s, achieving a sustained two-digit growth for two decades on the basis of a less liberalized and more regulated economic system (capitalism/socialism with Chinese characteristics).

The Asian financial crisis in 1997–98 caused distress in many Asian economies, even including Hong Kong and Singapore which are known to adopt very prudent macroeconomic policies. Asian capitalism was then blamed for its cronyism, corruption, patron–client exchanges, rent-seeking activities and macroeconomic mismanagement, though there were other economists like Jeffrey Sachs and Joseph Stiglitz who would put the blame more on the international financial architecture and the mismanagement of the International Monetary Fund (IMF).[13] Asian capitalism and the East Asian model of economic development had to shy away from the limelight of the global economy for a while.

The 2008–09 global financial crisis (tsunami) with its origin in the United States (US) casts serious doubts on the economic and financial operations under American capitalism. Many were talking about the end of American capitalism.[14] There was in the US, probably for the first time, diminishing public support for the American system. There were severe criticisms of the overdeveloped financial sectors and the predominance of a few financial giants undermining the spirit of American capitalism. On the other hand, China did not seem to have been affected by the global financial crisis at all; growth and development continued. Moreover, East Asia in general and China in particular have played an important part as the growth engine for economic recovery from the global recession. There is no question that after the rise and fall of Asian capitalism, we now witness the resurgence of Asian capitalism.

3.3 BEIJING CONSENSUS VERSUS WASHINGTON CONSENSUS

The Washington Consensus (WC) refers to a set of 'standard' policy reforms recommended by the Washington DC-based institutions (the World Bank, the IMF and the US Treasury Department) for developing countries, as summed up by Williamson (1990). In brief, the WC has a set of ten recommendations (which are just commonsense, free-market fundamentals and were familiar to many even at that time), as follows:

1. Prudent fiscal policy.
2. Public expenditure directed to promote growth and equality instead of providing subsidies indiscriminately.
3. A widened tax base with only moderate progressive tax rates.
4. Market-determined interest rates.
5. Market-determined exchange rates.
6. Trade liberalization (removal of tariff and non-tariff barriers).
7. Investment liberalization of inward foreign direct investment across the board (not selectively by sector).
8. Privatization of state-owned enterprises.
9. Legal protection for private property rights.
10. Deregulation of market controls for promoting competition and efficiency, except in the cases of significant public interest.

The WC was mainly advocated for Latin American countries during the global economic turbulence in the 1980s. The import-substitution Latin American countries found it very difficult to cope with the shortage of foreign resources arising from the sharp rise in US interest rates and oil prices in the early 1980s. It was much easier for the export-oriented East Asian economies to make ends meet under such circumstances, though they also encountered various degrees of difficulty. The WC was therefore simply a package of policies largely for the structural transformation of the import-substitution development strategy to an export-orientated strategy. The WC met with varied degrees of acceptance and criticism at the theoretical level. In practice, those countries which followed the WC had varied results. For example, the Argentine economic crisis of 1999–2002 was often related to adopting the WC policy recommendations; on the other hand, the economic success story in Chile was often attributed to its reforms based on the WC. In retrospect, the WC had a historical role to play in guiding the formulation of development strategies in the 1980s and early 1990s, though such a list of policies certainly lacks implementation details. The fact is however that the global economy has changed significantly, and the question is therefore whether the WC reform package is still useful for the 21st century.

The Beijing Consensus (BC) has been used to describe China's model of development since its policy reforms in the late 1970s. It is also meant as an alternative policy prescription to the WC for developing countries, in view of the fact that the WC is probably out of date and lacks theoretical vigor and implementation details. The tremendous economic success of China in the past 30 years has made the BC model extremely attractive to policymakers in developing countries. China's model of development is different in some ways from that of the East and Southeast Asian economies. It was believed that the term 'Beijing Consensus' was used by journalists from the late 1990s, but the term has become popularized after the publication of Ramo's monograph in 2004. However, it should be noted that Ramo (2004) does not actually spell out a model of economic development or a set of policy guidelines.[15] The theme of Ramo's essay is more on politics, security and defense than economics. The substance of the BC described by Ramo is expressed in terms of three theorems:

1. Development is based on continuous innovation.
2. There is an emphasis on equity and life quality; non-GDP indicators are used as measures of economic progress.
3. Development is based on self-determination (finance and military) largely for security reasons; globalization with Chinese characteristics.

The first theorem on innovation is largely economic, and is a familiar concept for development in the new economic era of constant change. The second theorem is for securing national support for growth and development. The third theorem is for using the minimum effort to achieve the greatest security in the international balance of power. The third theorem can probably generate the most interesting discussion, but it is not really about economic development per se. In sum, the BC as discussed by Ramo cannot be taken as an economic development model; it simply discusses some economic, political and security issues that developing countries should take into consideration. Most importantly, these three theorems do not seem to match China's development experience in the past three decades. China's rapid economic growth has not really been based on continuous innovation, and the existence of huge inequality among regions and within cities is well known. In terms of geopolitics, China's strategy of self-determination is perhaps a reality, but in terms of economic activities China has been depending heavily on foreign direct investment and technology transfer.

In this chapter, an attempt is made to redefine the BC as an economic development model based on the Chinese experience since China's implementation of policy reforms in 1979.[16] Let us call this model the Chinese Economic Model (CEM). Unlike the WC, the CEM is not just a list of policy guidelines but also puts great emphasis on the actions taken to implement the policies. The policy reforms in the CEM are not novel, but their implementation is laudable. In the CEM, policy reforms are undertaken: (1) in accordance with a well-planned sequencing; (2) with an incremental, gradual or evolutionary approach, in contrast to the 'shock' or 'big bang' approach of Russia, the Commonwealth of Independent States (CIS) and East European countries; and (3) on the basis of an experimental approach with pilot projects tested before nationwide applications – 'crossing the river by groping the stones'. A good policy could produce very bad results if it is implemented at the wrong time and at the inappropriate pace. Unlike Ramo's BC, the CEM is about economics and the mechanics of economic development with only little reference to politics and security.[17]

The CEM can be described as follows:

1. A country for economic development should at the beginning adopt an outward-looking and export-oriented strategy. This is indeed what the World Bank has been advocating for decades.
2. Different from the World Bank prescriptions, the CEM demonstrates that the timing, speed and sequencing of reforms are crucial in ensuring success. In implementing export-oriented strategy, the steps are: (a) to establish some carefully selected special economic/free trade/industrial/export processing zones along the east coast as starting and experimental projects, with strong and dedicated central government support to set examples for other regions or zones in due course,[18] implying a sequence of opening up the coastal regions before the inland regions; (b) to introduce exchange rates reforms for export

competitiveness in the form of a one-off devaluation under a managed fixed exchange rate regime; this is in contrast to the WC of introducing a flexible exchange rate system as soon as possible;[19] (c) liberalization of foreign exchange control has to be gradual and in the right sequence: liberalization of the trade account long before the capital account; (d) gradual liberalization of inward foreign direct investment in selected regions (mostly in the special economic zones) and selected sectors,[20] in contrast to the WC of across-the-board liberalization for avoiding resources allocation distortions.

3. Rural reforms are undertaken before urban reforms. The first step in improving the utilization of resources is to change the incentive system in agriculture. The household responsibility system is implemented step by step, resulting in drastic increases in agricultural output and its share in GDP. Rural industrialization of setting up township and village enterprises (TVEs) plays an important part in absorbing the agricultural labor released, in aligning industrial production to China's comparative advantage, and in providing capital for further agricultural development.
4. Urban reforms start with state-owned industrial enterprise reform, giving enterprises greater autonomy and paving ways for a market economy. While the central government continues to play a vital role in allocating resources, local governments are also given a greater say on the direction of industrialization. Privatization and the development of private sector business are only undertaken at a later stage using a step-by-step approach. The idea of allowing some people to get rich first is accepted; a bigger pie should be created before consideration is given to how the pie should be divided.
5. A very prudent approach to reforms in the financial sector is adopted. Liberalization of financial services is very gradual in terms of interest rate deregulation,[21] foreign ownership and foreign operation in RMB businesses. Similarly, the privatization of state-owned financial institutions is gradual and prudent. The development of the capital markets should also be gradual. Derivatives and futures markets should only be developed long after establishing the sound operation of the spot markets.[22]

3.4 CONCLUSION: THE CEM AS A DEVELOPMENT MODEL FOR THE 21ST CENTURY

In terms of the theoretical and practical substance in the CEM, and in view of a new and changing global economic environment in the 21st century, there is little doubt that the CEM as a redefined Beijing Consensus would supersede the Washington Consensus as an economic development model for the following reasons:

1. In the latter half of the 20th century, the NIE (newly industrialized economy) model of export-oriented, small, natural-resources-scarce, open economies[23] was predominant, largely explaining the economic success of developing countries. In the 21st century, we witness the rise of the BRIC (Brazil, Russia, India and China) countries which are export orientation cum import substitution, large and natural-resources-rich. The BRIC model (if one can derive one) will replace the NIE model as the predominant model of development.[24] In the 21st century, it is expected that large, natural-resources-rich developing countries will have a much better chance of success than small, open economies. Within the BRIC countries, China evidently has the most relevant experience for developing countries. The CEM will therefore be much more relevant than the NIE model and the Washington Consensus for this century.
2. Globalization has resulted in a much more integrated global economy than before. At the same time, the financial sector has become increasingly important in the domestic and international economy. Financial services are now globally integrated, and as a result the financial sector has to be regulated not only by nation-states but also by international bodies through international coordination and cooperation. The CEM in which the state imposes tight control over the financial sector and recognizes that measures of deregulation and liberalization need to be gradual, experimental and in the correct sequence, becomes more relevant than the Washington Consensus. As guidance for economic development, the CEM is much more useful than the Washington Consensus. The CEM is more than a list of policies: it has an underlying model of economic development spelling out the basic strategy (export-orientation and open-door) and the concomitant reforms (incentive systems, utilization of foreign resources, export promotion and comparative advantage alignment, rebalancing the production structure, price and enterprise reforms, privatization, macroeconomic management of exchange rates, interest rates and the financial sector at large) to be undertaken in an evolutionary manner based on trial and error and in accordance with a well-thought-out sequencing.

NOTES

1. The original version of this chapter was published in *Journal of Northeast Asia Development*, **12**, December 2010.
2. Hall and Soskice (2001) make a distinction between the liberal market economies (the US, the UK, Australia) and the coordinated market economies (Germany, Japan, France, Sweden).
3. For the development of American capitalism, see Weinberg (2002).
4. See Zingales (2009) for a good exposition on the roots and characteristics of American capitalism.
5. According to Hall and Soskice (2001), American capitalism characteristics are largely shared by the United Kingdom (UK) and Australia, and they are all called liberal market economies. On the other hand, capitalist countries such as Germany, France, Sweden and Japan are categorized as coordinated market economies.
6. In Orru et al. (1997), Part III ('Comparative Analysis of Business Networks') by Orru is devoted to analyzing the institutional features of capitalism in some European countries in comparison with some Asian countries. European capitalism here largely refers to Northern and Western European countries, or Hall and Soskice's coordinated market economies.
7. For an excellent study on East Asian capitalism, see Orru et al. (1997). For a comparative analysis of East and Southeast Asian capitalism, see MacIntyre (1994), Park (2000) and Safarian and Dobson (1996).
8. A good reference for the role of the state in the economic development of East Asia is Wade (1990).
9. Weber (1905) asserted that the origin of capitalism was related to Protestant ethics developed in 17th-century England.
10. See the arguments of Krugman (1994) on inspiration versus perspiration in explaining economic growth.
11. An early study on the NIEs (newly industrializing or industrialized economies) was undertaken by Chen (1979). Chen (1988) presented a model integrating economic, political and cultural elements to explain the economic success of East Asia. The World Bank study undertaken by Stiglitz (World Bank, 1993), is certainly the authoritative work on the success stories of East and Southeast Asian economies up to the early 1990s.
12. See Orru et al. (1997) for an interesting and insightful comparison of Asian capitalism in Japan, Korea and Taiwan with Western capitalism in Germany, Italy and France.
13. The debate on this subject was heated. Some important and interesting writings can be found in the 1998 volume of *Brookings Papers on Economic Activities* and the 1998 volume of *Foreign Affairs*. See also Chen (2000) for regarding the Asian financial crisis as a result of 'international failure'.
14. See for example Zingales (2009), Phelps (2009) and Schramm and Litan (2009).
15. Joshua Ramo is basically a journalist by profession. His monograph, *The Beijing Consensus* (Ramo, 2004), was also written in a journalistic way. There is no theoretical vigor nor is there a formal model or a set of policy recommendations as in the Washington Consensus. The monograph contains a lot of story-telling and anecdotes, and also reports on his meeting important people and government officials.
16. For an excellent exposition on China's reforms before and after 1979, see Lin et al. (1996).
17. One implication of the CEM is that a stable internal political environment is important for development at the early stages. Economic reforms should well precede political reforms; this is in contrast to the 'shock' approach adopted by Russia which implemented privatization, marketization and democratization all at the same time.
18. Special economic zones were actually set up in many developing countries before China's experiment. The success of China is explained by the carefully chosen locations, the strong support given by the central government, and a dynamic view of the zones

in the sense that the first zones should become 'role models' for the next tiers of zones, and the original zones would graduate and transform. Of course, by luck or by design, the success of the first tier of zones can also be linked to the part played by investment from Taiwan and Hong Kong, and other overseas Chinese.

19. If China had liberalized its exchange rate regime early and fast, China's economic success would have been ruined by the Asian financial crisis, 1997–98, as in the case of many other Asian developing countries.
20. To promote export, foreign capital and technology were utilized in an evolutionary manner – from compensation trade to original equipment manufacturing (OEM) to original product manufacturing (OPM) and then original design manufacturing (ODM).
21. As is demonstrated in the cases of Taiwan, South Korea and China, the implementation of market-determined interest rates can be postponed to a much later stage of development without damaging growth. Curbing market activities can help pave the way eventually to a fully market-oriented financial sector.
22. If China had developed futures markets and introduced financial innovations à la America, China would not have escaped the serious impacts of the global financial crisis in 2008–09.
23. See Chen (1979) and (1988).
24. See Chen (2007).

REFERENCES

Chen, Edward K.Y. (1979), *Hyper-Growth in Asian Economies*, London: Macmillan.

Chen, Edward K.Y. (1988), 'The Economics and Non-economics of Asia's Four Little Dragons', *Supplement to the Gazette*, University of Hong Kong, **35**(1), 21 March.

Chen, Edward K.Y. (2000), 'The Asian Financial Crisis of 1997–8: A Case of Market Failure, Government Failure or International Failure?' in Brigitte Granville (ed.), *Essays on the World Economy and its Financial System*, London: Royal Institute of International Affairs, pp. 49–65.

Chen, Edward K.Y. (2007), 'From the NIEs to the BRICs: Development Theory Revisited', *Edward K. Y. Chen Distinguished Lecture Series*, Inaugural Lecture, University of Hong Kong, 15 June.

Hall, P.A. and D. Soskice (2001), *Varieties of Capitalism: The Institutional Foundations of Comparative Advantage*, New York: Oxford University Press.

Krugman, P. (1994), 'The Myth of Asia's Miracle', *Foreign Affairs*, **73**(6), 62–78.

Lin, J.Y.L., F. Cai and Zhou Li (1996), *The China Miracle: Development Strategy and Economic Reform*, Hong Kong: Chinese University of Hong Kong.

MacIntyre, A. (ed.) (1994), *Business and Government in Industrializing Asia*, St Leonards, NSW: Allen & Unwin.

Orru, M., N.W. Biggart and G. Hamilton (1997), *The Economic Organization of East Asian Capitalism*, Thousand Oaks, CA: Sage Publications.

Park, D. (2000), 'The Dichotomy between Northeast Asian Capitalism and Southeast Asian Capitalism', *Journal of the Asian Pacific Economy*, **5**(3), 234–54.

Phelps, E.S. (2009), 'Refounding Capitalism', *Capitalism and Society*, **4**(3), 1064–5.

Ramo, J.C. (2004), *The Beijing Consensus*, London: Foreign Policy Centre.

Safarian, A.E. and W. Dobson (1996), *East Asian Capitalism: Diversity and*

Dynamism, Hong Kong Bank of Canada Papers on Asia, Vol. 2, Toronto: University of Toronto Press.
Schramm, C. and R.E. Litan (2009), 'The End of American Capitalism?' *American*, 6 February.
Wade, R. (1990), *Governing the Market: Economic Theory and the Role of Government in East Asian Industrialization*, Princeton, NJ: Princeton University Press.
Weber, M. (1905), *The Protestant Ethic and the Spirit of Capitalism* (trans. Talcott Parsons), New York: Scribner.
Weinberg, M. (2002), *A Short History of American Capitalism*, available at www.newhistory.com.
Williamson, J. (1990), 'What Washington Means by Policy Reform', in J. Williamson (ed.), *Latin American Readjustment: How Much Has Happened*, Washington, DC: Institute for International Economics, pp. 25–32.
Williamson, O.E. (1985), *The Economic Institutions of Capitalism: Firms, Markets, Relational Contracting*, New York: Free Press.
World Bank (1993), *The East Asian Miracle: Economic Growth and Public Policy*, Oxford: Oxford University Press.
Zingales, L. (2009), 'Capitalism after the Crisis', *National Affairs*, Inaugural Issue, 22–35.

4. The renminbi debate: a review of issues and search for resolution

Yoonbai Kim and Gil Kim

4.1 INTRODUCTION

The value of China's currency, the renminbi (RMB), has become a contentious issue. Many argue that the currency is undervalued and has been the main source for the country's large current account surpluses especially with the United States (US). There has been mounting external pressure on China to allow the RMB to appreciate against the US dollar. A number of economists also argue that the exchange rate regime in China should change to market-based floating from heavy intervention in the foreign exchange market.

In this chapter, we review some important issues related to the RMB. China has so far been resisting the pressure, permitting only gradual and small changes in its exchange rate policy. Apparently, the main concern for China seems to be that currency appreciation would have detrimental effects on its crucial export sector and create a host of economic problems, including worsening the unemployment problem in the rural sector and reducing economic growth. The Japanese experience of prolonged appreciation and decades-long recession has often been invoked as a reason for the resistance. The heated contention between the United States and China has pushed the world economy into a situation of competitive devaluations or 'currency wars' among many developed and emerging market economies.

In this chapter, we briefly review two among the most contentious issues regarding the RMB. One is whether China should move to a float or at least an exchange rate regime with greater flexibility. The other is whether and how much the RMB is undervalued. We find irreconcilable differences around the two issues of the RMB debate. Important questions underlying the contentions are about: (1) whether RMB appreciation is necessary to reduce current account imbalances in China and the US; and (2) whether the appreciation will induce recessionary impacts on the Chinese economy. Admittedly, both are empirical issues. However, to our surprise, they are not dealt with in a unified framework.

We employ a vector autoregressive (VAR) model to assess the role of the exchange rate in Japan and China. We then present empirical evidence that shows some important differences between the experiences of Japan and China. Currency appreciation in Japan appears to reduce current account surpluses and induce economic downturn, as the Chinese government argues. On the other hand, RMB appreciation is not likely to have any significant effects on the current account balance, while (insignificantly) raising real income instead of reducing it. The results imply that pressuring China to undertake RMB appreciation for the purpose of current account adjustment is ill guided. At the same time, refusing the request for exchange rate adjustment on the grounds of avoiding the Japan-like experience is not supported by the data.

The rest of this chapter is organized as follows. Section 4.2 briefly reviews the literature on the two main issues involving the RMB exchange rate. Section 4.3 presents a VAR model and empirical results that can deal with the key issues in a unified manner. Section 4.4 concludes with policy implications.

4.2 A REVIEW OF THE LITERATURE

Regarding the exchange rate of the RMB, two questions surface most often. One is whether it is undervalued or overvalued (and by how much). The other is whether China would be better off with a floating exchange rate. We review the second issue first in the following.

4.2.1 Should the RMB Float?

Many economists argue that China should allow its currency to appreciate significantly and should move to a regime of more flexible exchange rate. According to Roubini (2007), the RMB is grossly overvalued and it is in China's interest to move to a more flexible exchange rate regime. A failure to allow a nominal appreciation poses significant risks and potential costs such as protectionist backlashes from the US and Europe, and increasingly costly foreign exchange market intervention. He offers five reasons: (1) protectionist backlashes from the US and Europe such as branding China as a 'currency manipulator' by the US Treasury or protectionist legislation such as the Schumer–Graham proposal of a 27.5 percent tariff on Chinese goods; (2) foreign exchange market intervention becomes increasingly costlier due to the interest cost (with sterilization) or excessive liquidity credit and asset bubbles (without sterilization); (3) 'the imbalanced composition of aggregate demand' leading to excessive reliance on net exports and real investment and a very low level of consumption; (4) greater capital losses on holdings of foreign reserves when the RMB appreciates; (5) the risk of a surge in inflation. He also argues that risks of an RMB appreciation – such as a slowdown of growth, worsening unemployment problems in the rural sector, and deflationary pressures – would be modest and that their costs could be reduced by appropriate policies.[1]

As the logic goes, floating the renminbi will free up the monetary policy from maintaining the exchange rate at a target level. The resulting appreciation of the RMB would reduce the inflationary pressure in China. More importantly, the appreciation would reduce the current account surpluses. The notion that a flexible exchange rate regime would facilitate a faster current account adjustment is in fact not well supported by empirical evidence. Chinn and Wei (forthcoming) call such a maintained hypothesis without firm empirical evidence 'a faith-based initiative'. They also show that the real exchange rate adjustment is not systematically related to how flexible a country's nominal exchange rate regime is. It suggests that there will be no guarantee that the yuan will appreciate under a flexible regime. For instance, until October 2003 the market actually expected RMB depreciation, as measured by the non-deliverable forward rate. The virtue of a flexible exchange rate regime in enhancing the effectiveness of China's macroeconomic policy may also be overrated.

McKinnon (2007, 2009) argues that a (more or less) fixed exchange rate has served China well, and China would be better off keeping it the way it has been. He disputes important elements of arguments made by pro-floaters as 'Three Misconceptions' about exchange rate stabilization: MC1: the exchange rate can affect the trade balance; MC2: ongoing exchange rate appreciation reduces inflation; MC3: floating the rate would equilibrate the foreign exchange market. McKinnon maintains that a current account balance is the result of savings being greater than investment, and that the exchange rate has little to do with it. Although the beneficial effect of currency appreciation on domestic inflation can be a reality in the long run, he continues, the short-run loss of monetary control can outweigh the deflationary impact of a higher exchange rate. McKinnon maintains that exchange rate floating would expose Chinese banks to excess exchange risk due to their immature creditor status. Drawing from the experience of Japan, he argues that currency appreciation – by creating asset bubbles and their bursting – could trigger a deflation in China similar to the one that dogged Japan for most of the 1990s and in the early 2000s. Instead of exchange rate adjustment, McKinnon argues that global rebalancing can be done via 'expenditure reduction' policies.

4.2.2 Is the RMB Undervalued? By How Much?

Those who argue that the RMB is undervalued usually point to the following as evidence: (1) the current account is greatly in surplus; (2) reserves are huge and accumulating fast; (3) the reserve accumulation is driven by hot money inflows as well as current account surpluses and inflows of foreign direct investment (FDI); hot money is flowing into China in expectation of an RMB appreciation driven by massive trade surpluses and FDI flows; (4) without foreign exchange market intervention, the RMB would have appreciated sharply.[2]

Various methods have been employed to assess more rigorously the extent of exchange rate adjustment for the RMB. The most popular ones employ some variations of purchasing power parity (PPP) and fundamental equilibrium real exchange rate. According to the absolute version of PPP, equilibrium exchange rate is related to the ratio of price levels between two countries: $\widetilde{S}_t = p_t/p_t^*$, where $\widetilde{S}_t$ is the equilibrium nominal exchange rate (also called the PPP rate) and p_t and p_t^* are the domestic and foreign price levels. (The nominal exchange rate is defined as the price of foreign currency in terms of domestic currency. Thus, an increase is depreciation of the domestic currency.) *The Economist* magazine compiles the PPP rates based on the prices of Big Macs around the world. In the report published on 22 July 2010, the RMB was 47 percent undervalued.

An extended-version PPP takes into account the tendency that the relative price of non-traded goods tends to be higher in high-income countries. According to the Balassa–Samuelson hypothesis, the tendency is due to the phenomenon that productivity differential is greater in traded goods than in non-traded goods, as economic growth is more likely concentrated in productivity growth of such sectors as manufacturing that are classified as traded goods. With the extended PPP approach, Frankel (2009) estimates that the RMB was undervalued by 36 percent in 2000.

Another popular line of estimating the equilibrium is the fundamental equilibrium exchange rate (FEER) also called the macroeconomic balance approach. According to this approach, the equilibrium real exchange rate is the one that solves both internal balance and external balance. Internal balance is usually defined as full employment with price stability. External balance is more controversial, but very often defined as the current account balance close to zero or long-term sustainable capital flows. The macroeconomic balance approach generally involves assessing the change in the real effective exchange rate that is needed to close the gap between the actual or 'underlying' current account balance of a country and its 'equilibrium' level. This approach comprises three steps: (1) estimating the underlying current account balance; (2) estimating the equilibrium current account balance; and (3) estimating a trade model to calculate the exchange rate adjustment that is required to close the gap between the underlying and equilibrium current account balances, with key parameters being the price elasticities estimated for exports and imports (Dunaway et al., 2009). Employing the FEER approach, Cline and Williamson (2010) estimate that the RMB was 32.8 percent undervalued as of March 2009, while Goldstein and Lardy (2009) come up with a smaller estimate of 20–25 percent as of the end of 2008. Table 4.1 presents a brief summary of estimates of RMB under- or overvaluation. GAO (2005) provides a comparison of the older academic and policy literature.[3]

Although most of the measures summarized in Table 4.1 point to the direction of RMB undervaluation, most methods suffer from conceptual flaws or ambiguities. For instance, PPP or its extended version – including Balassa–Samuelson the (BS) effect – is intended to be a long-run model; the horizon is of limited usefulness to policymakers. Few would expect it to hold in the short run in economies with low inflation. Moreover, there does not seem to be an unambiguously clear choice for the best way to measure currency misalignment. That is because different criteria relate to different models:

> The large variance in the estimates for equilibrium real exchange rates raises serious questions about the robustness of the results. The basic conclusion is that, at least for China, small changes in model specifications, explanatory variable definitions, and time period used in estimation can lead to very substantial differences in equilibrium real exchange rate estimates. Therefore, such estimates should be treated with great caution. (Dunaway et al., 2009)

Given the host of uncertainties in determining the equilibrium exchange rate, it is no surprise that we have such a bewildering array of estimates for RMB valuation. Thus, it should be admitted that while we cannot reject the no-misalignment null, we also cannot reject the 20 percent undervaluation null hypothesis at conventional significance levels. This outcome highlights the lack of precision of our estimates (Cheung et al., 2010).

4.3 THE MODEL AND EMPIRICAL EVIDENCE

Key reasons for controversies around the extent of RMB undervaluation and the appropriate exchange rate regime are: (1) skepticism about the role of exchange rate changes in the process of external adjustment; and (2) the fear that the suggested appreciation of the RMB may induce a Japan-style long-term stagnation in China. See McKinnon (2007, 2009) for details. On the other hand, Eichengreen and Rose (2010) find little evidence of serious

Table 4.1 A summary of estimates for RMB under- or overvaluation

Authors	Method (data)	Year	Undervaluation (overvaluation if −)	Comment
The Economist	Absolute PPP	2010	47	Big Mac standard
Frankel (2006)	PPP with B–S effects	2000	36	
Coudert and Couharde (2005)	PPP with B–S effects	2003	43–50	
	FEER	2003	23	
Garton and Chang (2005)	PPP with B–S effects	2005	25	
Subramanian (2010)	PPP with B–S effects	2005	14.5–47.5	
Cheung et al. (2009)	Productivity approach (1988–2004)	2004	1.4–6.1	
Cline and Williamson (2010)	FEER	March 2009	32.8	Macroeconomic balance approach
Goldstein and Lardy (2009)	FEER	End 2008	20–25 (level)	CA balance for China
Cheung et al. (2010)	Relative PPP (1980–2009)	2009	7.5	Without trend
			36	With trend
	Relative PPP (1990–2009)	2009	13.5	Without trend
			1.6	With trend
	Absolute PPP (1980–2009)	2008	50	
	Absolute PPP/Penn effect (1980–2009)	2008	(−) 5	
Funke and Rahn (2005)	Relative PPP	April 2003	56	Big Mac standard
Cheung et al. (2007)	Absolute PPP (1975–2004)	2004	53	

economic and financial damage as a result of appreciating the domestic currency from a fixed exchange rate regime.[4] In this section, we attempt to offer an alternative assessment to these questions. It is important to recognize that the nominal exchange rate is an endogenous variable. If it is controlled by the government through foreign exchange market intervention, some other variables such as money supply or the price level have to change to accommodate the pressure in the foreign exchange market. The exchange rate also affects and is affected by the current account and other macroeconomic variables.

For this purpose, we consider a small VAR model that includes as endogenous variables the capital account–output ratio (*KAR*), real income (*RY*), relative price ratio (*RCP*), real money supply (*MR*), the current account–output ratio (*CAR*), and the nominal exchange rate (*NX*). The model also includes two measures of external shocks to control for exogenous shocks: the foreign interest rate (*RF*) and trading-partner real income (*YF*). Variables such as capital flows, real money supply and the current account balance, as well as two external variables, are included to eliminate the effects of third factors that may generate spurious correlation between output and the real exchange rate, and contribute to a reverse causality problem.

Variables are defined as follows: the capital account (*KAR*) and current account (*CAR*) are measured as ratio to gross domestic product (GDP).[5] Real output (*RY*) is real GDP. The relative price ratio (*RCP*) is calculated by dividing the domestic price level by the foreign price level. The price level is represented by the consumer price index. The real money balance (*MR*) is calculated by dividing the money supply (M1) by the domestic price level. The nominal exchange rate (*NX*) is the price of a US dollar in terms of the domestic currency. Foreign output (*YF*) is similarly defined as US real GDP. The real exchange rate (*RX*) can be obtained by subtracting *RCP* from *NX*. The US three-month Treasury bill interest rate is used as the foreign interest rate (*RF*). All variables are in logarithm except for the interest rates and the capital and current account ratios.

The six endogenous variables are ordered as listed in the following reduced form:

$$\begin{pmatrix} KAR_t \\ RY_t \\ RCP_t \\ MR_t \\ CAR_t \\ NX_t \end{pmatrix} = \begin{pmatrix} a_1 \\ a_2 \\ a_3 \\ a_4 \\ a_5 \\ a_6 \end{pmatrix} + A_{ij}(L) \begin{pmatrix} KAR_{t-1} \\ RY_{t-1} \\ RCP_{t-1} \\ MR_{t-1} \\ CAR_{t-1} \\ NX_{t-1} \end{pmatrix} + B_{ij}(L) \begin{pmatrix} YF_t \\ RF_t \end{pmatrix} + \begin{pmatrix} \varepsilon_{1t} \\ \varepsilon_{2t} \\ \varepsilon_{3t} \\ \varepsilon_{4t} \\ \varepsilon_{5t} \\ \varepsilon_{6t} \end{pmatrix}$$

where $A_{ij}(L)$ and $B_{ij}(L)$ are 6×6 and 6×2 matrices of polynomials in lag operator L.

The ordering of the endogenous variables can be justified as follows. First, capital flows are treated as the driving force of the macroeconomic variables. Empirical evidence indicates that capital flows are one of the important determinants of output and the exchange rate in a world of globalized capital movement, and capital flows are strongly influenced by external shocks such as the world interest rate and US business cycle.[6] By positioning the capital account at the top of the variables, we assume that it is the most exogenous variable among the endogenous variables.[7]

Second, the real exchange rate is separated into the nominal exchange rate and the relative price. With this separation, we can examine the hypothesis whether the behavior of the real exchange rate is invariant with respect to the exchange rate regime. The hypothesis implies, for instance, that a depreciation of the real exchange rate can be obtained by a depreciation of the nominal exchange rate or a decline in the domestic price level.

Third, real money supply is included since the behavior of real money can be an important key to understanding the effects of devaluation. The identification assumption is that output does not contemporaneously react to money supply changes. This assumption is based on real business cycle theory that the money supply may not affect output or at least take a lag to be effective.

Fourth, in this model, the nominal exchange rate is placed at the bottom. This means that the effects of contemporaneous changes in the exchange rate due to other variables in the system are removed from innovations in the nominal exchange rate. This arrangement is designed to extract 'pure' exchange rate shocks by eliminating the exchange rate changes that can be considered to be endogenous reactions to other variables. Relatively exogenous changes such as those induced by the change in the value of currencies of major trading partners should remain as innovations. The methodology is adapted from Kim and Roubini (2000) and is also used in Kim and Ying (2007).[8]

We apply the model for Japan and China. In both cases, we treat the US as the sole trading partner whose real income and the interest rate are taken as exogenous for each country. In the following, we present empirical results with impulse responses and variance decompositions.

4.3.1 Japan

The model is estimated for Japan using quarterly data from 1977Q1 through 2009Q4. (The estimation period was determined by the availability of the capital account data.) The lag length is set at four. For the

Table 4.2 Granger causality tests on CAR and KAR

	Dependent variable	Bilateral test		Multivariate test	
		KAR	CAR	KAR	CAR
Japan					
	CAR	0.945		0.576	
	KAR		0.681		0.818
China					
Quarterly data	CAR	0.929		0.975	
	KAR		0.161		0.883
Annual data	CAR	0.065		0.055	
	KAR		0.994		0.491

two exogenous variables, two lags along with the current value are used. In Table 4.2, we first present the test results of Granger causality between the current and capital accounts. The p-values indicate that Granger causality is insignificant in all cases in the bivariate setting or the multivariate case with all the variables in the system included. It suggests that neither precedes the other.

Variance decompositions are reported in Table 4.3 for the 4- and 24-quarter horizons, representing short-run and medium-run interactions. Capital flows are mainly driven by own shocks and shocks to real money supply in the short and medium run. They explain 45 and 32 percent of variations in capital flows in the medium run. For the current account balance, while own shocks are dominant, exchange rate movements and shocks to real money supply become more important, explaining 25 and 13 percent, respectively. Real income is mainly driven by own shocks, while real money supply becomes important in the medium run. For the exchange rate, own shocks are dominant in the short run, supported by capital flows and money supply movement; shocks on real money supply and real income become the second and third most important shocks after own shocks in the medium run, explaining 25 and 18 percent, respectively.

Impulse responses are reported in Figure 4.1. An increase in capital inflow appreciates the domestic currency and, with some delay, raises real income. An increase in the current account appears to have qualitatively similar effects on real income and the domestic currency. Depreciation of the yen generates an inflationary pressure as indicated by rising relative price and declining real money supply. With some delay of a few quarters, it also significantly improves the current account. Rather surprisingly, however, yen depreciation seems to give contractionary effects on real income, albeit insignificant.

Table 4.3 Variance decompositions

Japan

	ε^{KAR}		ε^{RY}		ε^{RCP}		ε^{MR}		ε_t^{CAR}		ε^{NX}	
	(4)	(24)	(4)	(24)	(4)	(24)	(4)	(24)	(4)	(24)	(4)	(24)
KAR	69.3	45.4	2.6	8.0	2.7	3.3	18.8	32.1	0.7	5.6	5.8	5.5
RY	3.7	4.2	77.7	51.5	2.6	1.6	11.2	33.9	1.2	7.1	3.7	1.7
RP	0.8	0.8	1.0	13.0	85.7	55.1	1.5	4.1	3.3	4.9	7.8	22.1
RM	0.1	2.1	0.5	41.3	1.3	1.6	95.9	44.2	0.5	8.8	1.7	2.0
CAR	1.9	1.2	0.7	4.1	13.3	8.8	4.2	25.0	78.4	48.0	1.5	13.0
NX	11.7	7.3	0.5	18.9	0.6	0.6	14.9	25.4	1.9	5.9	70.3	41.8

China (Quarterly data)

	ε^{KAR}		ε^{RY}		ε^{RCP}		ε^{MR}		ε_t^{CAR}		ε^{NX}	
	(4)	(24)	(4)	(24)	(4)	(24)	(4)	(24)	(4)	(24)	(4)	(24)
KAR	53.6	7.6	9.8	5.1	3.0	35.1	4.4	5.3	2.3	46.3	26.9	0.5
RY	19.1	6.9	72.7	6.4	0.7	37.6	6.7	5.4	0.2	42.6	0.7	1.0
RP	3.5	7.0	18.6	5.2	46.5	36.5	6.8	5.3	13.5	45.8	11.1	0.3
RM	8.1	7.4	6.5	4.8	30.9	33.0	13.2	5.1	36.5	49.6	4.9	0.2
CAR	22.2	8.9	10.4	5.3	1.4	29.7	9.8	5.4	38.1	48.7	18.1	2.0
NX	2.5	6.7	0.5	5.4	8.1	37.9	0.4	5.3	3.9	43.7	84.7	0.9

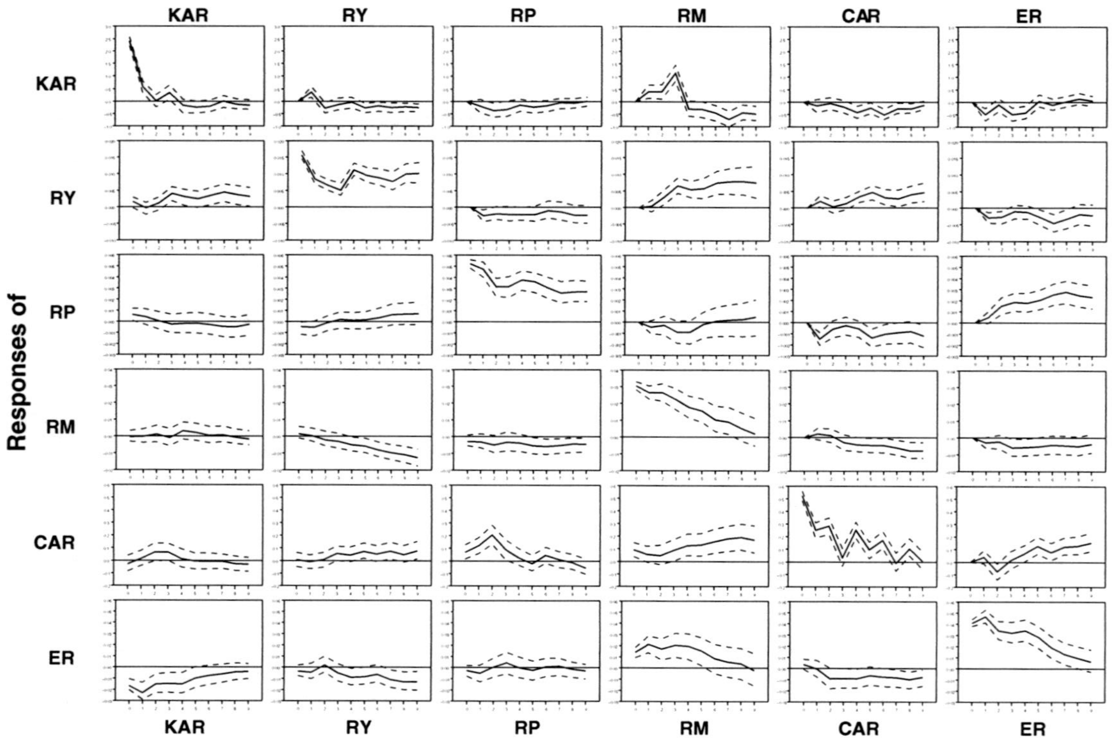

Note: Point estimates of the impulse responses are bounded by one standard deviation band on either side, which is obtained by Monte Carlo simulation with 2000 draws.

Figure 4.1 Impulse responses: Japan

4.3.2 China

For China, most relevant quarterly data are available only from 1999Q1 to 2009Q4. We thus estimate the same model using annual data, which are available from 1982 to 2009. Due to the small sample, the quarterly model is estimated with two lags.[9] The main results are as follows: Table 4.2 shows that, with the annual data, the capital account Granger-causes the current account in the negative direction (with the p-value at 6.5 percent). Thus an inflow induces a deficit on the current account. However, Granger causality in the opposite direction is not significant. With the quarterly data, Granger causality is significant in neither direction at the conventional significance level. These results suggest that over the long haul, the capital flows–current account relationship in China appears similar to those of other emerging market economies in which capital flows drive the current account instead of passively financing current account surpluses or deficits.[10] Over the last decade employed in the quarterly data, however, the two are only insignificantly related, perhaps due to the existence of capital controls.

For the rest, we focus on the quarterly data. Table 4.3 reports variance decomposition. Capital flows in China are mostly explained by own innovations and exchange rate changes in the short run, but the relative price ratio and the current account become more important in the medium run. Other variables are insignificant.[11] For real income, own shocks (presumably reflecting productivity growth) are dominant in the short run while shocks to the relative price ratio and the current account are surprisingly important, explaining 38 percent and 43 percent, respectively, in the medium run. Capital flows appear only marginally important in the determination of real income. For the current account, other than own shocks, capital flows and nominal exchange rate movement are important determinants in the short run. For the nominal exchange rate, other than own shocks, the current account and relative price movement plays a significant role in the medium run.

Panels of Figure 4.2 show impulse responses for China. Reflecting the small size of the sample, most responses are insignificant. An increase in the capital account has little or no effect on real income. The capital inflow also raises money supply. The current account balance seems to improve in the short run. The exchange rate is little affected by capital flows, however.

The effects of exchange rate changes are somewhat surprising. Real money supply and relative price decline insignificantly, along with lagged increases in capital inflows. Currency depreciation has a small positive effect on the current account only in the short run, and reverses within two or three quarters. More surprisingly, real income also declines, reversing

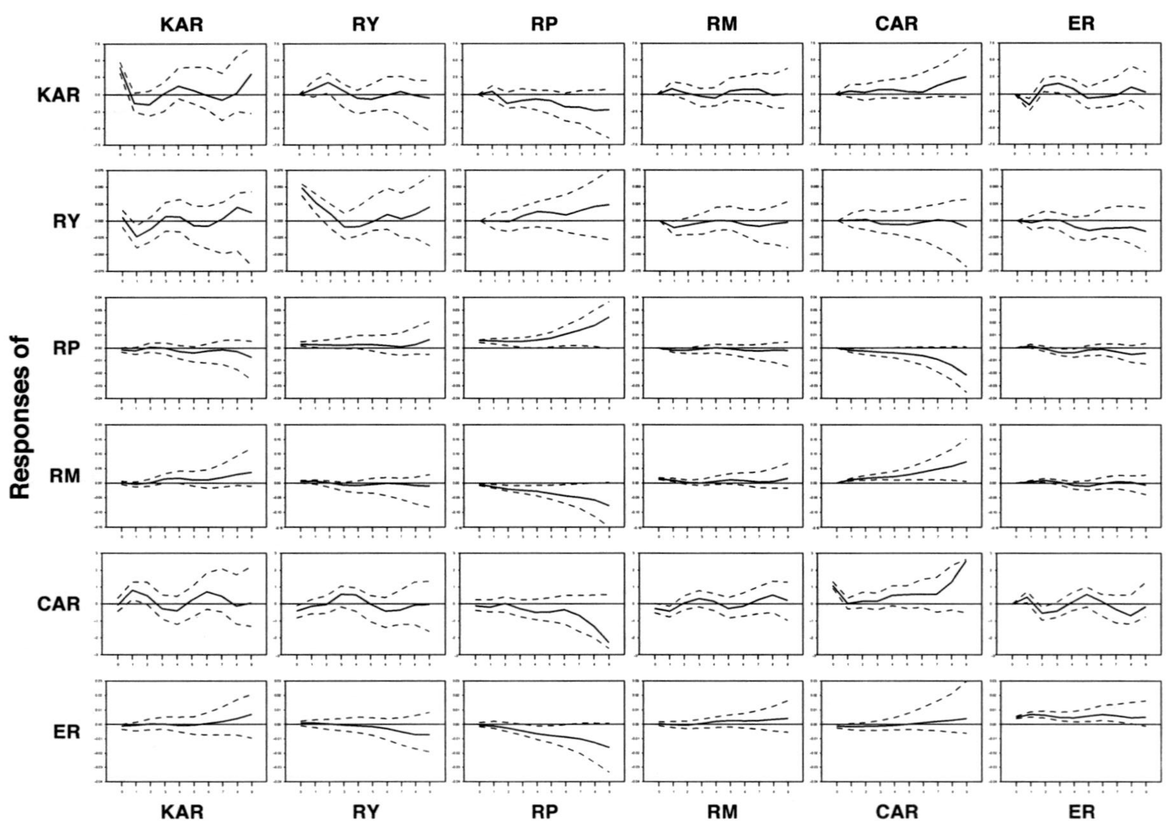

Figure 4.2 Impulse responses: China

small initial increases within two or three quarters.[12] This means that an RMB appreciation would in fact give expansionary effects on the Chinese economy, contrary to the position taken by China's government. It is important to note, however, that all these effects of exchange rate changes are statistically insignificant. Drawing strong conclusions with limited data seems inappropriate.

4.4 CONCLUDING REMARKS

China has been under tremendous pressure to appreciate its currency and move to a floating exchange rate regime. Many argue that the renminbi is undervalued and causes huge imbalances in the current account balances with the United States. China has been resisting the pressure to change its own exchange rate policy on the grounds that RMB appreciation will handicap its crucial export sector and create a host of economic problems, including worsening the unemployment problem in the rural sector and reducing economic growth. The Japanese experience of prolonged appreciation and decades-long recession has often been invoked as a reason for the resistance. The heated contention between the United States and China has pushed the world economy into a situation of competitive devaluations or 'currency wars' among many developed and emerging market economies.

In this chapter, we have briefly reviewed the ongoing debates. Existing studies show a bewildering array of estimates of RMB undervaluation or even overvaluation. Recommendations for the desirable exchange rate in China appear to be equally confusing too. Against this backdrop, we have presented empirical evidence that shows some important differences between the experiences of Japan and China. Currency appreciation in Japan appears to reduce current account surpluses, and induces deflationary pressure with falling prices. However, there is little evidence that real income falls with yen appreciation. On the other hand, RMB appreciation is not likely to have any significant effects on the current account balance. The effects on income are not significant either. If anything, a RMB appreciation may in fact induce some increase in real income. The results imply that pressuring China to undertake RMB appreciation for the purpose of current account adjustment is ill guided. At the same time, rejecting the external pressure on the grounds of avoiding Japan-like experience is not supported by the data.

Of course, some caveats are in order. The sample period for Chinese data is perhaps too short to be used in a VAR model. Consequently, most estimates are statistically insignificant as a result of the small sample problem. Moreover, given the strong possibility of structural breaks due to regime changes and rapid growth in a transition economy, one must exercise due caution in interpreting the results.

What do the empirical results show? Both sides of the debate have little empirical support at the crucial point. A more flexible stance is warranted on both sides. The results raise serious doubts as to the claims of both sides. Would currency appreciation work as the cure for global imbalance, as argued by many economists and the US government? Our empirical results suggest that RMB appreciation would not induce a recession in China. However, there is no evidence that the current account surplus would decline with currency appreciation. If the sole basis of recommending currency appreciation for China is to reduce the surplus on the current account, we may be disappointed with the outcome.

Policymakers in an open economy face three mutually inconsistent objectives: (1) monetary policy independence to stabilize the economy; (2) stable or fixed exchange rate; (3) an open capital account to benefit from international capital mobility. Faced with the trilemma, major industrial countries have given up objective (2) and moved to adopt floating exchange rates. This was not the universal choice: 16 European countries have decided to forgo monetary policy independence and become part of the euro zone. Among emerging market economies, exchange rate regimes are even more diverse. Unlike the stark choices suggested by the trilemma hypothesis, many countries are still in the gray zone called the 'intermediate regimes'. This is despite the dire prediction made by Stanley Fischer (2001) in the aftermath of the Asian financial crisis in 1997.

It is well known that China has adopted a unique policy combination. It has chosen to impose capital controls as a solution to the trilemma, while keeping monetary policy independence and exchange rate stability. The choice was made as early as 1994 (or perhaps even before that), when China did not even face the issue of the current account surplus. One should remember that China's decision to keep its exchange rate against the US dollar during the 1997 Asian financial crisis provided much-needed stability to the regional currencies and helped the world economy to get out of the crisis more quickly than expected. Also, it is increasingly admitted that unregulated capital movements have caused numerous financial crises around the world. Capital controls may be leaky and ineffective. However, they may be a lesser evil than free floating with unregulated capital flows. The global financial crisis of 2008 shows that no country, developed or developing, can be free from the hazards of unregulated capital flows.

China has maintained a fixed or heavily managed exchange rate in the past two decades. The de facto peg to the US dollar has served China well as it provided an anchor for its monetary policy. China's choice regarding the trilemma may have been a wise one. China's recent monetary history clearly shows bouts of double-digit inflation. It is not certain whether an inflation-targeting framework would have worked equally well in China. Wei (2007) suggests that China's monetary policy still has room for maneuver. China's capital controls are binding at the margin. China's fiscal policy also still has room for maneuver. State-owned firms collectively are making profits that are not currently counted in the government budget. The state could require these firms to pay up more dividends to augment exiting fiscal management tools.[13]

The world and economic science are full of uncertainties. Exchange rate economics has long been known for its inability to explain and forecast exchange rate movement. It is no wonder that economists cannot agree on the extent or even the existence of RMB undervaluation. We are not certain whether greater flexibility will promote the external adjustment for China. 'China bashing' must stop, as the world economy may have more to lose than to gain. It creates the expectation of currency appreciation for the RMB. In an environment with near zero world interest rates, China faces acute pressure to liberalize capital flows and float the currency. Instead of quarreling over an unsolvable problem of the equilibrium exchange rate issue, we can start with something we can address, or things we agree on. To be sustainable, the global economy needs some major adjustment or rebalancing. On the part of the US, a substantial reduction in fiscal deficits would be necessary. For China, structural adjustment to increase household consumption is called for. These would be some of the more productive approaches to solving the problem of the global imbalances.

NOTES

1. Frankel (2006) also offers a similar list of reasons why it is in China's interest to allow greater flexibility of the RMB. They are: (i) overheating of the economy; (ii) excessive reserve accumulation; (iii) long-run need to use the exchange rate for expenditure-switching; (iv) avoiding future crashes; (v) low price level by international standards.
2. On the other hand, those who dispute the undervaluation arguments argue that US current account deficits and China's surpluses are structural and induced by such factors as large fiscal deficits in the US and high Chinese savings rate. The latter is due to funding needs for education and health care, the absence of a sound social security system and social safety network, and an underdeveloped credit market.
3. We omit the estimates based on another popular methodology called the behavioral equilibrium exchange rate (BEER). These models incorporate a variety of channels

through which the real exchange can be related to other macroeconomic variables. Since each author selects different variables to include, the implied misalignments will necessarily vary. See Dunaway et al. (2009).

4. Eichengreen and Rose (2010) find, however, weak evidence for a deceleration in economic growth from relatively high levels: 'The average annual growth rate falls by roughly a percentage point between the five years before and after the policy event' (p. 2). They also add that as long as China moves gradually with currency appreciation, it need not worry about a crash.
5. We use the fitted value of GDP obtained from a regression of the nominal GDP (seasonally adjusted) to a linear trend. The financial account of the balance of payments consists of direct investment abroad, direct investment, portfolio investment assets, portfolio investment liability, financial derivatives assets, financial derivatives liabilities, and other investment assets and liability.
6. See Calvo et al. (1996), Kamin and Rogers (2000) and Kim (2000).
7. In other words, innovations on the capital account have contemporaneous effects on the other endogenous variables in the system, but innovations from the other variables have no contemporaneous effects on the capital account.
8. Kim and Ying (2001) also show that a change in the US real GDP and the interest rates explain more than 50 percent of capital inflows to Korea and Mexico.
9. With four lags, estimation fails due to too few degrees of freedom. Seasonal factors are added to address strong seasonality in real income.
10. See Kim and Ying (2007) for similar findings.
11. With annual data, real income becomes gradually more important, suggesting that capital inflows are induced by long-term growth potential of the country.
12. Although the contractionary effect of currency depreciation is surprising in the context of the RMB debate, it is frequently observed in developing countries. See Kim and Ying (2007) and Shi (2006) for more about this.
13. Wei (2007) admits that the benefits of moving to a more flexible exchange rate regime likely outweigh the costs for China. Still, China faces many challenges such as rising income inequality, pervasive corruption and the threat of massive unemployment. How much priority this particular reform of the exchange rate regime shift should be given is in doubt.

REFERENCES

Calvo, Guillermo A., Leonardo Leiderman and Carmen M. Reinhart (1996), 'Inflows of Capital to Developing Countries in the 1990s', *Journal of Economic Perspectives*, **10**(2), 123–39.

Cheung, Yin-Wong, Menzie Chinn and Eiji Fujii (2007), 'The Overvaluation of Renminbi Undervaluation', *Journal of International Money and Finance*, **26**(5), 762–5.

Cheung, Yin-Wong, Menzie Chinn and Eiji Fujii (2009), 'Pitfalls in Measuring Exchange Rate Misalignment: The Yuan and Other Currencies', *Open Economies Review*, **20**(2), 183–206.

Cheung, Yin-Wong, Menzie Chinn and Eiji Fuji (2010), 'Measuring Misalignment: Latest Estimates for the Chinese Yuan', in S. Evenett (ed.), *The US–Sino Currency Dispute: New Insights from Economics, Politics and Law*, A VoxEu.org publication, pp. 79–90.

Chinn, Menzie and Shang-Jin Wei (forthcoming), 'A Faith-based Initiative Meets the Evidence: Does a Flexible Exchange Rate Regime Really Facilitate Current Account Adjustment?' *Review of Economics and Statistics*.

Cline, William and John Williamson (2010), 'Estimates of Fundamental Equilibrium Exchange Rates, May 2010', Washington, DC: Peterson Institute for International Economics.
Coudert, Virginie and Cécile Couharde (2005), 'Real Equilibrium Exchange Rate in China', CEPII Working Paper, 2005-01.
Dunaway, Steven Vincent, Lamin Leigh, and Xiangming Li (2009), 'How Robust are Estimates of Equilibrium Real Exchange Rates: The Case of China', IMF Working Paper, 6(220), Washington, DC: IMF.
Eichengreen, Barry and Andrew Rose (2010), '27 Up: The Implications for China of Abandoning its Dollar Peg', UC Berkeley, Mimeo.
Fischer, Stanley (2001), 'Exchange Rate Regimes: Is the Bipolar View Correct?' *Journal of Economic Perspectives*, **15**(Spring), 3–24.
Frankel, Jeffrey (2006), 'On the Yuan: The Choice Between Adjustment Under a Fixed Exchange Rate and Adjustment under a Flexible Rate', in Gerhard Illing (ed.), *Understanding the Chinese Economy*, Oxford University Press, pp. 246–75.
Frankel, Jeffrey (2009), 'New Estimation of China's Exchange Rate Regime', *Pacific Economic Review*, **14**(3), 346–60.
Funke, Michael and Jörg Rahn (2005), 'Just how Undervalued is the Chinese Renminbi?' *World Economy*, **28**, 465–89.
Garton, Phil and Jennifer Chang (2005), 'The Chinese Currency: How Undervalued And How Much Does It Matter?' *Economic Roundup*, Spring, 83–109.
Goldstein, Morris and Nicholas R. Lardy (2009), *The Future of China's Exchange Rate Policy*, Washington, DC: Peterson Institute for International Economics.
Government Accountability Office (GAO) (2005), 'International Trade: Treasury Assessments Have Not Found Currency Manipulation, but Concerns about Exchange Rates Continue', *Report to Congressional Committees* GAO-05-351, Washington, DC: Government Accountability Office, April.
Kamin, Steve B. and John H. Rogers (2000), 'Output and the Real Exchange Rate in Developing Countries: An Application to Mexico', *Journal of Development Economics*, **61**, 85–109.
Kim, S. and N. Roubini (2000), 'Exchange Rate Anomalies in the Industrial Countries: A Solution with a Structural VAR Approach', *Journal of Monetary Economics*, **45**(3), 561–86.
Kim, Yoonbai (2000), 'Causes of Capital Flows in Developing Countries', *Journal of International Money and Finance*, **19**, 235–53.
Kim, Yoonbai and Yung-Hsiang Ying (2001), 'An Empirical Analysis on Capital Flows: The Case of Korea and Mexico', *Southern Economic Journal*, **67**(4), 954–68.
Kim, Yoonbai and Yung-Hsiang Ying (2007), 'An Empirical Assessment of Currency Devaluation in East Asian Countries', *Journal of International Money and Finance*, **26**, 265–83.
McKinnon, Ronald (2007), 'Why China Should Keep Its Dollar Peg', *International Finance*, **10**(1), 43–70.
McKinnon, Ronald (2009), 'The Case for Stabilizing China's Exchange Rate: Setting the Stage for Fiscal Expansion', *China and World Economy*, **17**(1), 1–32.
Roubini, Nouriel (2007), 'Why China Should Abandon Its Dollar Peg', *International Finance*, **10**(1), 71–89.

Shi, Jianhuai (2006), 'Are Currency Appreciations Contractionary in China?', NBER Working Paper, 12551.

Subramanian, Arvind (2010), *New PPP-Based Estimates of Renminbi Undervaluation and Policy Implications*, Policy Brief 10-8, Washington, DC: Peterson Institute for International Economics.

Wei, Shang-Jin (2007), 'Don't Over-sell the Benefits of a Change in the Chinese Exchange-Rate Policy', available at www.voxeu.org/index.php?q=node/675.

5. Weathering the financial storms: the government of China

Jing Ma and Lihui Tian*

5.1 INTRODUCTION

Since 1978, when the economic reforms were taken, China's gross domestic product (GDP) has grown ten times. In 2011, the GDP of China was $8.789 trillion based on purchasing power parity, and China ranked at number two in GDP in the world, although the GDP per capita of China was $6600 which comes under the lower-middle-income group. In 2007, the growth rate of the country was as high as 13 percent. The rapidly growing economy of China is now facing certain issues which may hinder its economic growth, including the increase in unemployment, economic corruption, environmental damage, lack of arable land and a rapidly aging population. In spite of these challenges, there are severe external shocks to China's economic development.

Indeed, the global financial crisis has slowed China's economy considerably. In the final quarter of 2008, the Chinese economy registered one of its slowest growth rates, of 6.8 percent. However, by comparing China's GDP growth with other Asian economies, China's economy holds up well despite being badly hit by the financial crisis. China's impressive economic performance during the 1997 regional financial crises and the 2008 American financial storm was not achieved easily. Besides the sound fundamentals of China, we argue that the active role played by the government in managing economic activities and effective government intervention has helped China to weather the global crisis.

5.2 FREE MARKET VERSUS GOVERNMENT INTERVENTION

Formulated at the time of the Latin American debt crisis in 1980s, the Washington Consensus promotes the retreat of government intervention in economic activities, including privatization of state enterprises, trade liberalization, financial liberalization and deregulation, depreciation of the exchange rate, reduction of government spending, macroeconomic stabilization and institutional reform for better protection of property rights. During the 1997 Asian financial crisis, this Consensus was subject to heavy criticism, particularly when the International Monetary Fund (IMF) asked the Thai government to cut government expenditures and tighten monetary policies. However, the problem of Asia's fall in 1997 is mainly attributed to the twisted government–business relationship at the firm level (World Bank, 2001). It is argued that the problem was not derived from the global free capital markets, but from political interference with that free flow of funds. Such government interference was derisively branded as 'crony capitalism' or 'moral hazard'. At the heart of the Washington Consensus is the ideology of the free market.

Indeed, the neoclassical economists as well as the mainstream of economics argue that free markets are efficient and can promote growth everywhere (for example Hayek, 1952 [2010]; Friedman, 2002; Plant, 2009). They propose the best path of economic development to be trade and financial liberalization with market opening at the macro level, and privatization of state-owned enterprises at the micro level. Advanced technology and global capital come with market opening. A vast literature exists on the imperfections of government in allocating resources. Sappington and Stiglitz (1987) further initiate the application of the theory of incentives to privatization issues. They argue that the main difference between private and public firms centers on the ease of government intervention in firms' production activities, and that government intervention results in inefficiency and corruptions. Although Arrow (1962) contended that free-enterprise economies underinvest in research and invention because of their aversion to risk, and that markets are not perfect aggregators of information (Grossman and Stiglitz, 1976), Demsetz (1969) argues that government institutions are worse than the market.

On the other hand, the economists of dependence schools argue that the government needs actively to forge policies and shape market forces in order to promote economic growth (Wallerstein, 1979; Johnson, 1994, 2010). Keynes advocates government interventions in the advanced countries (Hayes, 2008). Gerschenkron (1962) emphasizes the role of the state in substituting for the market in backward countries trying to catch up. The government may be helpful when there are market failures with externalities, information asymmetry and cases of natural monopoly. The economists of dependence schools view economic development as a process of dynamic, non-marginal change, and contend that the market mechanism cannot be relied upon to guide the investment process. More importantly, the market is subject to crashing when global capital flows out in a very short time frame. With the stronger influence of global capital, the role of the government becomes rather complicated.

In its policy research report on the East Asian miracle, the World Bank (1993) acknowledges the frequent occurrences of sectoral intervention in the East Asian growth processes, even though it tries to argue that industrial policy was not effective. It concedes by saying that government intervention was not harmful, though still not helpful. Besides getting the fundamentals right, should government selectively intervene in economic activities, particularly when there is a financial crisis?

5.3 INTERNATIONAL TRADE, FOREIGN INVESTMENT AND CHINA'S ECONOMIC GROWTH

China is the world's fastest-growing major economy, with average growth rates of 10 percent for the past 30 years. China's growth comes from huge state investment in infrastructure and heavy industry, from private sector expansion in light industry, and from exports. Similar to other Asian economies, the Chinese economy has grown fast with an accumulation of physical and human capital, technological progress through international technology spillovers and domestic research, and the construction of infrastructure. Different from some Latin American countries in previous decades, the Chinese government remains a strong government, tightly controlling the monetary and fiscal tools and owning many large firms. Although the economic planning system has been abolished and the economic market system has been installed, the government heavily and frequently intervenes in economic activities.[1]

After its three-decade reform and opening-up. China's economy is rather globalized. As a major factor of openness, international trade has made an increasingly significant contribution to economic growth. Chinese international trade has experienced rapid expansion together with dramatic economic growth, which has made the country target the world as its market. In fact, China's foreign trade has grown, on average, faster than its GDP between 1984 and 2009, and it became the second-largest trading nation in the world, and the largest exporter and second-largest importer of goods, in 2009 (see Table 5.1). As its role in world trade has steadily grown, international trade is playing a significant role in China's economic growth. China's exports of goods and services as a share of GDP rose from 9.1 percent in 1985 to 37.8 percent in 2008, and its net exports contributed to one-third of its GDP growth in 2008. The Chinese

Table 5.1 Economic growth, international trade and foreign investment

	GDP index	GDP per capita index	Total volume of international trade	Total volume of exports	Total volume of foreign investment
1993	114	112.7	123.6	113	122.9
1994	113.1	111.8	180.8	197.2	110.9
1995	110.9	109.7	115.3	119.5	111.4
1996	110	108.9	102.7	101	113.9
1997	109.3	108.2	111.7	120.5	117.5
1998	107.8	106.8	99.6	100.4	90.9
1999	107.6	106.7	111.3	106.1	89.9
2000	108.4	107.6	131.4	127.7	112.7
2001	108.3	107.5	107.4	106.7	83.7
2002	109.1	108.4	121.8	122.4	110.7
2003	110	109.3	137.2	134.7	102.1
2004	110.1	109.4	135.5	135.3	114.1
2005	111.3	110.7	122.4	127.6	99.6
2006	112.7	112	120.6	123.9	105.1
2007	114.2	113.6	118.3	120.4	116.8
2008	109.6	109.1	107.9	107.4	121.6
2009	109.1	108.6	83.7	81.7	96.4

Note: This table reports the growth of China's GDP, GDP per capita, total volume of international trade, total volume of export and total volume of foreign investment. After adjusting for inflation, we compare the number of the current year with the last year, which means the numbers of last year are taken as 100.

Source: National Bureau of Statistics of China.

government estimates that the foreign trade sector employs more than 80 million people, of which 28 million work in foreign-invested enterprises. The consequence of this deep linkage to the foreign economies is that any large external shock would inevitably have a tremendous negative impact on China's economic growth.

China's economy is heavily dependent both on global trade and on investment flows. Foreign investment flows to China have been a major factor behind its productivity gains and rapid economic growth. As shown in Table 5.1, the growth of foreign investment is generally faster than the GDP growth. Foreign direct investment (FDI) flows to China in 2007 totaled $75 billion, making it the largest FDI recipient among developing countries and the third-largest overall, after the European Union (EU) and the United States (US).

The 1997 Asian financial crisis and the 2008 US financial storm resulted in regional and global economic slowdown, respectively, and the exports of China and foreign investment in China have plummeted sharply. In 1998, the growth rate of export was 0.4 percent, compared with 20.5 percent in 1997; and the growth rate of foreign investment was negative at −9.1 percent, compared with 17.5 percent in 1997. The GDP growth was 10 percent in 1996, 9.3 percent in 1997 and 7.8 percent in 1998. The aftermath of the 2008 American financial storm is more significant, with export growth dropping from 7.4 percent in 2008 to −18.3 percent in 2009, and with growth of foreign investment dropping from 21.6 percent to −3.6 percent.[2] The shocks from the reduction in exports and foreign investment are significant, but China's GDP growth was 14.2 percent in 2007, 9.6 percent in 2008 and 9.1 percent in 2009.

In recent years, China's capital markets have developed fast, particularly its stock market (see Table 5.2). The number of public listed firms grew from 53 in 1992 to 1718 at the end of 2009, and the number of share trading accounts grew from 2.3 million in 1992 to 17.2 million in 2009. The market capitalization was 3.9 percent of total GDP in 1992, 22.2 percent in 1997, 123.1 percent in 2007 and 71.6 percent at the end of 2009. The stock market plays an important role in China's economy, and external financial crises can have an influence on China through the contagion of stock markets. In fact, the market index of the Shanghai Stock Exchange decreased by 3.9 percent year on year in 1998, and by 65.4 percent in 2008.

Consequently, the real estate market in several Chinese cities has exhibited signs of a bursting bubble, including a slowdown in construction, falling prices and growing numbers of unoccupied buildings. This has increased pressure on the banks to lower interest rates further to stabilize the market. In addition, the current crisis has greatly shrunk external demand, which has resulted in the closure of thousands of factories and a rise in unemployment, especially in developed coastal areas. The Chinese government in January 2009 estimated that 20 million migrant workers had lost their jobs in 2008 because of the global economic slowdown. According to an official survey on the confidence of investors and senior management of enterprises conducted in the fourth quarter of 2008, the index of business confidence was 30 percent lower than in the previous quarter.

In summary, China did suffer from the regional and global financial crises significantly, but we argue that China managed to go through the crises rather well, with a strong government. In the following section, we discuss the role of government in weathering the financial storms.

Table 5.2 China's capital markets

	Issuance of public debt	Issuance of corporate bond	Trade volume of bonds	Trade volume of futures	Issuance of common stock	Trade volume of common stock	Shanghai Stock Market Index	Shenzhen Stock Market Index
1992	46.1	68.4			9.4	68.1	780	241
1993	38.1	23.6			37.5	362.7	834	238
1994	113.8	16.2			32.7	812.8	648	141
1995	151.1	30.1			15	403.6	555	113
1996	184.8	26.9	1803.9	8411.9	42.5	2133.2	917	327
1997	241.2	25.5	1647.7	6117.1	129.4	3072.2	1194	381
1998	380.9	14.8	2166.2	3696.7	84.2	2354.4	1147	344
1999	401.5	15.8	1828.4	2234.3	94.5	3132	1367	402
2000	465.7	8.3	1911.9	1608.2	210.3	6082.7	2073.5	635.7
2001	488.4	14.7	2041.8	3014.5	125.2	3830.5	1646	475.9
2002	593.4	32.5	3325	3949	96.2	2799	1357.7	388.8
2003	628	35.8	6213.6	10839.7	135.8	3211.5	1497	378.6
2004	692.4	32.7	5032.4	14693.5	151.1	4233.4	1266.5	315.8
2005	704.2	204.7	2836.8	13446.3	188.3	3166.5	1161.1	278.8
2006	888.3	393.8	1827.9	21006.3	559.4	9046.9	2675.5	550.6
2007	2313.9	505.9	2066.7	40974.1	868	46055.6	5261.6	1447
2008	855.8	843.5	2860.1	71917.3	385.2	26711.3	1820.8	553.3
2009	1792.7	1586.4	4005.9	130514.3	496.8	53598.7	3277.1	1201.3

Note: This table reports the development of China's stock market. The numbers of issuance of public debt, issuance of corporate bond, trade volume of bonds, trade volume of futures, issuance of common stock and trade volume of common stock are in billions of Chinese yuan (renminbi).

Source: National Bureau of Statistics of China.

5.4 KEYNESIANISM AND GOVERNMENT INTERVENTION

Keynesian economics argues that private sector decisions sometimes lead to inefficient macroeconomic outcomes, and therefore advocates active policy responses by the public sector, including monetary policy actions by the central bank and fiscal policy actions by the government, to stabilize output over the business cycle. Keynes further contended that during economic downturns, aggregate demand for goods might be insufficient. Therefore, government policies could be used to increase aggregate demand, thus increasing economic activity and reducing unemployment and deflation. Likewise, during economic overheating, government policies could be used to eliminate inflation to balance and stabilize the economy.

Following Keynes, China has responded to the 2008 US financial storm on a number of fronts, quickly and effectively.[3] On 8 October 2008, China's central bank announced plans to cut interest rates and the reserve requirement ratio in order to help stimulate the economy. On 21 October, China's State Council announced a new economic stimulus package, which would include an acceleration of construction projects, new export tax rebates, a reduction in the housing transaction tax, increased agriculture subsidies, and expanded lending to small and medium-sized enterprises. This stimulus package was confirmed as a two-year, 4 trillion yuan one (about US$586 billion) on 9 November. Table 5.3 reports the distributions of the government fund, which is mainly dedicated to infrastructure

Table 5.3 Components of the fiscal-stimulus package

Item	Amount (RMB bn)	Share (%)
Transportation and power grids	1800	45
Post-earthquake reconstruction	1000	25
Rural infrastructure	370	9.25
Environment projects	350	8.75
Public housing	280	7
R&D	160	4
Healthcare and education	40	1
Total	4000	100

Note: This table reports the distribution of the 4 trillion yuan fiscal stimulus package, made by the Chinese government in 2008. The numbers are in billions of Chinese yuan (renminbi).

Source: National Bureau of Statistics of China.

and infrastructure-related projects. The package finances programs in ten major areas, including affordable housing, rural infrastructure, water, electricity, transport, the environment, technological innovation and rebuilding areas hit by disasters. This is the typical approach of Keynesianism, to extend domestic demand and stimulate the domestic market by increasing infrastructure projects.

The Keynesian economists argue that fiscal stimulus increases the market for business output, raising cash flow and profitability, and spurring business optimism. To Keynes, this accelerator effect means that government and business could be complements rather than substitutes in this situation. Government spending on such things as basic research, public health, education and infrastructure could help the long-term growth of potential output. The $586 billion economic stimulus spending package includes developing infrastructure projects as a means of sustaining the Chinese economy. As shown in Table 5.3, the government budget is 7.6 trillion yuan, up 22.1 percent from the previous year, and the budget deficit is about 8.6 times the 2008 budget deficit, although it is merely 3 percent of GDP.

China also made important adjustments to relax its monetary conditions. Some of these measures include cutting interest rates and lifting lending limits on commercial banks. The lending rates were adjusted quite significantly downwards from 7.2 percent to 5.6 percent from August 2008 to November 2008. The lending rate was further revised to 5.3 percent in December 2008. Similarly, the central bank also cut half a percentage point on the reserve requirement ratio for banks from an all-time high of 16.5 percent to 16 percent in December 2008. As shown in Table 5.4, the money supply increased quickly. In December 2008 and January 2009, China's money supply registered its highest year-on-year percentage changes since May 2008, of 17.9 percent and 18.8 percent, respectively. In addition, the massive foreign reserves and favorable trade surplus also allow China to maintain the stability of its currency, both of which are important monetary factors for China to maintain the competitiveness of its economy and its attractiveness to FDI inflow. China made use of the macroeconomic tools aggressively and reinforced the domestic market as a way to fend off the global reverberations from the economic downturn under Keynesianism.

5.5 GOVERNMENT OWNERSHIP OF BANKS AND FIRMS

Indeed, besides the opening of foreign trade and investment in China, the rapid growth of the non-state sector and the foundation of a diversified

Table 5.4 Government deficits, investment of fixed assets and monetary supplies

	Fiscal deficits or surplus	Growth of fixed assets (%)	Growth of M2 (%)	Growth of M1 (%)
1993	−29.3	61.8	31.3	35.9
1994	−57.5	30.4	34.5	26.2
1995	−58.2	17.5	29.5	16.8
1996	−53.0	14.5	25.3	18.9
1997	−58.2	8.8	17.3	16.5
1998	−92.2	13.9	14.8	11.9
1999	−174.4	5.1	14.7	17.7
2000	−249.1	10.3	12.3	16.0
2001	−251.7	13.1	14.4	12.7
2002	−315.0	16.9	16.8	16.8
2003	−293.5	27.7	19.6	18.7
2004	−209.0	26.8	14.7	13.6
2005	−228.1	26.0	17.6	11.8
2006	−216.3	23.9	17.0	17.5
2007	70.7	24.8	16.7	21.1
2008	−20.2	25.9	17.8	9.1
2009	−778.2	30.0	27.7	32.4

Note: This table reports the national fiscal deficits (or surplus) with units as billions of Chinese yuan (RMB), the percentage growth of investment of fixed assets, the percentage growth of M2 and the percentage growth of M1. Money supply definition 1 (M1) refers to the sum of legal tender notes and coins held by the public plus customers' demand deposits placed with licensed banks. Money supply definition 2 (M2) refers to the sum of M1 plus customers' savings and time deposits with licensed banks, plus negotiable certificates of deposits issued by licensed banks held by non-authorized institutions.

Source: National Bureau of Statistics of China.

banking system have benefited China's reform a great deal. However, the government still owns a large proportion of banks and firms, which allows it to intervene with economic activities at the micro level.

Meanwhile, the government is also the controlling shareholder of Chinese banks, which makes government monetary policies very effective. At a time when other economies remain pinched by the global credit crunch, China is awash in liquidity. As the government pushed banks to free up credit to hard-hit sectors of the economy, Chinese bank lending more than doubled in January 2009. New loans rose a record amount in January 2009 to 1.62 trillion yuan ($237 billion) from December 2008's 771.8 billion yuan, which was also a year-on-year increase of over 800 billion yuan or 104 percent, given the figure of bank lending as 814.1 billion yuan in January 2008. It means that banks lined up to provide funds to developers for the stimulus-package projects, which largely benefited cash-strapped domestic enterprises trying to stay afloat amid shrinking overseas demand and waning consumer confidence.

Although thousands of private companies closed down in 2008, the government responded with plans to expand the public sector to take up the slack caused by the global financial crisis. Due to career concerns, the managers of the state-controlled enterprises closely follow the instructions of the government (Tian and Estrin, 2008). For instance, the central government tightly controls 159 large state-owned enterprises (SOEs), and through these has provided key inputs from utilities, heavy industries and energy resources that has facilitated private sector growth and driven investment, the foundation of national growth. These firms have actively expanded their corporate operations and assist other firms even at the cost of profitability. They even use retained cash to purchase land in order to boost the real-estate market, even if their major operation has nothing to do with real-estate development. Therefore, China's corporate sector has turned bullish in a very short time, which is shown by an increase of 41 percent in China's Purchasing Management Index (PMI) in December 2008 (Table 5.5).[4] This has put a stop to the slide in the country's PMI index for the first time since May 2008. It has consequently resulted in boosting market confidence and raising aggregate demand.

5.6 SUMMARY

Despite going through the 1997 Asian financial crisis and the 2008 US financial storm, China has developed rather well during the past two decades. Indeed, these two crises have hit China quite hard, but China handled them better than other economies, with the active role of its government. China's government is reasonably rich, strong and powerful and it keeps intervening in economic activities in China, which is against the doctrine of Washington Consensus and neoliberal economics.

Indeed, China's economic growth in the last 30 years is the result of introducing more market-oriented economic policies. The rapidly growing private sector, and its role as a major player in the global economy, could not have been possible with China's centrally planned system. However, we argue that the Chinese government has significantly contributed to dealing with the external shocks from world financial markets, particularly

Table 5.5 FDI, investment and confidence in 2008

	Growth of actual foreign direct investment	Growth of fixed asset investment	Index of market confidence	Purchase management index
Jan-08	109.78	24.30	102.59	53.00
Feb-08	75.19	24.30	102.60	53.40
Mar-08	61.25	25.90	102.48	58.40
Apr-08	59.32	25.70	103.31	59.20
May-08	54.96	25.60	103.43	53.30
Jun-08	45.55	26.80	103.53	52.00
Jul-08	44.54	27.30	102.84	48.40
Aug-08	41.60	27.40	101.99	48.40
Sep-08	39.85	27.60	100.75	51.20
Oct-08	35.06	27.20	99.01	44.60
Nov-08	26.29	26.80	97.80	38.80
Dec-08	29.67	26.10	97.11	41.20

Note: This table reports the monthly data of growth of actual foreign direct investment, growth of fixed asset investment, index of market confidence, and purchase management index. The data is compared with the corresponding month of 2007, after adjusting for inflation.

Source: National Bureau of Statistics of China.

with the stabilization of domestic stock markets, its real-estate policies and the promotion of confidence among producers and consumers. The evidence from China during market failures supports the theories of developmentalists on the active role of governments in economic development. Keynes still helps.

NOTES

* This research was financially supported by 'the Fundamental Research Funds for the Central Universities'.

1. China generally implements reforms in a gradualist fashion.
2. Exports in May 2009 were down 26.4 percent on a year-on-year basis, the biggest monthly decline ever recorded. FDI flows to China dropped by nearly a third in January 2009 (year-on-year basis).
3. On 27 September 2008, Chinese Premier Wen Jiabao reportedly stated in a speech that 'What we can do now is to maintain the steady and fast growth of the national economy and ensure that no major fluctuations will happen. That will be our greatest contribution to the world economy under the current circumstances' (Wen, 2008).
4. The Purchasing Management Index (PMI) measures new orders made by the manufacturing sector.

REFERENCES

Arrow, Kenneth (1962), 'Economic Welfare and the Allocation of Resources for Invention', *The Rate and Direction of Investment Activity: Economic and Social Factors*, Princeton, NJ: Princeton University Press, pp. 609–25.

Demsetz, Harold (1969), 'Information and Efficiency', *Journal of Law and Economics*, **12**(4), 1–21.

Friedman, Milton (2002), *Capitalism and Freedom*, Chicago, IL: University of Chicago Press.

Gerschenkron, A. (1962), *Economic Backwardness in Historical Perspective*, Cambridge, MA: Harvard University Press.

Grossman, Sanford J. and Joseph Stiglitz (1976), 'Information and Competitive Price Systems', *American Economic Review*, **66**(2), 246–53.

Hayek, Friedrich (1952 [2010]), *Studies on the Abuse and Decline of Reason: Text and Documents edited by Bruce Caldwell*, Chicago, IL: University of Chicago Press.

Hayes, M.G. (2008), *The Economics of Keynes: A New Guide to the General Theory*, Cheltenham, UK and Northampton, MA, USA: Edward Elgar Publishing.

Johnson, Chalmers A. (1994), *Japan: Who Governs?: The Rise of the Developmental State*, New York: Norton & Company Books.

Johnson, Chalmers Ashby (2010), *Dismantling the Empire: America's Last Best Hope*, New York: Metropolitan Books.

Plant, Raymond (2009), *The Neo-liberal State*, Oxford: Oxford University Press.

Sappington, D.E. and Joseph E. Stiglitz (1987), 'Privatization, Information, and Incentives', *Journal of Policy Analysis and Management*, **6**(4), 567–81.

Tian, Lihui and Saul Estrin (2008), 'Retained State Shareholding in Chinese PLCs: Does Government Ownership Always Reduce Corporate Value?' *Journal of Comparative Economics*, **36**(1), 74–89.

Wallerstein, Immanuel (1979), *The Capitalist World-Economy*, Cambridge: Cambridge University Press.

Wen, J. (2008), 'Reform and Opening up: The Eternal Driving Force for China's Development', available at: http://news.xinhuanet.com/english/2008-09/27/content10122832.htm.

World Bank (1993), *The East Asian Miracle: Economic Growth and Public Policy*, Oxford: Oxford University Press.

World Bank (2001), *Rethinking the East Asian Miracle*, Oxford: Oxford University Press.

6. The global financial crisis and its implications for East Asian financial integration

Pilhyun Kim

6.1 INTRODUCTION

A few years have passed since the subprime crisis in 2008, which later morphed into the biggest financial crisis in history, first started to grasp media headlines. And the global economy is still suffering from its aftermath, posting only anemic recoveries around the world. Among those countries affected by this crisis, the East Asian region stands out in a sense that it went through two major financial crises in just ten years. No other region has had a similar experience. People in East Asia collectively thought that they learned a valuable lesson from the 1997 crisis. This time around, they realized, to their grief, that the talk of financial integration thereafter did not really amount to anything. A greater need for financial cooperation by building closer economic and financial ties among the East Asian countries was recognized by all but was not appreciated truly enough to materialize into concrete policy measures. There are many reasons for this failure, that range from political unwillingness to economic imbalances. However, if anything, the current crisis brought to the surface that financial cooperation and integration in East Asia can no longer be put off until the time is perfectly right. It is essential that East Asia advances its integration and cooperation process in order to secure sustained economic growth. To this aim I review, in this chapter, what damage the current global financial crisis has wreaked on East Asia's economies and their prospects. Then I suggest policy measures to help avoid future catastrophes such as this.

6.2 THE IMMEDIATE AFTERMATH OF THE GLOBAL CRISIS

6.2.1 The Real Sector

The onset of the global financial crisis, symbolized by the Lehman Brothers' collapse, dealt a heavy blow to highly export-dependent East Asian economies, as Table 6.1 shows. A financial scare quickly translated into withdrawal of demand for their products. As a result, the exports of the East Asian countries began to show significant decline in the fourth quarter of 2008. Six months into the crisis, Korea posted a 22 percent decline in its export sector. Taiwan and Singapore experienced even more severe declines. Their exports declined by more than 30 percent in March 2009. China seemed an exception in the early stage of the crisis. However as the crisis propagated, it started to feel the strain and saw exports decrease in double digits in the first quarter of 2009. As exports declined, the amount of imports going into the region also dropped significantly. Part of this decline was due to a drop in the prices of raw materials, which comprise a large part of imports. However, it was mostly a result of shrinking domestic demand in the region.

Achieving economic growth through exporting has been a mixed blessing for the East Asian region. While it allowed countries in the region to take full advantage of rises in global demand when the global economy was sailing smoothly, it also made them particularly vulnerable to changes in the economic mood overseas. Since most of these economies are geared toward the export sector, even minor changes in global economic conditions could pose a serious challenge to them. The subprime crisis was a perfect storm for them. As the panic spread, uncertainties faced by the East Asian countries amplified. Consequently industrial production declined significantly in the region, as can be seen in Table 6.2. China was the only exception, although its industrial production growth fell from double digits to single. Also, Indonesia saw a relatively minor drop in its industrial production, as its external sector was comparatively small.

6.2.2 Financial Sector

The East Asian financial markets shared a similar experience. In 2007, East Asia posted a collective surplus of $100 billion on capital accounts. However, things started to change pretty quickly as the global financial crisis sent foreign investors scurrying for safer assets, causing the East Asian financial markets to tumble. As a result, East Asia's capital account suffered a $172 billion deficit in just a year. It is interesting to note that

Table 6.1 Trends in the trade sector of the East Asian economies during the sub-prime crisis (%)

	Export							Import						
	2008				2009			2008				2009		
	Sep.	Oct.	Nov.	Dec.	Jan.	Feb.	Mar.	Sep.	Oct.	Nov.	Dec.	Jan.	Feb.	Mar.
Korea	27.6	7.8	−19.5	−17.9	−34.2	−18.5	−22.0	42.8	29.6	11.3	−8.9	−22.9	−28.1	−32.9
China	21.5	19.2	−2.2	−2.8	−17.6	−25.8	−17.3	25.7	19.8	5.5	−9.1	−27.5	−29.7	−30.9
Japan	1.5	−7.8	−26.7	−35.0	−45.7	−49.4	−45.5	32.6	28.8	19.3	6.0	−8.1	−18.6	−29.3
Taiwan	−1.6	−8.3	−23.3	−41.9	−44.1	−28.6	−35.7	19.7	13.4	−3.5	−22.9	−39.6	−45.3	−47.2
Hong Kong	3.5	9.4	−4.9	−10.8	−21.3	−22.6	−21.5	6.9	5.6	2.5	−3.9	−16.5	−19.9	−22.4
Philippines	1.1	−14.8	−11.4	−40.3	−40.6	−39.1	−30.9	7.1	2.5	−13.5	−25.4	−33.3	−33.5	N/A
Malaysia	15.9	−6.8	−10.9	−20.1	−34.0	−15.9	−15.6	14.4	3.7	−4.4	−17.3	−26.3	−33.0	N/A
Singapore	17.7	−5.1	−15.5	−21.9	−40.4	−29.1	−32.7	32.9	19.3	6.9	−9.1	−22.8	−27.1	−32.5
Indonesia	28.5	4.9	−2.4	−20.6	−36.1	−32.9	−32.1	50.5	41.5	22.9	7.6	−13.9	−26.1	−34.1
Thailand	20.7	3.8	−21.0	−12.8	−28.3	−13.7	−20.6	39.8	28.8	20.2	6.05	−15.2	−29.2	−37.6
USA	7.6	4.1	−3.7	−13.8	−21.1	−23.8	−20.8	10.7	2.3	−15.7	−14.9	−26.9	−33.9	−88.9
EU	11.9	−7.7	−25.6	−15.7	30.4	−33.6	−29.0	11.8	−6.8	−24.1	−15.4	−30.0	−32.5	−29.2

Source: IMF, ADB, Bank of Korea.

Table 6.2 Responses of industrial production of East Asia to the sub-prime crisis (%)

	2008		2009		
	Nov.	Dec.	Jan.	Feb.	Mar.
Korea	−12.5	−21.2	−21.1	−15.2	−11.5
China	5.4	5.7	3.8	3.8	8.3
Japan	−15	−24.4	−30.2	−36.6	−34.2
Taiwan	−49	−50.2	−43.3	−27.2	−26
Singapore	−6.7	−13.3	−27.6	−15.1	−33.8
Philippines	−7.1	−15.4	−19.9	−21.1	N/A
Malaysia	−8.2	−15.6	−19.8	−14.6	−14.4
Indonesia	0.5	−3.9	−4.6	−2.4	N/A
Thailand	−7.7	−18.5	−21.1	−20.3	−15.4

Source: IMF, ADB, Bank of Korea, MITI.

other emerging markets did not experience similar events. The difference comes from short-term portfolio investment. In 2007, the emerging markets in Asia, Europe, Latin America, Africa and the Middle East collectively saw a net outflow of $8 billion from their portfolio investment accounts as can be seen in Figure 6.1. However, emerging Asian markets saw a net outflow of $35.7 billion from their portfolio investment accounts at the time, which means that only they experienced the net outflow. As a matter of fact the emerging markets excluding Asia experienced a net inflow of $28 billion in portfolio investments. The situation was similar in 2008, when the net outflow from the emerging Asian markets took up 61.3 percent of total net outflow from the emerging markets. The lopsided experience is largely due to the fact that foreign investors had already received a relatively high rate of return from their investments in East Asia by the time the crisis hit the world. Between 2002 and 2007, gains in the Korean, Chinese and Indonesian stocks were 204, 222 and 546 percent, respectively. Indeed the average gain in the major Asian stock markets was more than 200 percent.

The sudden and massive exodus of foreign capital from the East Asian financial markets sent the region's stock prices and currencies plunging despite the fact that the region's financial markets were least exposed to risks associated with the subprime mortgages in the US. Table 6.3 shows that stocks in China, Korea and Japan, the three biggest economies in the region, lost half of their value by March 2009 when compared to December 2007. Other countries shared a similar experience as investors' confidence

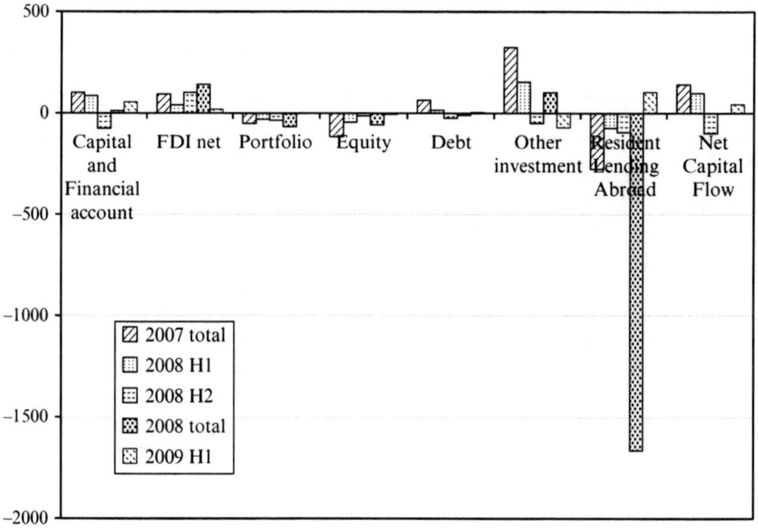

Notes:
H1: first half of year; H2: second half of year.
Includes NIEs and China, Indonesia, Malaysia, the Philippines and Thailand.

Source: World Bank.

Figure 6.1 Trends in capital accounts of the East Asian countries ($ billion)

was shattered by the global financial crisis. The bond markets in the region did not fare so well either. Bond issues in 2008 fell significantly in 2008. The net amount of bonds issued increased only by 15 percent, significantly lower than the average growth rate of 20.3 percent between 2005 and 2007. Corporate bonds issuance rose by 18 percent, but it merely reflects difficulties Asian firms had with raising funds in the international financial markets dominated by advanced countries.

What was more pressing for policymakers in the region was rapid depreciation of their currencies. To those who experienced the exchange rate markets turmoil translating into total collapse of their economies, it presented a truly grim prospect. Most major currencies in the region except the Japanese yen and Chinese yuan saw their values dropping precipitately. Among them, the Korean won saw the biggest drop in its value as its exchange rate against the US dollar fell by more than 67 percent in March 2009 when compared to January 2008. Table 6.4 shows the reaction of exchange rates to major news events.

Table 6.3 Stock prices in Asia after the global financial crisis

	2007	2008				2009
	Dec.	Mar.	Jun.	Sep.	Dec.	Mar.
China	100	66	52	43.6	34.6	45.1
Indonesia	100	89.1	85.6	66.7	49.4	52.2
Malaysia	100	86.3	82.1	70.5	60.7	60.4
Philippines	100	82.4	67.9	71	51.7	54.8
Thailand	100	95.2	89.6	69.5	52.4	50.3
Vietnam	100	55.8	43.1	49.3	34	31.2
Hong Kong	100	82.2	79.5	64.8	51.7	48.8
Korea	100	89.8	88.3	76.3	59.3	63.6
Singapore	100	86.8	85.1	68.1	50.8	49.1
Taiwan	100	100.8	88.4	67.2	54	61.3
Japan	100	81.8	88.1	73.5	5.9	53

Note: Stock prices as of end of each month.

Source: World Bank.

Table 6.4 Trends in exchange rates of Asian currencies (against USD, %)

Date / Currency	2/1/2008	19/2/2008	16/9/2008	27/10/2008	3/2/2009	8/4/2009
Korean	936.9	943.9	1160	1442.5	1570.3	1354.5
won		0.7	23.8	54	67.6	44.6
Chinese	7.2981	7.155	6.8425	6.8511	6.8428	6.8361
yuan		(−2.0)	(−6.2)	(−6.1)	(−6.2)	(−6.3)
Japanese	109.67	107.77	105.66	92.79	97.45	99.76
yen		(−1.7)	(−3.7)	(−15.4)	(−11.1)	(−9.0)
Malaysian	3.3095	3.2182	3.4438	3.58	3.732	3.6293
RM		(−2.8)	4.1	8.2	12.8	9.7
Indonesian	9390	9161	9440	11024.5	12080	11390.5
rupia		(−2.4)	0.5	17.4	28.6	21.3
Thai bhatt	30	31.69	34.58	34.82	36.26	35.493
		5.6	15.3	16.1	20.9	18.3
Philippines	41.16	40.64	47.0965	49.37	49.24	47.981
peso		(1.3)	14.4	19.9	19.6	16.6

Note: The number in the parenthesis is the growth rate against the start of the year. The dates represent nationalization of Northern Rock, the collapse of Lehman Brothers, rescue of AIG by the Federal Reserve, IMF assistance to Iceland, and emergence of Eastern European financial panic (in order).

Source: Korea Center for International Finance.

Table 6.5 Capital inflows to emerging markets ($ billion)

	2006		2007		2008	
	Emerging Asia[1]	Emerging economies[2]	Emerging Asia	Emerging economies	Emerging Asia	Emerging economies
Private capital net inflow	258.9	564.9	314.8	928.6	96.2	465.8
Equity investment net inflow	122.6	222.3	112.9	296.1	57.9	174.1
Direct investment	87.2	170.9	148.6	304.1	112.7	263.4
Portfolio investment	35.5	51.5	−35.7	−8.0	−54.7	−89.3
Private credit net inflow	136.3	342.6	201.9	632.4	38.2	291.7
Commercial bank	90.5	211.9	155.7	410.3	29.8	166.6
Non-bank	45.8	130.7	46.2	222.2	8.4	125.1

Notes:
1. Emerging Asia includes China, India, Indonesia, Malaysia, the Philippines, Korea and Thailand.
2. Emerging economies include emerging Asia, 8 Latin American countries, 8 emerging European countries, and 5 countries in Africa and the Middle East.

Source: Institute of International Finance.

The main culprit of the large currency devaluations was the drastic change in inflows of capital to the region. The net inflow of private capital to the emerging countries in East Asia declined significantly from $315 billion in 2007 to $96 billion in 2008. Most of this decline was driven by large drops in equity investment and private credit. What is interesting is that the capital outflow was more severe in emerging Asia compared to other non-Asian emerging markets, as Table 6.5 shows. Short-term capital flew out of emerging Asia at a much faster rate with the onset of the global financial crisis. For instance, emerging Asia saw a drop of $35.7 billion in its portfolio investment account in 2007. On the contrary, the emerging economies as a whole experienced only an $8 billion net outflow in the same year, which means that emerging Asia was singled out for withdrawal of funds. The pattern was repeated in 2008. In that year, 61.3 percent of net outflows from the portfolio investment account was from emerging Asia.

The reason emerging Asia suffered more severe capital outflow seems rather clear. Economies in this region posted economic growth that was twice as great as that of the developed economies between 2002 and 2007. The average growth rate of real gross domestic product (GDP) for emerging Asia was more than 5 percent, while Organisation for Economic Co-operation and Development (OECD) countries and the euro zone economies grew around 2 percent in the same period. Fast economic growth guaranteed comparatively higher returns from portfolio investment in emerging Asia. Between 2002 and 2007, the average investor investing in the stock markets of Korea, China and Indonesia enjoyed returns of 204, 222.4 and 546.2 percent, respectively. On the contrary, the rate of return for the United States (US) stock market was only 59 percent. Therefore, international investors had less incentive to remain in emerging Asia's stock markets as they had already achieved their targets.

6.3 WHAT IS WRONG WITH EAST ASIA'S ECONOMY

6.3.1 High Level of External Dependence

Thanks to rapid economic growth, East Asia's share in world trade has grown significantly. In 2007, the trade volume of the region reached more than $7 trillion, which is a quarter of the world's total trade volume. Twenty-seven percent of the world exports came from East Asia. With booming export sectors, the collective GDP of ASEAN+3[1] reached 19 percent of the world GDP, making the region the third largest economic bloc after the European Union (EU) and North America. However, this growth in size is largely attributable to growth in external demand. Sixty-five percent of EU trade is between member countries. On the other hand, the figure is only 39 percent for East Asia. Intra-regional trade has been increasing recently, but this is largely due to increases in trade of intermediate goods that are used to manufacture final goods to be sold outside the region. This feature of the East Asian economies is a result of the so-called export-oriented growth strategy mentioned earlier. Another characteristic of East Asian trade is the formation of a production network with China at its center. In this framework, China supplies an ample supply of cheap labor and serves as an endpoint for East Asia's exports to other regions, which is why a recent rise in intra-regional trade has been mainly due to a rise in intermediate goods trade. As a result, the region's economies are highly susceptible to external market conditions. As Figure 6.2 shows, the correlation between the global economic conditions and the region's export sectors is more than 0.5 on average, while the average for the world is 0.475. If one excludes China, Indonesia

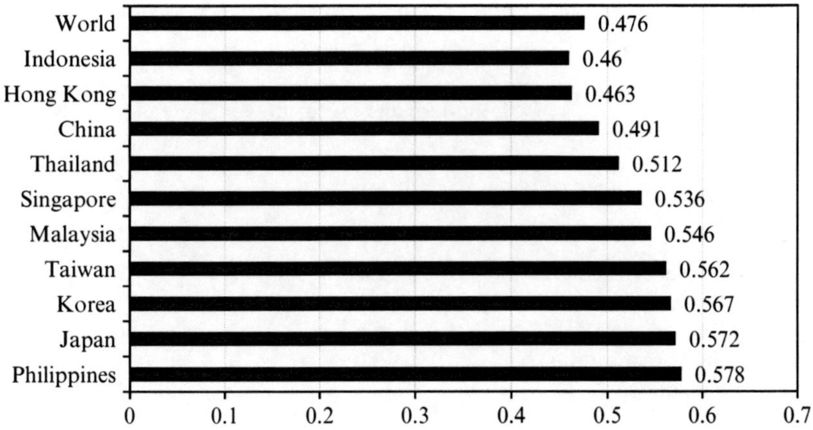

Source: Mizuho Research Institute.

Figure 6.2 Correlation between East Asian exports and global economic conditions

and Hong Kong, economies with either large domestic markets or no significant manufacturing sector, the correlation rises to 0.55. The sensitivity of the region's export-dependent economies to external demand partly explains why the current financial crisis has affected the region disproportionately.

6.3.2 Weak Financial Sector

A more fundamental structural problem lies with the financial markets in the region. Underdeveloped financial markets in East Asia were not able to distribute a huge pool of savings by households and corporations in an efficient manner. Instead, the extra funds were recycled into asset markets in the US and other Western countries, contributing to the global asset bubble. Had the Asian financial markets found a way to direct the funds to domestic markets by offering more competitive investment opportunities, investment in the Asian markets would have been more active and consumption more robust as a consequence. Nowhere can this be seen more clearly than in the region's bond markets. The bond markets in East Asia have grown significantly since the Asian financial crisis of 1997. The overall size of the regional bond market rose from 20 percent of the regional GDP to 60 percent between 1997 and 2007 (Murphy et al., 2007). However, when compared to other regional markets such as the US and the EU, the East Asian bond market is still fairly small. In terms of the

Table 6.6 Foreign holdings of US long-term securities by region (2007) ($ billion)

Region	Long-term debt securities	Share of total (%)
Europe	1007	34
Euro area	664	23
Asia	1092	37
Americas	397	14
Caribbean financial centers	260	9
Australia/Oceania	20	1
Africa	4	0
International organization	33	1
Countries unknown	385	13
Total	2939	100

Source: Terada-Hagiwara (2008).

volume of transactions, the US bond market is by far the biggest in the world, comprising 83 percent of total bond transactions. Since US treasury bills and notes are considered the safest assets, this seems only natural. However, when one considers that the EU, similar in size in terms of GDP to ASEAN+3, takes up 11 percent of total transactions, it is evident that the East Asian bond markets are less developed than the economic size of the region warrants.

Development of the regional bond markets in East Asia has been delayed, since most countries in the region suppressed their financial sectors and used the banking sector to distribute funds. By centralizing the movement of funds through banks, these countries could more efficiently have channeled massive amounts of funds to those industrial sectors that the policymakers deemed necessary to promote economic growth. This policy environment left few choices for personal investors in the region. As a result, the regional investors found it more attractive to invest in the overseas markets, particularly the US bond market, and they bought, for example, 37 percent of all long-term US bonds in 2003 as shown in Table 6.6.

Given the degree of development of the US financial market and the variety of safe assets it provides, the regional investors' decision to concentrate heavily on that specific market can be considered purely rational. However, it should be noted that this pattern of investor behavior is hampering development of regional bond markets and serves as an indirect impetus to cause further outflow of regional funds to overseas markets, making the region more vulnerable to external shocks.

There are additional factors that are preventing the regional bond markets from making progress. First, the existence of robust demand for and supply of a commodity or service is essential for any market to form and develop. Unfortunately, that is not the case for the East Asian region. Demand for East Asian bonds is lacking due to the weak roles played by institutional investors. Due to costs associated with information gathering and transactions, individual investors have only a limited role to play. It is the institutional investors with supposedly better knowledge and expertise that need to pick up the slack. However, pension funds and insurance industries that could serve as a breeding ground for institutional investors are not well developed. Consequently, institutional investors in this region are comparatively less sophisticated than their counterparts in other regions. Also, the supply of private bonds is dominated by a small number of large corporations which do not actively use bond markets as their source of funds. Second, infrastructure that is needed to support bond market transactions is seriously lacking. There are still many regulations that impede efficient flow of funds across borders so that investors do not have an effective tool to hedge against exchange rate risks associated with bond transactions (Murphy et al., 2007). A more serious problem is the shortage of professionals equipped with expertise in bond markets. The East Asian economies are relatively new to financial markets as most of them have in the past preferred banks to manage capital flows. Therefore, they have had less time to accumulate the relevant human capital. What makes it difficult is that those with financial talent have an incentive to move to other financially sophisticated countries where they could expect much higher incomes.

Foreign exchange markets are among the most vulnerable parts of the region's economies. Underdeveloped foreign exchange markets make the regional economies extremely sensitive to capital fluctuations in the international financial markets. This sensitivity is mainly due to the small size of the region's foreign exchange markets. The United Kingdom (UK) foreign exchange market took up 34.1 percent of the total transactions in the world in 2007. The second largest was the US, with 16.6 percent. Japan was a distant fourth with 6.0 percent. However other Asian countries' foreign exchange markets were just specks in the whole picture. Korea, the thirteenth-largest economy in the world, had a foreign exchange market that took up only 0.8 percent of the total volume. Compared to the real sectors, it can be clearly seen that the financial markets in the region are very much underdeveloped. Because of their small size, a relatively small movement of capital across borders could potentially disrupt the whole system in the region. Another weakness of the region's foreign exchange markets is that exchange-related derivatives are not in active use. Because

Table 6.7 Comparison of size of foreign exchange markets

	Spot	Outright forward	Foreign exchange swaps	% of currencies used in transactions
US dollar	29.7	10.9	59.4	86.3
Euro	36.9	12.1	51.1	37.0
Yen	40.4	12.1	47.5	16.5
Pound sterling	32.5	10.0	57.4	15.0
Swiss franc	42.2	10.1	47.7	6.8
Australian dollar	25.7	10.0	64.3	6.7
Canadian dollar	29.7	11.8	58.6	4.2
Swedish krona	20.7	10.0	69.3	2.8
Hong Kong dollar	18.4	7.0	74.6	2.8
Norwegian krone	18.4	9.7	71.9	2.2
New Zealand dollar	29.4	11.3	59.3	1.9
Mexico peso	37.4	11.7	50.9	1.3
Singapore dollar	22.5	7.9	69.6	1.2
Won	44.7	29.4	25.9	1.1
Rand	19.9	12.1	68.0	0.9
Danish krone	21.8	10.3	67.9	0.9
Rouble	70.7	5.0	24.3	0.8
Zloty	20.0	10.9	69.1	0.8
Indian rupee	42.6	27.5	29.8	0.7
Renminbi	61.4	31.3	7.4	0.5
New Taiwan dollar	47.1	40.6	12.3	0.4
Brazilian real	50.2	47.3	2.5	0.4
Forint	34.1	15.7	50.2	–
Czech koruna	23.8	20.9	55.3	–
Baht	18.9	13.3	67.8	–
Turkish lira	61.4	11.4	27.2	–
Philippine peso	36.9	32.5	30.5	–
Rupiah	43.7	39.3	17.0	–
All currencies	32.6	11.7	55.6	200.0

Note: Percentage shares of average daily turnover in April.

Source: BIS (2007).

of this, Asian firms and financial institutions find it relatively harder to manage the exchange rate risk. In particular, the swap markets in Asia are considerably less developed when compared to advanced countries, as Table 6.7 shows.

6.4 POLICY RECOMMENDATIONS

6.4.1 Form a Robust Free Trade Zone

Economic integration in East Asia is essential to reduce its dependency on external demands. The idea first gained credence after the 1997 financial crisis, and the East Asia Vision Group consequently submitted a report to the ASEAN+3 committee in 2001 to build an East Asian Free Trade Area (EAFTA). However there are a few obstacles to overcome before the idea can be realized in practice. Firstly, there are too wide gaps among the regional economies in terms of economic and institutional development. Secondly, the region has no clear lead country similar to Germany in European integration. China and Japan are clear candidates for this role, but neither of them seems ready either politically or economically. Their strategies for integration differ significantly as China prefers ASEAN+3 while Japan prefers ASEAN+6, which also includes Australia, New Zealand and India.

Due to the lack of a comprehensive roadmap for economic integration, each individual country is left to its own devices to promote free trade in the region. As a result, what appears to be a 'noodle bowl' of free trade arrangements is emerging, as Table 6.8 shows. Korea, Japan and China are vying for closer economic ties with ASEAN. Japan, in particular,

Table 6.8 Regional free trade agreements in Asia

	Under review	Under negotiation	Completed
Korea–China	❍		
Korea–Japan		❍	
Korea–Singapore			❍
Korea–ASEAN			❍
China–ASEAN			❍
China–Singapore			❍
China–Thailand	❍		
Japan–Thailand			❍
Japan–Brunei			❍
Japan–Indonesia			❍
Japan–Malaysia			❍
Japan–Philippines			❍
Japan–Singapore			❍
Japan–Vietnam			❍
Japan–ASEAN			❍
AFTA (ASEAN FTA)			❍

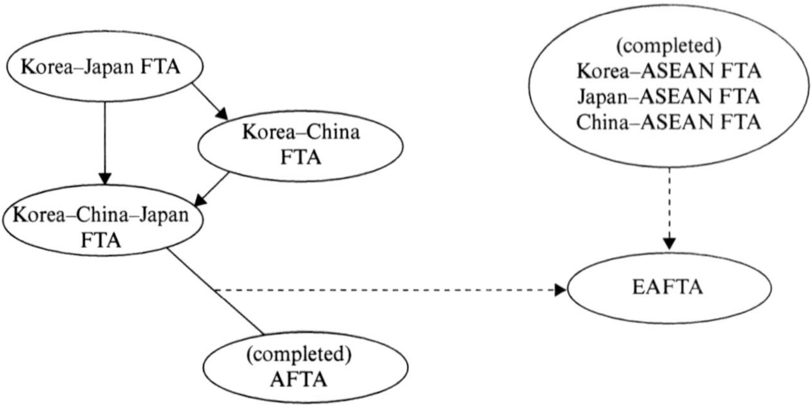

Figure 6.3 A road to free trade in East Asia

completed individual free trade agreements with ASEAN member countries and also has another free trade agreement with ASEAN as a collective. It seems that China has followed a somewhat similar path. As one can see, the free trade agreements in the region are highly disaggregated and lack strategic integrity. What is more, the three biggest economies in the region – namely Korea, China and Japan – do not have free trade agreements with each other. Given their economic significance in the region, it is crucial for them to reach a free trade agreement in order to advance regional economic integration. To this aim, it is necessary to install a secretarial office to oversee and harmonize the overall integration process in the region. The office should be permanent until the integration is complete, in order to guarantee policy continuity. Furthermore, Korea, Japan and China should play a more prominent role in the integration process.

The optimal economic integration process is one in which Korea, Japan and China first form free trade agreements with each other. This process is illustrated in Figure 6.3. To maximize the benefits of a free trade agreement, EAFTA should not be based on the current ASEAN+1 paradigm. Since the ASEAN+1 type of free trade agreement is a low-grade arrangement just proclaiming the principles of free trade, its expansion to the entire region will not be a bona fide answer to the regional integration. Therefore, a robust free trade agreement needs to be made among Korea, Japan and China and then expanded to incorporate the ASEAN Free Trade Area (AFTA) to complete the economic integration of the region (EAFTA).

6.4.2 Develop Regional Bond Markets

The initiative to develop the regional bond markets drew serious attention in the wake of the 1997 Asian financial crisis. The argument was that a well-developed regional bond market would enable regional economies to borrow from each other rather than from 'outside' investors, thus shielding the region from external shocks. However, as the world came back to normalcy in the early 2000s, the idea seemed to lose steam as liquidity based on low interest rates flooded the globe. The 2008 global financial crisis underlined the importance of having a robust bond market in the region once more. But the idea behind it is a bit different this time. This time, the fundamental problem on each side of the Pacific was the so-called 'global imbalance', which is another way to say that Asian savings were being used to fuel US consumption. A growing number of Asians began to think that only if they had some form of robust bond market in place that would channel the savings to regional corporations rather than to the US, the disaster could have been at least manageable.

As a matter of fact, the initiative to develop regional bond markets was one of the more successful initiatives that came out of the 1997 crisis. Between 2002 and 2008, the size of bond markets in Korea, China and Thailand grew by 170 percent, 650 percent and 300 percent, respectively. Granted that they are still fairly small when compared to bond markets in advanced countries, yet no one can deny that the Asian economies have come a long way since the 1997 crisis.

East Asia took a two-pronged approach to develop its bond market. Firstly, it was necessary to build the necessary infrastructure for the smooth functioning of the bond market. To this end, the Asian Bond Markets Initiative (ABMI) was started in 2003. Its stated goal was to focus policy efforts toward providing, among other things, credit guarantees and credit ratings. These efforts bore fruit as early as 2004 when the Asian Development Bank and International Finance Corporation jointly issued bonds denominated in Malaysian ringgit. In May 2008, treasury secretaries from ASEAN+3 countries agreed to accelerate the momentum of the ABMI and set specific policy targets. These include promoting and facilitating the issuance of local currency-denominated bonds, and improving the regulatory framework and the related infrastructure for the bond markets. Four task forces were set up to pursue these targets, and an ABMI steering group was put in place to supervise them. Secondly, certain measures to stimulate demand were implemented. EMEAP[2] pooled $1 billion to establish the Asia Bond Fund (ABF) to this end in June 2003. Encouraged by the success of the ABF, EMEAP set out to establish a second fund of $2 billion, called ABF2. This fund

Table 6.9 Shares of bonds issued by private and public sectors in the East Asian bond markets (%)

	China	Hong Kong	Indo-nesia	Japan	Korea	Malay-sia	Philip-pines	Singa-pore	Thai-land	Vietnam
Public	88.4	22.0	90.6	89.9	45.1	54.5	92.0	56.5	79.5	96.0
Private	11.6	78.0	9.4	10.1	54.9	45.5	8.0	43.5	20.5	4.0

Source: ADB.

was designed to invest in those bonds issued by governmental entities in the region.

Despite the great strides East Asia has made so far, serious challenges remain. The foremost obstacle to robust development of the regional bond markets is the overwhelming dominance of public bond issues in the regional markets, as shown in Table 6.9. When the public sector plays a dominant role in the bond market, it could potentially raise the borrowing costs for private enterprises that must compete with the government sector to secure funds. As a result, they will have less incentive to use the bond market as an alternative source of funds. Lukewarm participation by the private sector, in turn, discourages incentives to provide such infrastructure as credit rating services. If there exists no objective entity to entice private firms to improve transparency and accountability by the threat of credit degradation, investors will also have less incentive to invest in privately issued bonds. In this way, the presence of a dominant public sector could cause a vicious cycle.

One way to break the cycle is to exogenously impose a third-party credit rating agency, since no endogenous formation of such an entity can be expected in the current setting. Viewed in this light, the agreement reached in May 2009 by ASEAN+3 treasury secretaries to kick-start the Credit Guarantee and Investment Mechanism (CGIM) can be regarded as a policy breakthrough. The CGIM is funded to the extent of $5 billion, and is to reduce risks associated with investing in regional bonds with less than optimal transparency by providing credit guarantees. The mentality here is similar to that found in the export-led growth strategy, in that the government used to provide credit guarantees to exporting firms that were not able to obtain trade finance. It was quite successful with the export sector, but whether it can pull off the same result with the financial sector remains to be seen.

One factor is that the size of the fund to back the guarantee is too small compared to the volume of bond transactions in the region. For it to have any meaningful impact, the size of the fund should be at least $100 billion.

Another factor that could derail the process is the heterogeneity that exists across bond markets in the region. Bond markets in most countries in the region are still relatively closed to outside investors, for fear of destabilizing their domestic economies. In order to facilitate the efficient flow of funds between countries in the region, it is necessary to have common standards as to issuance and transaction of bonds. How this will be harmonized remains largely unresolved.

6.4.3 Enhance Financial Cooperation

Since the 1980s, financial globalization has mainly occurred with the advanced countries in the lead and central to the process. As a result most emerging markets, including the East Asian economies, have been marginalized by the changes and have become more dependent on financial markets in the advanced countries such as the US and UK. Also, doubts about the International Monetary Fund's (IMF) ability to provide assistance in a timely manner when the regional market is in trouble are finding more supporters. Recent experiences in the aftermath of the global financial crisis only make these doubts stronger.

In order to maintain stability of the region's financial markets, what is most needed is a system for liquidity provision similar to the IMF, but specifically designed for the region. The idea was popular right after the 1997 crisis but soon lost appeal as the region enjoyed a huge pool of liquidity. The fact that the US objected to the idea of having a regional entity independent of the IMF did not help the matter either. However, the Chiang Mai Initiative (CMI), an arrangement of liquidity provision among the regional economies, provides a basis for closer financial cooperation in the region. In 2008, when the world was in a collective liquidity straightjacket, the regional economies had an opportunity to appreciate once more the value of having a handy liquidity provision arrangement. The appreciation led to further advancement of the CMI and resulted in the Post CMI in 2009. The Post CMI is a milestone achievement in that it raised the total swap agreement from $80 billion to $120 billion. What is more significant is that the liquidity will now be provided collectively in a relatively short period of time, and that procedural details have been clarified. Considering that under the previous CMI one had to go to each individual country to ask for assistance, the Post CMI is very significant progress in the right direction.

Still, more needs to be done to make the current financial cooperation concrete. Firstly, there is a question about the adequacy of liquidity to be provided in an emergency: $120 billion is a lot of money, but not when compared to the economic size of the region. The question gains more traction among pessimists when one considers the fact that the amount of funding a liquidity-shocked country can get without the IMF-imposed conditionality is a mere $24 billion. Therefore, serious thought needs to be given to the idea of expanding the amount of liquidity provision to make it more useful in an emergency.

Secondly, liquidity provision can inadvertently create moral hazard among member countries. In order to avoid this possibility and guarantee sustainability of the system, it is necessary to enhance the Economic Review and Policy Dialogue (ERPD) currently in place. The ERPD was first introduced in 2000 and has been jointly run with the CMI since 2005. Accordingly, policymakers from around the region get together every two years to exchange information on both foreign and domestic financial market activities. However sharing information is strictly voluntary, and the collection and analysis of information is done by individual countries. Hence, the credibility of the whole process comes into question. In order to make financial cooperation more effective, sharing information needs to be made compulsory. Information collection and analysis also needs to be done by a third-party entity to boost credibility and confidence of the regional economy. Finally, there is a strong need to found a 'neo-AMF' (Asian Monetary Fund) to oversee the whole process. It should be given a role to monitor the regional financial markets and maintain the stability of the region's foreign exchange markets.

NOTES

1. ASEAN+3 comprises the ten member nations of the Association of Southeast Asian Nations (ASEAN) and Korea, China and Japan.
2. EMEAP stands for the Executives' Meeting of East Asia and Pacific Central Banks. Its members are Korea, China, Japan, Hong Kong, Thailand, Malaysia, the Philippines, Indonesia, Australia and New Zealand.

REFERENCES

Murphy, Cherelle, Amy Auster and Katie Dean (2007), *Asia Bond Markets: 1997 and Now*, ANZ Investment Bank, Australia.

Terada-Hagiwara, Akiko (2008), 'Asian Holdings of US Treasury Securities: Trade Integration as a Threshold', ADB Economics Working Paper Series, 137.

7. The G20 and the role of Asia in the future

Deok Ryong Yoon

7.1 INTRODUCTION

The G20 has emerged as a new economic steering group through the crisis. The G20 played a vital coordination role during the 2008 global financial crisis and contributed clearly to preventing the expansion of economic recession in the world. As the global economy recovers, there is a growing concern about the weakening spirit of collaboration. Recently, the global economy faced the so-called 'currency war' which can be exports-aid through competitive currency devaluations. Almost all the member countries of the G20 were drawn into the war, criticizing each other. The Group of Twenty seems to be standing at a crossroads to becoming a global governance body.

Even with the concern about the future of the G20, Bradford and Linn (2009) argue that the change of global governance to the G20 is based on broad and fundamental changes of economic environment. The factors that have driven the G20's emergence are as follows.

First, the shifting of the global demographic and economic balance has called for a new system of governance. After the Cold War ended, the eastern hemisphere joined the market economy. With globalization, large emerging economies such as China, Russia, India and Brazil have revealed themselves as new economic powers. The increasing influence of emerging economies shifted the economic balance from the developed economies to emerging economies. Second, the growing global interdependencies across borders and different economic sectors required global responses to the changes. Globalization has enlarged economic interconnectedness and deepened the impact of economic incidents such as financial crisis, so that a policy failure of one country could destabilize the global economy. Third, growing recognition of the ineffectiveness of the current system of global governance made a new system of governance necessary. The world has suffered from persistent stalemate on many pressing issues, such as global poverty, climate change and the Doha trade round. The existing international institutions including the United Nations, World

Trade Organization (WTO), International Monetary Fund (IMF), World Bank and G8 could not solve any of the acute global problems. The global financial crisis triggered a process of change in global governance.

Asia stands at the center of the power shift in the new global governance. Six countries from Asia constitute the second-largest delegation to the G20, after Europe. The global economy is becoming more and more influenced by the Asian economy, owing to its fast annual growth rate of 7 percent on average, and huge foreign reserve stock occupying two-thirds of the entire volume in the world. Moreover, the economic policies of China and India may have an impact on the economic environment of other countries due to the sheer volume of their population.

The world has acknowledged the global importance of the Asian economy. Asia has obtained six seats on the new global steering committee. However, the power shift to Asia requires a sharing of responsibilities. Due to the huge potential economic influence of the Asian economy, the world economy cannot be stabilized without its cooperation. The role of Asia is regarded as one of the most crucial factors in managing the global economy.

The problem with Asian countries is that they do not have any institutional arrangement to coordinate the Asian voice. Asian countries have made their own paths until now, without close consultation with neighboring countries even though they face similar problems. They all suffer from exchange rate problems: they are hoarding huge amounts of foreign reserves, and they run mostly export-oriented economies. Now is the time for the Asian countries to be equipped with an institutionalized cooperation mechanism. It is the first step to responding to the requirements from outside, and to coordinate regional economic policies.

This chapter studies two main questions, mentioned above. First, what is the role of the G20 in the post-crisis future? Second, what is the role of Asia in the G20, and how will Asia respond to expectations?

The chapter is structured as follows: section 7.2 deals with the possible role of the G20 and section 7.3 describes the conditions of the role. Section 7.4 identifies the role of Asia in the G20 and considers how the Asian countries should respond to the expectation. Finally, section 7.5 brings all this together to provide a conclusion.

7.2 THE FUTURE ROLE OF THE G20

7.2.1 The G20's Emergence and its Achievement

As we now enter the age of globalization, the demand for global governance is greater than ever. Interconnectedness has bound the world together,

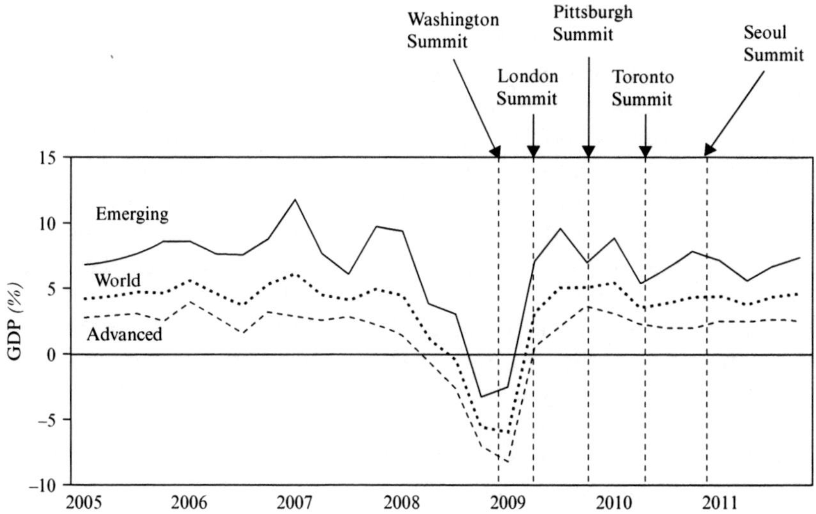

Source: IMF, World Economic Outlook.

Figure 7.1 Economic growth and G20 Summits

and issues that happen in the domestic arena draw international attention and response. The recent financial crisis affected not only its epicenter, but the rest of the world – a reminder that global economic governance is very necessary, over and above the existing international financial institutions.

In this respect, the G20 has come a long way in becoming central to discussions on global financial and economic issues since it was launched following the Asian financial crisis of 1997. It has been successful in many aspects, such as maintaining its neutral and cooperative relationship with the G8 and other global governance organizations, preventing the recession from worsening into a full-fledged economic depression and bringing about a quick recovery.

Furthermore, the G20 has succeeded in passing the baton from Washington to London, and from London to Pittsburgh, Toronto and Seoul. The transition from one summit to another has been smooth, with the organization successfully responding to the immediate crisis and releasing the global economy from its lethargic state, followed by steps toward achieving the Framework for Strong, Sustainable and Balanced Growth and promoting further development across nations (see Figure 7.1). Every G20 summit concludes with a declaration. The declaration is considered as the official result of the meeting. The worthiness of each meeting is evaluated therefore by the declaration.

7.2.2 The G20 as the Premier Economic Forum

The good news is that the global economy has survived the worst of the recession. The recovery is under way and slowly gaining momentum, with most Organisation for Economic Co-operation and Development (OECD) and emerging markets growing once again. However, the pace of the recovery has been uneven and significant challenges that underscore the importance of international cooperation remain, leaving little room for progress in narrowing macroeconomic imbalance. This calls for a premier economic forum with greater authority and clout. With a number of fastest-growing economies as members of the group, the G20 is an appropriate platform to discuss the issue of representation of the under-represented, and the achievement of global equality and economic soundness throughout the global community.

The idea that the G20 has emerged as the world's premier economic forum has gained credence as it created Working Groups to deal with several specific issues regarding the crisis. The G20 has managed to bring under control emergencies that arose following the financial crisis – arguably in a more effective manner than existing international organizations. This is partially because the G20 is a unique group that includes emerging powers that are not properly represented in other organizations. It is also notable that it is a summit of actual leaders, who have the authority to execute measures that would be difficult or impossible for diplomats or technocrats to achieve.

Regardless of some of the strengths that the G20 possesses, status as the world's premier economic forum will not materialize automatically even though the Seoul Summit ended successfully. Achieving legitimacy and assuming a role as *the* principal forum for financial discussion would still remain a strenuous task for the G20. It will be especially difficult for the G20 to justify its own existence after the global economy revives and stabilizes. But the G20 should not be forgotten and must not be dismantled even after it reaches its goal of relieving the global financial crisis, just as it did with the Asian crisis. Furthermore, it will be crucial that the G20 continues its efforts to broaden its scope and assign to itself more meaningful agendas; to establish its position as not just another forum for debate, but as a global steering group, a role which also includes many other subordinate roles explained in the following paragraphs.

7.2.3 The G20 as a Global Macroeconomic Coordinator

One of the criteria that the G20 must possess as a global steering group is to deliver its commitments by their actual implementation. One of the most effective measures that the G20 continues to use is the Framework for

Table 7.1 Main agendas for G20 Summits in Toronto and Seoul

Toronto Summit	Seoul Summit
Main objectives • Searching for a new order	Main objectives • Establishing a new order
Agendas • Framework for Strong, Sustainable and Balanced Growth • Reform of the Financial Sector and International Financial Institutions • Fighting Protectionism and Promoting Trade and Investment • Other Issues and Forward Agenda	Follow-up agenda • The Strong, Sustainable and Balanced Growth: – Exchange Rate, – Guidelines for Current Account Balance • Reform of IFIs • Reform of financial regulations
	New agenda • Global Financial Safety Net • Development Issues

Strong, Sustainable and Balanced Growth first proposed at the Toronto Summit (see Table 7.1). This framework has been particularly successful in widening its scope and including not only economic recovery and resilience, but also fiscal, social and environmental sustainability and balance – within countries and across the globe in the G20 agenda. It has rendered beggar-thy-neighbor policies – such as manipulation of exchange rates, trade barriers and conditionalities – open to active discussion, giving developing countries an opportunity to relieve their long frustration. It will also continue to put critical issues regarding food, fuel and financial shocks, as well as environmental concerns, on the G20 table. Moreover, with the successful implementation of the first stage of the MAP (Mutual Assessment Process), the leaders at the Toronto Summit were able to discuss the outcomes and set future policy goals that will bring the world economy closer to realizing the G20's shared objectives of a stronger, more sustainable and balanced growth.

Although the outcome of the first MAP was a success, many also voiced the need to implement these measures on a national level, tailored to circumstances of individual countries. Group-based policies in the first round were highly generic and eventually these policies would have to be implemented at the country level. Therefore, the second stage of the MAP would be conducted at the country and European level, to enhance the usefulness of the Framework. Analyses from the IMF and the World Bank would therefore provide more specificity on development of policy options, with a special focus on policy options for emerging markets in the G20. The leaders at the summit will discuss the endorsement of recommended policy initiatives and announce a comprehensive policy action plan including specific collective policy commitments by members, to help the global economy reach or get closer to the agreed, shared objectives of strong, sustainable and balanced growth.

Likewise, through the MAP, which is to become an annual exercise with continued assistance from organizations like the IMF and the World Bank, and in close collaboration with finance ministers and central bank governors of various countries, the G20 should continue to provide successive summits with future tasks for further consideration and implementation. It is also critical that the G20 continue discussions of ways to institutionalize this macroeconomic framework further and consider all effective ways of continuing the ongoing improvement. In this case, the G20 would have to play a role of a global coordinator – monitoring the commitments made by members of the G20, ensuring an active flow of proposals between member countries, and promoting close collaboration with other international organizations – to follow up future successful summits.

7.2.4 The G20 as a Global Financial Regulator

Although cooperation with other international institutions is crucial for the G20 to play an active role as a global coordinator, it is equally important to evaluate existing systems critically and make efforts toward making necessary improvements. When the 2008 financial crisis broke out, it was fairly evident that other economic governance structures like the World Bank and the IMF had not functioned to their full extent. The inadequate regulation of global banks and financial markets resulted in the magnitude of the crisis, and its impact on the developing countries further demonstrated that crises are unfortunately inevitable in deregulated financial systems. Although it is too early to dismiss the functionality of existing international institutions, the consensus on the need for effective global financial regulations is stronger than ever before.

Acting upon this consensus, the G20 leaders reached an agreement on new capital and liquidity requirements and called on the Financial Stability Board (FSB) to consider and develop concrete policy recommendations to deal with SIFIs (systemically important financial institutions). Such measures should include more intensive supervision and consideration of financial instruments to encourage market discipline. Moreover, the G20 mandated the FSB and BCBS (Basel Committee on Banking Supervision) and other relevant organizations to report on progress and reforms made to date, in the areas of supervision, hedge funds, credit rating agencies, and so on. The FSB was asked to make recommendations for stronger supervision in order to identify and address risks, as well as recommending early

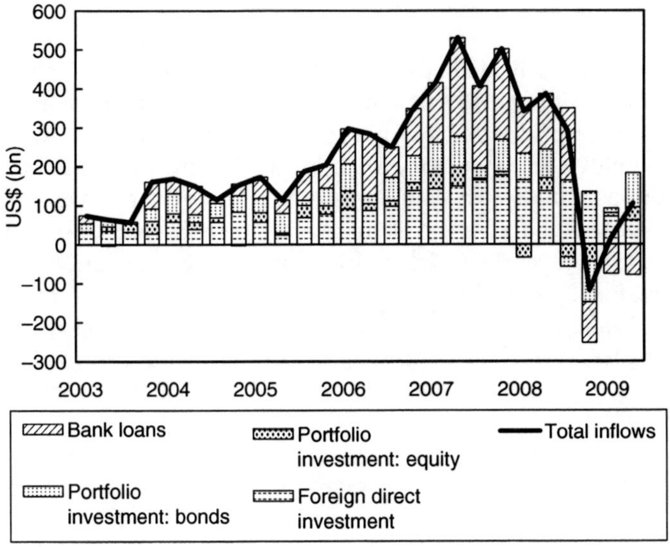

Source: IMF, Global Financial Stability Report.

Figure 7.2 Sudden reversal of capital flow

intervention. In addition, the G20 should also acquire status as a global financial regulator with a regulating domain that is equal in size to the global market it regulates, therefore reducing moral hazard and promoting comprehensiveness. The G20 should also seek ways to counter the procyclical nature of the financial system, which leads to excessive financial activity when the economy is good and insufficient financial activity when the economy is bad (see Figure 7.2).

The G20 should also redesign regulatory principles so that they would be adaptable and applicable to all developing countries. It must also be powerful enough that it can influence the decisions to be made by domestic financial regulators, especially in already developed, powerful countries. The G20 as a new organization for regulatory governance needs to coordinate a well-functioning network between national regulators, operate a prudential regulation of international financial organizations like the World Bank and IMF, and build on institutions like the Bank for International Settlements (BIS). Finally, the G20 should consider potential risks of financial instability and future crises on the real global economy. In this connection, an important task of the G20 would be to follow up on initiatives such as monitoring of the financial regulation agenda, and its compensation standards and principles, to ensure a more resilient global financial system.

7.2.5 The G20 as a Global Safeguard

The G20 can actually assume its role as a global safeguard quite naturally, as it operates as the world's financial regulator. Being an integrated global economy, the world is constantly exposed to financial crises, which have become highly contagious (see Figure 7.3). Countries that have experienced the potentially devastating impact of sudden reversals of capital flows have suffered serious disruptions in their domestic financial and foreign exchange markets. When domestic currencies are not widely used in international settlements, these problems may deteriorate into a foreign exchange liquidity crisis that threatens the soundness of respective domestic economies, even if the crises are external. In such times, the G20 must continue to emphasize the importance of collective efforts toward mitigating these risks.

Fortunately, progress is being made in this regard. The precautionary lending facilities of the IMF have been formed, in addition to enhancement of the FCL (Flexible Credit Line), introduction of a PCL (Precautionary Credit Line) and a GSM (Global Stabilization Mechanism), and strengthening of RFAs (Regional Financing Arrangements). At the Seoul Summit,

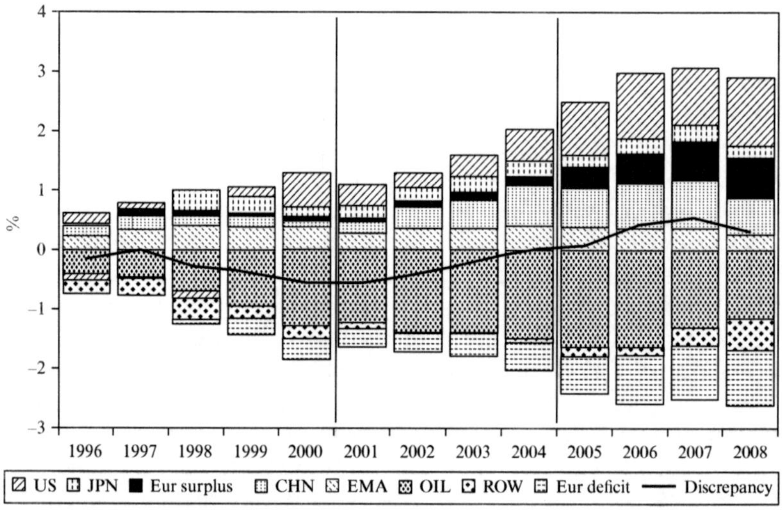

Note: EMA = European Monetary Agreement; OIL = Oil Exporting Countries.

Source: Blanchard and Milesi-Ferretti (2009).

Figure 7.3 Global imbalance current account balances (% of world GDP)

leaders have accepted the control of capital flow to reduce volatility under a few conditions.

To maintain the progress made so far, the G20 in the future must continue to monitor capital flows, foreign and financial markets closely, as well as the work of international financial institutions such as the IMF, and endorse appropriate outcomes as part of its broader work on strengthening global financial safety nets.[1]

7.3 CONDITIONS TO FULFILL THE ROLE OF THE G20

7.3.1 Institutionalization

At the Pittsburgh Summit, the leaders of the G20 announced locations of successive summits – Toronto, Seoul and Paris – signaling that starting in 2011, the G20 summits will be held on an annual basis. Based on the notion that institutionalization requires continuity, this can be seen as the first proof of ongoing institutionalization of the G20 Summit. However, it is hard to say that the G20 has gained unassailable legitimacy, which comes from a combination of effectiveness and representativeness.

One of the criticisms of the G8 was its lack of continuity and implementation monitoring. The G20 must prove that it can do a better job in terms of actual deliverance of commitments. It must also cooperate on a regular basis with non-member countries and other international organizations to ensure true global representativeness.

7.3.2 Establishment of a Global Network

Although there have been heated debates about whether the G20 Summit is an appropriate platform for discussing 'development', the newly added agenda is indeed a sensation in a sense that it marks the transition from a mere managing of crises to actively engendering global growth. In this case, it is important that the G20 create a global network in which the Group can freely communicate its messages and engage in efforts worldwide. Aid may often be fragmented or even unhelpful at times when it is not tailored to specific circumstances of recipient countries. It is therefore advisable that the G20 broaden its representation to small and medium-sized economies, and underdeveloped countries; not in terms of increasing its membership, but to give them a louder voice, for example, in international financial institutes (IFIs) and other international regulatory bodies.

As a group that includes emerging countries, the G20 must discuss the best ways in which the under-represented countries may effectively be taken into consideration. If the G20 is to support the developing world, it must ensure that the recipients have the capacity to use the support for their intended effects, making meaningful contributions to developing countries. Therefore, maintaining an intimate global network will facilitate information and communication flows across borders and broaden consultative mechanisms, creating an environment where voices of non-member countries, international institutions, and even non-governmental organizations (NGOs) can be heard.

7.3.3 Communication with Private Sectors

To achieve a strong, sustainable, and balanced growth, the G20 needs investment from both the public and the private sectors.[2] As such, Seoul hosted a pre-G20 Business Forum of more than 100 global chief executive officers (CEOs) on the eve of the November 2010 Summit. Issues at this forum included post-crisis growth, finance, trade, eco-friendly growth and development, and corporate social responsibility, all of which parallel the most prominent interests and objectives of the G20 Summit. After the meeting, the CEOs delivered 68 recommendations to the political leaders, and 60 were adopted. Though business summits are not a regular part of the G20 leaders' meetings, this forum will represent a new and important part of the G20 processes. It also represents another crucial step towards opening channels for other voices, for participation of the private sector. Likewise, in building and maintaining a global network with non-G20 countries and other international organizations, the CEOs discussing their economic concerns at a round table with political leaders on a regular basis will further solidify the G20's status as the premier forum for global economic cooperation.

7.4 ASIA'S ROLE IN THE G20

7.4.1 Expected Role of Asia in the World

In the G20 regime, Asia has entered into the limelight. Asia sends the second-biggest delegation to the G20 with six countries, following behind Europe with its seven delegates. The strong presence of Asia can be attributed to Asia's economic power. Asia is the fastest-growing region in the world, showing an average growth rate of more than 7 percent per year. Asia has the world's second- and third-largest economies: China and Japan. China and India also attract special attention due to their large populations – China with 1.3 billion and India with 1.2 billion. Their fast economic growth may change the world economic map through enormous production capacity as well as the large potential demand.

Asia has the greatest foreign reserve stock, holding over two-thirds of the world's entire reserves. Asia's trade volume is approximately 20 percent of the total trade volume. Population in Asia exceeds 60 percent of the total world population and is still growing fast. All these data regarding Asian economic fundamentals implies that the Asian economy will be expanding rapidly for the foreseeable future. The increase in Asia's economic power will undoubtedly influence the global economy more strongly in the future.

The expected role of Asia in the world will be as follows. First is the sharing of responsibility. The strong Asian presence in the G20 reflects the expectation of the world to share not only the power, but also the responsibility in managing the world economy. Since China and India commenced economic growth, the global economy has been influenced more and more by the demand for energy. The oil price and climate change are becoming more dependent on demand from these countries. These countries, however, support industries with energy subsidies. Asian countries are being required to pay more attention to the impacts of their policies on other countries in the world.

Second is providing dynamics of economic growth. Asian economic growth has reduced the poverty ratio in the region. For example, the goal of poverty reduction by 50 percent, according to the Millennium Development Goals (MDGs), has already been achieved in East Asia, while other countries showed aggravated absolute poverty and minimal economic growth of less than 2 percent (see Yoon, 2010). Even though the dynamics of economic growth overflows to neighboring Asian countries, it has yet to stimulate economic growth in other regions. The world hopes that Asian countries will open their economies more widely and liberalize the markets more actively.

Third is offering new markets and new demand. Asia is renowned for creating a 'saving glut'.[3] Asia's high savings have been criticized due to the negative impact on the global financial market, reducing the interest rate and creating an asset bubble. The high reserve stock of Asian countries also triggered disputes on global imbalance and exchange rate policy. The non-Asian countries hope that Asian countries will expand their domestic consumption and open their markets to the world. In fact, domestic markets in Asian countries have been growing fast, but investment has expanded more rapidly than the consumption to support high gross domestic product (GDP) growth. Even though the increasing purchasing power will definitely led to the expansion of domestic consumption, Asian countries may need to make efforts to contribute global economic growth by expanding domestic consumption.

7.4.2 Conditions to Assume Asia's New Role: Regional Cooperation

These days, Asia is being required to contribute to the world economy, rather than just make use of the world market. Even though the world expects a more active role of Asia in reviving the economy, it is not certain whether Asia will be able to comply, because there is not a single, coherent unit 'Asia'. Even though other countries refer to Asian countries as a collective unit, they do not have an institutional arrangement to behave as a unit. The six member countries of the G20 do not have any dialog channel to discuss their role in the G20. The response to the expectations of the world is left to the individual decision of each country.

The impediments to collective behavior are mostly based on internal diversity and political legacy (Lee and Yoon, 2007: 7). Asian countries show great differences in economic size, development level, income level, resource endowment, and so on. A broad spectrum of political systems from authoritarian to democratic systems may also make it difficult to reach an agreement on an institutionalized cooperation in the region. The historical legacy of invasion is a stumbling block in the road to regional cooperation.[4] A low profile of regional identity and a lack of experience in cooperation are counted as unfavorable conditions. The Confucian traditions in China, Japan and Korea may not mingle well with the Islamic cultures of some East Asian countries. East Asia cannot expect to receive external support, as the European countries did from the United States at the beginning of their regional integration. All these non-economic conditions reveal why Asian countries' institutional cooperation is lagging behind their degree of economic cooperation.

In the economic sphere, Asian countries have made great progress in cooperation and show a high degree of functional integration. First of all, functional economic integration has proceeded rather robustly. The share of intra-regional trade between East Asian countries has risen substantially since 1990 (see Figure 7.4). The share of intra-regional trade in Asia has increased continuously, reaching the level of the North American Free Trade Agreement (NAFTA). Intra-regional financial cooperation has increased too. Intra-regional foreign direct investment (FDI) has also increased in volume, while the share in total FDI has decreased recently in the years of global crisis (see Figure 7.5). Asian countries are accepting each other as business partners in order to produce products. The internal markets in the region are increasing in importance as the Asian countries' purchasing power grows. Intra-regional economic relation in Asia will grow rapidly as the income level increases.

China stands in the middle of the regional economic cooperation. China attracts investment as well as products produced in the region; some are

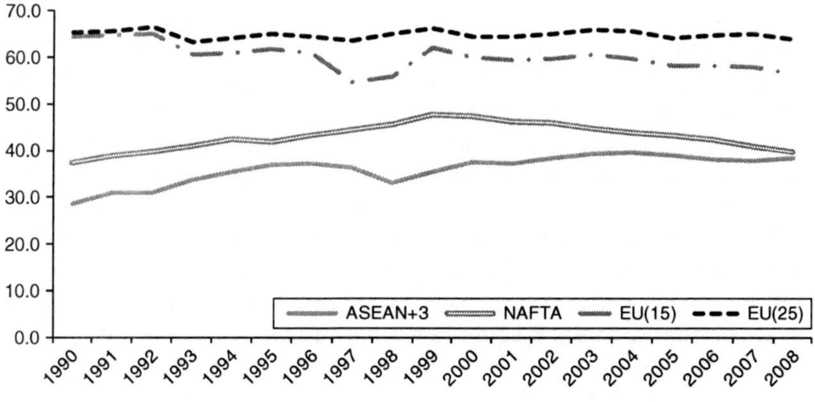

Figure 7.4 Share of intra-regional trade in major economic regions

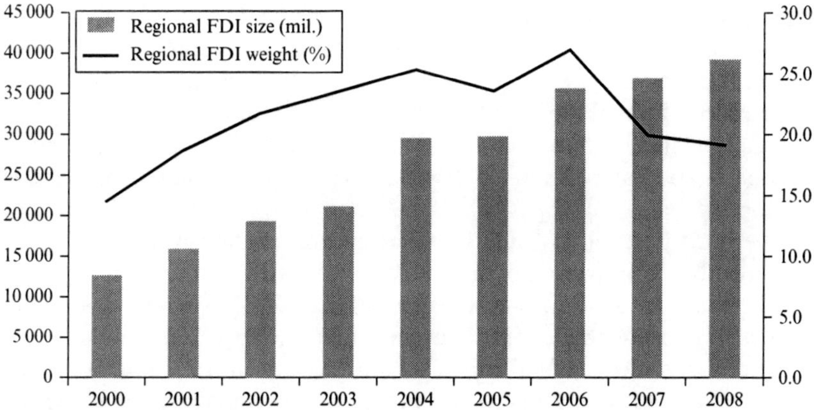

Figure 7.5 Intra-regional FDI (in volume – $ mil. and share – %)

for production and some for consumption. China's economic growth will strengthen the regional interdependency. Asian countries are becoming more and more interdependent economically.

7.4.3 Possible Ways for Assuming Asia's Role in the G20

Building an Asian regional caucus

Asia is being required to contribute to the world economy, rather than just making use of the external markets. Regarding the interdependency of the Asian economies, it is more effective to take collective action in assuming Asia's role in the G20. Because Asian countries do not have a regional consultation meeting, they could establish an Asian Caucus for the G20. Asian countries could get together to discuss the agendas and consider whether they need collective action regarding the given agendas. Firstly, the Asian caucus may have a regional meeting to find a common position so that they can be more influential in the meeting. Secondly, the caucus may represent Asia's regional opinion if needed. And thirdly, the regional caucus may try to achieve coordinated implementation of agreements.

Even if they cannot find a consensus, the member countries of the G20 could then at least deliver the opinions of non-member countries at the G20 summit. A collective channel in Asia could be useful for the Group of Twenty too, because it could save time and effort in cooperation with Asian countries.

There are various possibilities for forming the Asian Caucus. The first option will be to caucus just among the Asian G20 members. They could have a meeting before the G20 Summit to discuss possible cooperation and collective action. Even if they could not find a consensus for a collective action at times, the countries would at least have communicated their different positions, hopefully to reach a better understanding.

The second possibility would be to form a partial regional caucus. For instance, China, Japan and Korea could form one caucus and India, Indonesia and Saudi Arabia another. Australia could join one of these, if it chooses.

The third possibility would be an expansion of the caucus by inviting non-member countries. To raise efficiency, Asian countries may try a partial caucus at first, then establish a full caucus. They could expand the caucus to non-member countries according to the agendas.

Afterwards, the regional caucus could develop into a cornerstone for Asian economic integration. If the members of caucus accumulate experiences in cooperation and build up trust in each other, the countries could begin with economic integration in Asia. If the caucus works effectively, the Asian G20 members could establish a Secretariat for continuous consultations. In this case the member countries could expand economic cooperation among themselves, and the Secretariat may lead the economic integration process. The regional caucus should start as soon as possible, to deal with agendas requiring collective action.

Regional economic integration

The second possible way for collective action would be integrating Asian economies as the Europeans did. If individual economies are integrated, their interests will become more homogeneous than before. Then Asian countries will behave collectively and respond to the external world in a similar way.

The problem with this option is that it will take take too long to complete the regional economic integration. This integration took several decades from the beginning to the completion of economic and monetary integration for the European countries. It takes time because of the following reasons.

Firstly, the countries need time to find a common vision. There have been many talks about possible Asian economic integration. But the vision of economic integration has not been adopted by the leaders of Asian countries. There have been many attempts to create bilateral and multilateral free trade agreements (FTAs) among the East Asian countries. Some of the discussions have concluded in agreements to establish FTAs. The FTA-seeking countries pursue the reduction of barriers between national markets in this region to save transaction costs. The countries do not see and talk beyond the immediate economic gains. Therefore, it will take time to find a common vision among Asian countries.

Secondly, it takes time to realize economic convergence. The economic integration process will reduce the barriers between national markets and intensify competition among the companies in the Asian region. Asian countries show large gaps in productivity due to their different development levels. They need time to reduce the productivity gaps to avoid shocks from abrupt market integration.

Thirdly, the countries may need time to overcome historical legacies. The Asian region still suffers from disputes deriving from historical problems and territorial conflicts. Unresolved conflicts from the past still remain. Asian countries must find a way around these historical legacies.

If Asian countries can agree on regional economic integration, they may need to take a multi-track approach. Countries with relatively better conditions for economic integration could join the first group of economic integration. Then the rest of the countries could build up the next groups according to their economic condition and willingness to join. Hopefully the G20 members in Asia will join the first group for integration so that they may cooperate in the leaders' meeting from the beginning.

The first group may lead the integration process because they may have more opportunities to exchange their views and expand mutual understanding. They can also utilize the occasions and experiences of cooperation to further the integration process.

Steps to Take Now

It would be more efficient for a smaller group to design a monetary cooperation scheme and lay the initial foundations. The practical way would be for those countries with similar visions to lay the foundation, start the process and invite interested countries to join them afterwards.

Table 7.2 Economic relation between China, Japan and Korea ($ million, ranking in parentheses)

	Korea		China		Japan	
Trade	*To Japan*		*To Korea*		*To Korea*	
	Import	61 000(2)		112 200(2)		29 200(7)
	Export	28 300(3)		73 900(4)		59 000(3)
	Total	89 300(2)		186 100(4)		88 200(3)
	Deficit	32 700(1)		38 200(2)		29 700(3)
	To China		*To Japan*		*To China*	
	Import	76 900(1)		150 600(1)		142 300(1)
	Export	91 400(1)		116 200(3)		124 000(2)
	Total	1 683 000(1)		266 800(2)		266 300(1)
	Surplus	145 000(1)		34 500(3)		18 300(6)
Investment	To Japan	609(14)	To Korea	336(9)	To Korea	1420(2)
	To China	4850(2)	To Japan	37(14)	To China	6500(5)

Among the most important problems in pursuing regional integration in Asia may be that this region does not share any common vision; as well as that no country has stepped forward to lead this regional integration. Asia needs an engine for pushing the integration process forward.

Who then can lead the integration process? China, Japan and Korea may be the most favorable candidates to initiate the integration process. The three countries represent more than 87 percent of Asia's entire GDP in 2008. The three countries have already established a complex of cooperation networks. They have diverse cooperation channels and experiences. The rapidly increasing economic interaction among these countries shows the importance of more intensive cooperation (see Table 7.2). The existing trend of economic interaction among these countries implies that their economic relations will probably end up with a higher degree of economic integration. China, Japan and Korea have significant influence in the G20. All of this implies that significant progress toward Asian economic integration is difficult without the active engagement of these three countries.

All the data show that China, Japan and Korea are in the most favorable position to lead regional economic integration in Asia. They have been holding summit meetings every year since 2008, and the three countries agreed to establish a secretariat for their summit in Korea at the senior officials meeting in February 2010. The secretariat opened its office on 27 September 2011 in Seoul, Korea.

The three countries have made good progress on institutionalizing their cooperation. On this institutional basis, the three countries should initially form a core group for economic integration. They can then set up the idea of an economic community as a concrete vision. The secretariat of the China, Japan and Korea summit can play the role of the secretariat for their economic community. This group can function as a Northeast Asian regional caucus in the G20, and the secretariat for the summit can support the caucus too. This group can be expanded to other Asian G20 members. If these three countries proceed with these efforts, they might finally behave and be treated as one single economic entity.

7.5 CONCLUSION

The G20 was called in as a firefighter to respond to the global financial crisis. The G20 leaders met in Washington DC to respond to the world financial and economic crisis on 15 and 16 November 2008 – the first summit to tackle the financial crisis. The summit concluded in agreements to introduce expansive monetary policy to stabilize the financial turmoil. The leaders of the world's greatest economies agreed a set of principles and priorities for crisis management and an action plan for the next four months. They identified the longer-term agenda of reform for the global financial system as well. The first G20 Summit was a success. The second G20 Summit in London in April 2009 showed a high degree of international cooperation, because the leaders were better prepared than in the first meeting. The leaders sought ways to prevent the economic recession from worsening into a deep depression. In addition to the measures to stop the economic crisis, leaders started to fix the financial markets. The markets reacted positively to the agreements and engagements of the G20. The global economy started to recover.

At the Pittsburgh meeting, the G20 designated itself as the 'Premier Economic Forum for International Cooperation'. With this self-declaration as a global economic forum, the G20 has evolved from a crisis committee into a global economic steering committee. The role of the G20 in the global economy has changed since the Pittsburgh meeting. The G20 must take care of all the rules and frameworks of the global economy, albeit that member countries have different ideas on the current issues.

Today, the G20 is at a critical juncture in many respects, as the global economy recovers. It is becoming more difficult to find a consensus in the Group of 20 as the economy returns to a normal situation. Each country takes quite a different position on several important issues, such as the exit strategy, bank levy, global imbalance, exchange rate, and so on.

Even though there is strong concern about the effectiveness of the G20, the G20 is the right place to manage the global economy. The G20 has already shown its collaborative capacity in overcoming the crisis. It just needs to identify its role more clearly, and make institutional arrangements guaranteeing the effectiveness of the agreements.

Asian countries stand at the center of the G20 in terms of prestige and burden of responsibility. Asian countries have faced macroeconomic instability repeatedly, but an effective mechanism other than the accumulation of reserves has yet to be put forward. A more active macroeconomic cooperation in Asia might be cited as a possible way to stabilize Asian economies.

The Asian countries faced two problems concerning the global imbalance. One is the high external dependency, and the other is increasing criticism from outside the region due to the reserve hoarding. The expansion of the Asian market is being requested from the outside as well as inside.

The new challenge to the Asian economy is the high expectations of the world. Asia has the second-largest membership in the G20. However, Asian member countries lack a cooperation scheme. A regional caucus would at least be a useful instrument for effective cooperation.

China, Japan and Korea may initiate an Asian regional caucus, making use of their institutionalized summit. The existing secretariat can support not only the summit, but the caucus, and possibly an economic community among them in the future. Institutionalization of regional dialog may be the best way to vitalize economic cooperation and to overcome political disputes.

NOTES

1. Discussion Note: Framework Session, Sherpa Meeting, Seoul, 20–22 July 2010.
2. According to Sakong Il, Chairman of the G20 Organizing Committee Seoul, 'the global financial crisis is in a recovery stage, but what recovery has been possible was achieved in the public sector . . .We need to make the recovery more robust. To do that, we need to ensure that there is right investment and the right environment for the private sector.' Congratulatory Remarks, Dr Il Sakong, Chairman of the Presidential Committee for the G20 Summit, 7 July 2010, Seoul Economic Daily, Seoul Forum 'Korea in 2010 and Beyond: Reinventing Korea to Become a Global Economic and Technological Leader'.
3. 'Saving glut' is a term coined by Ben Bernanke (2005) to describe too much saving in comparison with investment demand.
4. The historical legacy is sometimes revived in territorial conflicts among the countries.

BIBLIOGRAPHY

Bernanke, Ben S. (2005), 'The Global Saving Glut and the US Current Account Deficit', March, available at http://www.federalreserve.gov/boarddocs/speeches/2005/200503102/default.htm.

Blanchard, O. and G.M. Milesi-Ferretti (2009), 'Global Imbalances: In Midstream', *IMF World Economic Outlook*, October.
Bradford, Colin and Johannes Linn (2006), 'Pragmatic Reform of Global Governance: Creating an L20 Summit Forum', Policy Brief, 152, Washington, DC: Brookings Institution.
Bradford, Colin and Johannes Linn (2009), 'Is the G-20 Summit a Step Toward a New Global Economic Order?' Policy Brief, 170, Washington, DC: Brookings Institution.
Bradford, Colin and Johannes Linn (2010), 'Taking Action at the Seoul G-20 Summit', in *The G-20 Seoul 2010 Summit – Strengthening the Global Recovery*. Washington, DC: Brookings Institution.
Bradlow, Daniel D. (2010), 'Reforming Global Economic Governance: A Strategy for Middle Powers in the G20', Vox, 13 August, available at http://www.voxeu.org/index.php?q=node/5403.
Drysdale, Peter (2008), 'East Asia and the Crisis in Global Governance', *East Asia Forum*, 11 September, available at http://www.eastasiaforum.org/2008/09/11/east-asia-and-the-crisis-in-global-governance/.
Eichengreen, Barry (2009), 'The G20 and the Crisis', Vox, 13 March, available at http://www.voxeu.org/index.php?q=node/3160.
Izvorsky, Ivailo (2010), 'Private Consumption in East Asia is Not Too Low', *East Asia & Pacific on the Rise*, 24 October, available at http://blogs.worldbank.org/eastasispacific.
Lee, Kyung-Tae (2010), 'Where is the Asian Community Going?' *Japan SPOTLIGHT*, March/April.
Lee, Kyung Tae and Deok Ryong Yoon (2007), 'A Roadmap for East Asian Monetary Integration: The Necessary First Step', KIEP Working Paper 07-04, Seoul: Korea Institute for International Economic Policy.
Woods, Ngaire (2010), 'The G20 Leaders and Global Governance', GEG Working Paper 2010/59, Global Economic Governance Programme, Center for International Studies, Oxford University.
Yoon, Deok Ryong (2010), 'The G20 and Development: The Korean Agenda', Policy Brief, September, FRIDE and Club de Madrid.

8. The G20 and Asian monetary cooperation

Woosik Moon[1]

8.1 INTRODUCTION

Along with globalization, emerging countries have had to suffer from the whims of radical inflows and outflows of international capital. For instance, sudden capital outflows brought about a currency crisis in Asian countries in 1997. Bilateral swaps were not available; the International Monetary Fund (IMF) bailout was too stringent to help Asian countries to overcome the crisis. Realizing the need for an emergency fund, Asian countries set out to build the Chiang Mai Initiative (CMI). In 2008, Asian countries were hit by the global financial crisis which originated from the US subprime mortgage market collapse. They were victimized again, although they did not cause the crisis. The CMI was not yet ready. The IMF turned out to be inefficient and did not play any meaningful role to prevent and overcome the crisis. In the absence of an international lender of last resort, Korea, for instance, relied on a currency swap with the US, leading to the multilateralization of the CMI. It is obvious that such experiences made the creation of a global financial safety net and insurance against future crisis the top policy priorities of the Korean government. Indeed, the Korean government made best efforts to make these priorities a major part of the agenda in the G20 Seoul Summit held in November 2010.

This chapter examines the strategies Korea should take to prevent financial crises and to contribute to the recovery of the world economy at global, regional and national levels. More precisely, this chapter asks the following three questions:

- Could the IMF be an international lender of last resort?
- Could the Asian Monetary Fund (AMF) be a regional lender of last resort?
- What is the desirable strategy for Korea?

This chapter argues that the prevention and containment of financial crises for a country like Korea necessitate efforts at national, regional and global levels. For instance, Korea needs bilateral swaps at the national level, the CMI at the regional level and a global safety net at the international level. Each of these is not complete by themselves – they are complementary. However, a bilateral currency swap is not always guaranteed; nor is the CMI sufficient. Furthermore, the establishment of a global financial safety net was insufficiently addressed at the G20, although it is essential to solve the global imbalances and to prevent the recurrence of crises in a world of free capital movement.

The organization of this chapter is as follows: section 8.2 asks about the need for a global safety net. Sections 8.3 and 8.4 examine whether the IMF could be developed into a global or regional lender of last resort. Section 8.5 explores the strategy for Korea. Finally, section 8.6 concludes.

8.2 WHY DO WE NEED A GLOBAL SAFETY NET?

Given that the economic recovery in the United States (US) and European markets is likely to be slow, global economic recovery depends on the growth of emerging economies, especially on those in Asia. Asia now accounts for one-fourth of the world gross domestic product (GDP) and it is the fastest-growing region in the world. But for emerging countries to play a 'locomotive' role in leading the world economy, they need to increase their spending and imports substantially.

However, it would be very difficult for them to assume this role because they are export-oriented economies and their currencies are not international. Take the example of Korea. In 1997, Korea was hit by the financial crisis that happened first in Thailand, spread to other Asian countries, and eventually embroiled Russia and Latin American countries. Korea and other Asian countries were blamed for their crony capitalism, excessive leverage, lack of transparency, and so on, and had to accept the prescription known as the 'Washington Consensus' that promoted market liberalization and fiscal responsibility. The 'conditionality' for emergency loans imposed by the IMF and the US (behind the IMF) was 'too harsh in the Korean crisis' (Siebert, 2008). Western states advanced 'their interests not at the point of a gun but at the tip of a cheque-signer's pen' (Rothkopt, 2008).

In 2008, Korea was hit again by a financial crisis. This time, the epicenter of the crisis was the US ('a made-in-the US-financial crisis'), but Korea and many other emerging economies were not immune from this crisis. In fact, they were suffering as innocent victims. Figures 8.1–8.4 summarize the situation in Korea. The exchange rate of the Korean won

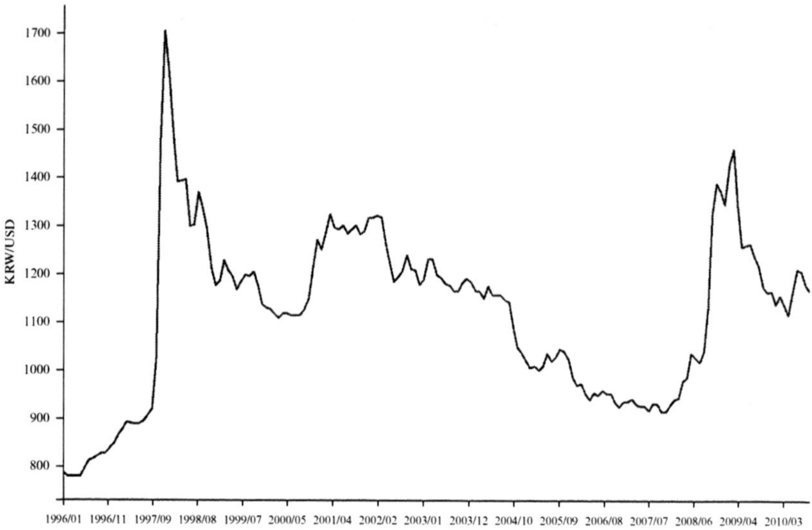

Figure 8.1 Won–dollar exchange rate (monthly)

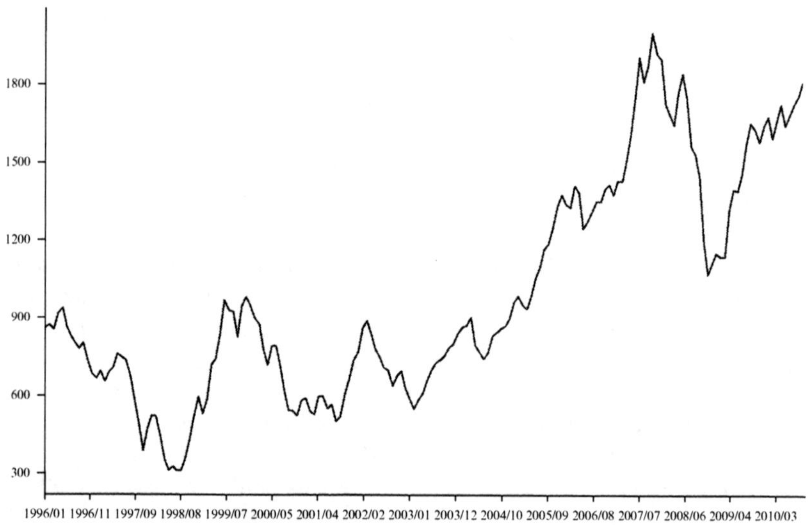

Figure 8.2 Stock price trend (KOSPI)

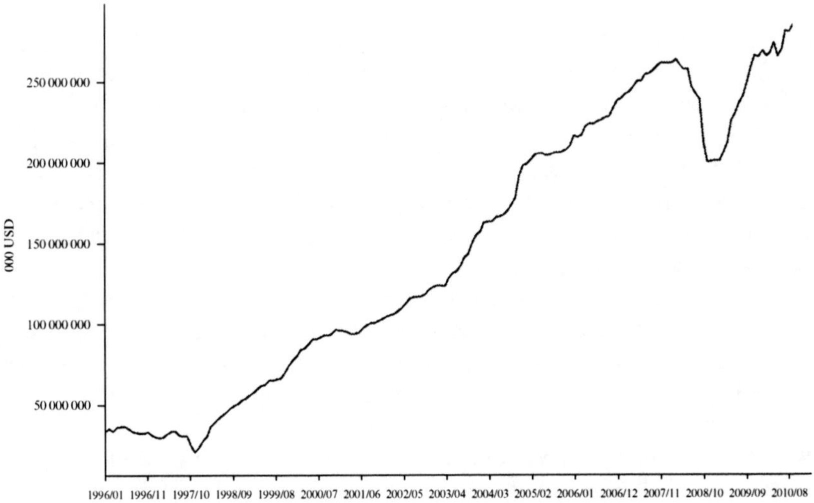

Figure 8.3 Foreign reserve holdings

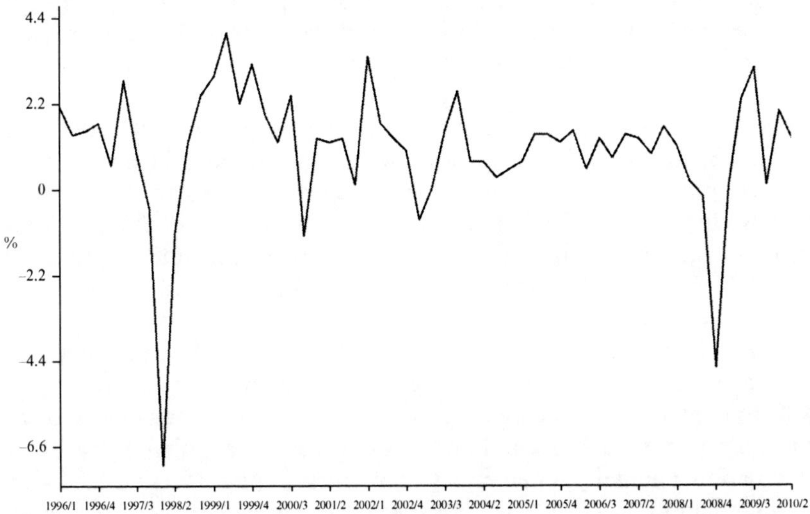

Figure 8.4 Growth rate of real GDP

vis-à-vis the US dollar soared to 1400, the highest since the 1997 currency crisis. At the same time, the stock price dropped to below 1000. Compared to the peak in December of the previous year, this was a drop of more than 50 percent. The skyrocketing of the Korean won was first of all triggered by the capital outflows as mutual and pension funds in industrialized countries were trying to scale back their emerging market exposure, but more importantly it was the result of the Korean banks' incapacity to borrow the US dollar in the one-sided and illiquid US money market generated by a global crisis.

As its foreign exchange market fell into major turmoil, the Korean government intervened to no avail. Korea had more than $250 billion worth of foreign exchange reserves, but this large stock of foreign exchange reserves (nine times as large as the foreign exchange reserves in 1997) did not help to stabilize the exchange market. However, the $30 billion currency swap with the US helped. It was eventually confidence in the continuing trade surplus that helped Korea to recover market trust and to stabilize foreign exchange markets.

It was obvious that under such a situation Korea could not actively promote domestic demand and imports to help the recovery of the global economy. The promotion of domestic demand and imports triggers the current account deficit and the threat of the capital withdrawal, which is leading Korea continuously to stockpile international foreign reserves. In fact, the fear of a dollar shortage was the main reason behind the foreign reserve hoarding by many Asian countries. The cost of such foreign reserve hoarding is huge (for example, see Moon and Rhee, 2009). Thus it is essential to establish a global financial safety net through which emerging countries can insure themselves against sudden capital outflows, and increase their spending. This is also an effective way to solve the so-called 'global imbalances' problem. If emerging countries increase their spending and reduce their current account surpluses, it helps the US and the global economy. It will be helpful to persuade China to do the same.

Here, there is a problem of asymmetry between the emerging and developed economies. Emerging countries turned out to be more vulnerable to global crises because of their need for external financing through the US dollar, euro and yen. However, the need for a global provision of international liquidity for emerging economies lacking cross-border dollar funding had been largely overlooked until the spread of the global crisis to emerging economies threatened the stability of the developed ones. This might be due to the fact that the shortage of the international currency is basically a problem of emerging countries, not of industrialized countries: 'The dollar is our currency but the crisis is your problem'. Also, this might be due to the fact that emerging countries had little voice to solve this problem.

Setting up a global safety net with regard to international capital flows is essential not only from the perspective of global prosperity, but also from that of equal burden sharing between developed and emerging economies. In short, the global financial safety net allows emerging economies to mitigate the impact of sudden reversals of capital outflow and to prevent a national crisis from spreading throughout the world.

8.3 COULD THE IMF BE AN INTERNATIONAL LENDER OF LAST RESORT?

Although the epicenter of this crisis is the US and the European Union (EU), these countries seem less affected by a possible shortage of liquidity. In fact, industrialized countries with international currency could rely on their central banks, which act as lenders of last resort, and they could also meet cross-border funding needs through a swap agreement between central banks. These countries did not even need the IMF.

The IMF was the sole source of dollar funding only for emerging countries. In cases of global crisis, however, it is obvious that the IMF cannot play a role as an international lender of last resort. Its financial resources were limited to US$250 billion. Furthermore, the provision of liquidity coordinated by the IMF came after the collapse of the system, rather than before, to pre-empt large currency swings (see Figure 8.5). Harsh conditionality was another factor making access to the IMF very difficult. Indeed, it is almost impossible for Korea and Asian countries that experienced the 1997 financial crisis to rely on the IMF, because the fact that they have to borrow money from the IMF suggests that their economic policies have failed (the stigma effect).

The G20 Summit meeting held in London on 2 April 2009 agreed to reform the lending and conditionality framework of the IMF, increasing the financial resources of the IMF from $250 billion to $750 billion and introducing the Flexible Credit Line (FCL) as a new lending facility. The aim of the FCL was to provide emerging market economies that had strong fundamentals with a line of credit that could protect them in case the crisis spread. Despite these measures, however, it is not obvious whether the IMF could be developed into an effective international lender of last resort.

The cooperation between central banks of industrialized and developing countries looks much more appropriate and effective (Sachs, 2008). Indeed, speaking on the difference compared with the Asian crisis, IMF managing director Strauss-Kahn said:

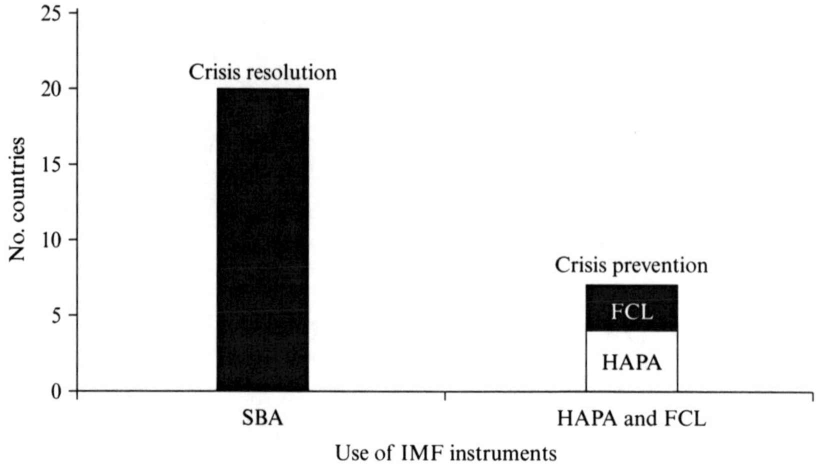

Source: Goretti and Joshi (2010).

Figure 8.5 Crisis resolution or prevention

> What originated in Thailand and spread to Korea, Indonesia, and other countries was mainly a balance of payments problem. That was our core business. This crisis, even if it is a huge crisis, is different. This is a different kind of crisis, so the solution to be applied is not the same. The main actors today are the central banks and treasuries; the main actors in the Asian crisis were institutions like the IMF. (IMF, 2008)

Tables 8.1 and 8.2 show that central bank swaps could mobilize much larger sums of money than the IMF did to cope with the 2008 global financial crisis. For instance, while the IMF provided a mere sum of 33 billion in special drawing rights (SDRs) to dozens of developing countries, the US Federal Reserve Board concluded a total of US$412 billion swaps with 14 developed and developing countries. In particular, the decision by the US Federal Reserve System to extend the swap agreements that had been limited to the central banks of developed countries to those of four emerging economies such as Korea, Singapore, Mexico and Brazil was an important step towards reinforcing a global financial safety net. Also, central banks' cooperation is more effective in stabilizing the financial system.[2] For instance, Figures 8.6 and 8.7 demonstrate that the central bank swap was much more effective in stabilizing foreign exchange markets in Korea, compared to IMF lending.

Since the US showed little interest in the extension of multilateral monetary swap deals suggested by developing economies, however,

Table 8.1 Stand-by facility of IMF as of 30 March 2009 (1000 SDR)

Country	Agreement date	Due date	Approval	Sums not used	Sums borrowed
Armenia	06-Mar-09	05-Jun-11	368 000	206 448	161 552
Belarus	12-Jan-09	11-Apr-10	1 618 118	1 100 320	517 798
El Salvador	16-Jan-09	31-Mar-10	513 900	513 900	0
Gabon	07-May-07	06-May-10	77 150	77 150	0
Georgia	15-Sep-08	14-Mar-10	477 100	189 200	287 900
Hungary	06-Nov-08	05-Apr-10	10 537 500	4 215 000	6 322 500
Iceland	19-Nov-08	18-Nov-10	1 400 000	840 000	560 000
Latvia	23-Dec-08	22-Mar-11	1 521 626	986 282	535 344
Pakistan	24-Nov-08	23-Oct-10	5 168 500	3 101 100	2 070 559
Serbia	16-Jan-09	15-Apr-10	350 775	350 775	0
Seychelles	14-Nov-08	13-Nov-10	17 600	11 440	6 160
Ukraine	05-Nov-08	04-Nov-10	11 000 000	8 000 000	3 029 625
Total			33 050 269	19 591 615	13 491 438

Source: IMF.

Table 8.2 Swap agreements of FRB as of the end of 2008 ($ billion)

Central banks	Agreement date	Due date	Amounts
ECB	18-Sep 2008	30 January 2009	110
Bank of Japan	18-Sep 2008	30 January 2009	60
Bank of England	18-Sep 2008	30 January 2009	40
Swiss National Bank	18-Sep 2008	30 January 2009	27
Bank of Canada	18-Sep 2008	30 January 2009	10
Reserve Bank of Australia	24-Sep 2008	30 January 2009	10
Sveriges Riksbank	24-Sep 2008	30 January 2009	10
Danmarks Nationalbank	24-Sep 2008	30 January 2009	5
Norges Bank	24-Sep 2008	30 January 2009	5
Reserve Bank of New Zealand	28-Oct 2008	30 April 2009	15
Banco Central do Brasil	29-Oct 2008	30 April 2009	30
Banco de Mexico	29-Oct 2008	30 April 2009	30
Bank of Korea	29-Oct 2008	30 April 2009	30
Monetary Authority of Singapore	29-Oct 2008	30 April 2009	30
Total			412

Source: IMF.

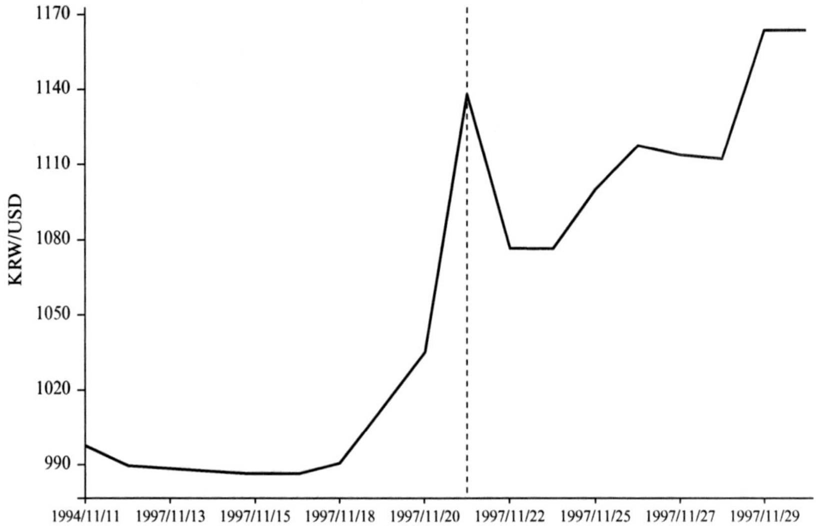

Figure 8.6 Won–dollar trend around the IMF bailout loan ($30 billion) at 21 November 1997

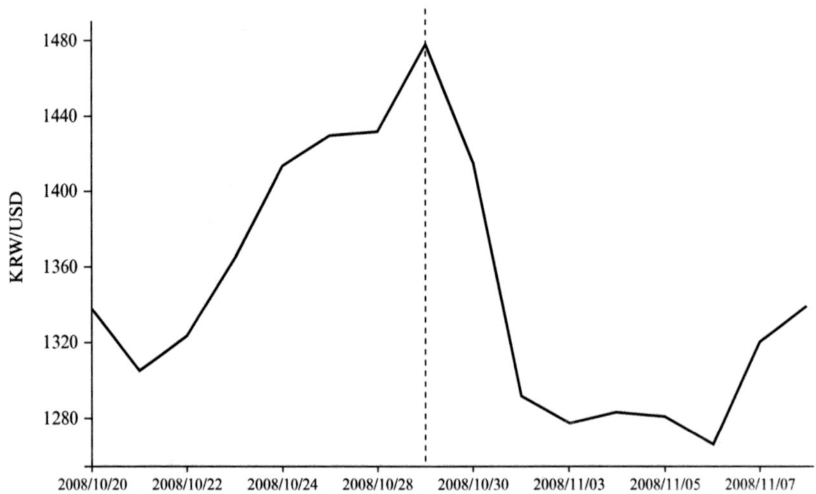

Figure 8.7 Won–dollar trend around the Kor–US currency swap ($30 billion) at 29 October 2008

governmental officials and delegates from the international organizations had to seek an alternative within the existing framework of IMF. As a result, to expand and reinforce the IMF's existing crisis prevention toolkit, another new crisis prevention credit line named the Precautionary Credit Line (PCL) was added, following the strong request of Korean government, ahead of the G20 Seoul Summit meeting to be held in November 2010. The PCL provides a large amount of up-front access to as much as 500 percent of a nation's IMF quota for those nations that cannot use the FCL. Although these new facilities will be helpful for emerging economies, the IMF will no longer monopolize the role of lender of last resort and will have to compete with regional institutions (Henning, 2008).

8.4 COULD THE AMF BE A REGIONAL LENDER OF LAST RESORT?

The idea to create an Asian Monetary Fund first came out of the need to support crisis-hit Asian countries during the 1997 currency crisis. To this end, the Japanese Ministry of Finance proposed to create it in September 1997. At least three arguments can be provided for a regional lender of last resort. One is that an international activity is not speedy enough to nip a crisis in the bud. When significant problems appear within a region, which are clustered due to intra-regional interdependence, a regional institution could redirect its resources better than a truly international institution which has numerous tasks. The second argument is that financial assistance from an international organization is not encompassing enough when compared to what ought to be achieved. For example, as we could witness in the recent global crisis, there was a shortage of disposable funds at the IMF, which eventually led to the increase in funding through G20 meetings. The third argument is that the activity of an international institution does not rest on regional peculiarities but on a general rule. Thus as long as East Asian peculiarities matter, there is an obvious need for a regional arrangement.

But this proposal faced strong opposition from the US government on the grounds that the AMF would be a duplication of the IMF and would only exacerbate the moral hazard behavior of borrowing countries. Amid the lukewarm responses from Asian countries themselves, this proposal was dropped.

However, debates over the need of emergency funds at the regional level subsisted (see for example Woo, 2008). In 2001, leaders of the Association of Southeast Asian Nations Plus Three (ASEAN+3) met together at Chiang Mai, Thailand and they agreed to create a set of bilateral swap arrangements. Under this initiative, named the Chiang Mai Initiative (CMI), countries in East Asia could borrow short-term liquidity in the event of a crisis or contagion. The CMI was undeniably an important step in establishing regional monetary cooperation. However, the CMI was far from being a regional arrangement, due to its limited capacity to conduct effective surveillance and monitoring of Asian economies, and its linkage to the IMF programs. In addition, the activation of CMI was extremely cumbersome due to the nature of its bilateral swaps. For instance, there were 17 bilateral swap agreements (BSAs) among eight Asian countries.

There were continuous efforts to multilateralize the CMI and expand its size. In May 2008, there was an agreement made to increase the total size of CMI to US$80 billion and to fix the proportion of contribution coming from ASEAN countries and the +3 countries at 20:80. Then the leaders of ASEAN+3 agreed on all the main components of the CMI multilateralization (CMIM) at the ASEAN+3 Finance Ministers' Meeting (AFMM+3) in May 2009 in Bali, Indonesia. The CMIM came into effect in March 2010. As a result, the existing multiple BSAs were replaced by a single contractual self-managed reserve pool agreement and the total size of the swap pool was again extended to US$120 billion. Member contributions and borrowing limits were decided in such a way that Japan and China (including both mainland China and Hong Kong) would contribute 32 percent each, Korea 16 percent and ASEAN 20 percent. Furthermore, in May 2010, ASEAN+3 agreed to establish an ASEAN+3 Macroeconomic Research Office (AMRO) in Singapore by May 2011, initially with a small number of professional staff who work with the ASEAN Secretariat to conduct an effective surveillance and monitoring of member states' economies. In a sense, the CMIM is heading towards an AMF, with a more institutionalized structure and an independent surveillance unit.

Kawai (2009, 2010) proposes to transform the CMIM into the AMF. This will require the improvement of the Economic Review and Policy Dialog (ERPD) so that lending conditionality, independently from IMF programs, can be formulated in the event of CMIM activation. Once these conditions are met, a de facto AMF can emerge, capable of conducting effective surveillance and handling regional financial crises. The benefits of such a regional monetary institution are twofold. Firstly, it will free East Asian countries from the monopoly of the IMF over emergency loans. Competition should always be welcomed. For example, in Europe, there are two parallel systems for supplying liquidity to member countries: the European Central Bank and the IMF. Secondly, the presence of a regional body will certainly solidify the position of individual Asian countries in international financial institutions.

Despite the possibility that the CMIM could be developed into the AMF, however, it is most likely that the CMIM would not be self-sufficient in protecting Asian countries. The amount of swap is still insufficient and therefore should be supplemented by both intra- and extra-regional institutions. In fact, the outbreak of the global financial crisis in 2008 revealed, again, the insufficiency of the CMIM as a regional lender of last resort. For Korea, for instance, the maximum fund it could finance through the CMIM is a mere $19.2 billion, or just $3.84 billion if only the fund unlinked with the IMF is considered (see Table 8.3). This sum will be insufficient to contain the crisis. Thus, no matter what happens as to the regional lender of last resort, it is clear that the appropriate coordination of global, regional and national institutions is essential to prevent the crisis. Indeed, in the case of global crisis, Korea relied on a US currency swap. Unwilling to go to the IMF or the CMI (which is tightly linked with the IMF), the Korean authority entered into a US$30 billion currency swap arrangement with the US Federal Reserve System (Fed) in October 2008. Furthermore, Korea had a swap agreement with the Bank of Japan for US $30 billion. Korea had also a yuan-based currency swap with China for the same amount (180 billion yuan, equivalent to US $30 billion).

8.5 WHAT SHOULD KOREA'S STRATEGY BE?

The prevention and containment of crises should be addressed at national, regional and global levels. Firstly, Korea should strengthen its bilateral cooperation, particularly with the US and the EU. There is no need to emphasize the importance of the bilateral swap that the Korean government entered into with the US to overcome the global financial crisis. Given that the dollar and the euro are the two most important international currencies, closer cooperation with the US and the EU is essential, and in this regard Korea should take full advantage of the newly concluded Korea–US and Korea–EU free trade agreements (FTAs) (see Moon, 2010). In fact, the Korea–US and Korea–EU FTA agreements are creating a huge opportunity for Korea to take full advantage of the newly emerging multipolar system and to develop its economy as a hub for the world economy as well as for the Asian one. Korea is the only country in East Asia that has been capable of concluding FTAs with the US and the EU, and it has an economy which is not too big, nor too small, so does not have to fear them. For example, Japanese industries are too competitive and large for the EU to open its market. China is also too big to be allowed to enter into the EU market. Obviously in the short run there will be an

Table 8.3 Structure of CMIM

Members	Financial contributions		Borrowing agreements			Voting power			
	$ Billion	Share (%)	Multiplier	Maximum swap amount ($ billion)	IMF delinked portion ($ billion)	No. of basic votes	No. of votes based on contributions	Total no. of votes	Share (%)
Plus Three Countries	96.00	(80.00)	0.69*	57.6	13.20	4.8	96.0	100.8	(71.59)
PRC and HKG	38.40	(32.00)	0.72*	19.2	5.52	1.6	38.4	40.0	(28.41)
PRC	34.20	(28.50)	0.50	17.1	3.42	1.6	34.2	35.8	(25.43)
Hong Kong, China	4.20	(3.50)	2.50*	2.1	2.10	0.0	4.2	4.2	(2.98)
Japan	38.40	(32.00)	0.50	19.2	3.84	1.6	38.4	40.0	(28.41)
Republic of Korea	19.20	(16.00)	1.00	19.2	3.84	1.6	19.2	20.8	(14.77)
ASEAN	24.00	(20.00)	2.63	63.1	12.62	16.0	24.0	40.0	(28.41)
Brunei Darussalam	0.03	(0.03)	5.00	0.2	0.03	1.6	0.0	1.6	(1.16)
Cambodia	0.12	(0.10)	5.00	0.6	0.12	1.6	0.1	1.7	(1.22)
Indonesia	4.77	(3.98)	2.50	11.9	2.39	1.6	4.8	6.4	(4.52)
Lao PDR	0.03	(0.03)	5.00	0.2	0.03	1.6	0.0	1.6	(1.16)
Malaysia	4.77	(3.98)	2.50	11.9	2.39	1.6	4.8	6.4	(4.52)
Myanmar	0.06	(0.05)	5.00	0.3	0.06	1.6	0.1	1.7	(1.18)
Philippines	3.68	(3.07)	2.50	9.2	1.84	1.6	3.7	5.3	(3.75)
Singapore	4.77	(3.98)	2.50	11.9	2.39	1.6	4.8	6.4	(4.52)
Thailand	4.77	(3.98)	2.50	11.9	2.39	1.6	4.8	6.4	(4.52)
Vietnam	1.00	(0.83)	5.00	5.0	1.00	1.6	1.0	2.6	(1.85)
ASEAN+3	120.00	(100.00)	1.16*	120.7	25.82	20.8	120.0	140.8	(100.00)

Note: *Hong Kong, China's borrowing is limited to the IMF delinked portion because Hong Kong, China is not a member of the IMF.

Source: The Joint Media Statement of the 12th ASEAN+3 Finance Ministers' Meeting, 3 May 2009, Bali, Indonesia; retaken from Kawai (2010).

important benefit from the rise in trade and FDI flows between Korea and the US and Korea and the EU, once these FTAs enter into force.

The Korean market itself is important enough because Korea is the world's fourteenth-largest economy. But, given that Korea is very likely to pursue FTAs even with Japan and China, Korea is expected to play a key role in helping global companies to advance in the ever growing Asian markets, particularly in the Chinese market. In fact, Korea will be a gateway for the American and European companies to penetrate into the Japanese and Chinese markets without tariff. In the same way, Japanese and Chinese companies will have a strong interest to advance into the US and European markets through Korea. To take advantage of this strategic position of the Korean economy as a gateway, both Asian and Western companies are expected to bring huge amounts of foreign direct investment (FDI) into Korea. Moreover, Korea has a solid manufacturing base, which means that the rules of origin related to its FTAs would strengthen Korea's merit as an FDI destination. In short, Korea is a gateway to the global markets for Asian companies, as well as to Asian markets for global companies. This strategic advantage of Korea will obviously allow Korea to cooperate more easily on monetary matters, including bilateral swaps.

Secondly, Korea should strengthen its monetary and financial cooperation with its neighboring Asian countries. In particular, it should strengthen the trilateral cooperation between Korea, Japan and China. So far, the most important challenge for Asian economic integration has been so-called 'ASEAN centrality', which means that ASEAN has played the leading role. However, ASEAN is an economic dwarf compared to the +3 countries in Northeast Asia. ASEAN accounts for only 10 percent of the region's GDP and 20 percent of the quota for the CMIM, while the +3 represent 90 percent of the region's GDP and 80 percent of the CMIM quota. Most of the ASEAN members except for Singapore are also receiving official development assistance from the +3 countries. It is not clear whether the ASEAN countries are really interested in regional integration, given the nature of ASEAN as a simple forum. It seems that the ASEAN countries just want to maximize their net benefit from the CMIM, taking advantage of the rivalry between Japan and China. The design of the CMIM proves that it is for ASEAN countries and not for the +3 countries.

Needless to say, successful regionalization in East Asia necessitates closer cooperation between the +3 countries. Fortunately, in December 2008, Japan held the first trilateral summit meeting between Korea, Japan and China, separately from the ASEAN+3 process, to acquire its own identity. Then at its third trilateral summit meeting held in Jeju, Korea, the leaders of the +3 agreed to establish a secretariat for the efficient promotion and management of the trilateral cooperative projects in Korea. This will be the first crucial step towards the institutionalization of the partnership among the +3, which few believed to be possible. And once this secretariat is in operation, the ASEAN secretariat and +3 secretariat are likely to compete and cooperate to further regional integration in East Asia. For example, separately from the CMIM, which turns out to be insufficient in preventing crises for a country like Korea, bilateral swaps between the central banks of the +3 countries could be considered. Furthermore, as the recent currency war between China, Japan, the US and EU shows, there is a need for closer exchange rate coordination among the +3 countries. The creation of a basket currency incorporating the Japanese yen, Chinese yuan and Korean won might be considered as well.

The establishment of the +3 secretariat will contribute to building sub-regionalism for Northeast Asia, paralleling ASEAN for Southeast Asia. More importantly, it will serve as a stepping stone for East Asian regionalism, given the economic and political importance of the +3 countries in Asia.

Thirdly, as a strategy at a global level, Korea should continue to emphasize the importance of a global financial safety net, just as it has done for the G20 Seoul Summit. As a host country of the G20 meeting, it seems that Korea has already had significant success in making the need for a global financial safety net one of the main agenda items for the G20 Seoul Summit.

8.6 SUMMARY AND CONCLUSION

The prevention and containment of financial crises for a country like Korea necessitate a solution at national, regional and global levels. Firstly, Korea should strengthen its bilateral cooperation, particularly with the US and the EU. Given that the dollar and the euro are the two most important international currencies, closer cooperation with these countries is essential, and in this regard Korea should take full advantage of the newly concluded Korea–US and Korea–EU FTAs. Secondly, Korea should strengthen its monetary and financial cooperation with its neighboring Asian countries. In particular, it should strengthen its bilateral swaps with Japan and China. Thirdly, as a global-level strategy, Korea should continue to emphasize the importance of a global financial safety net, as it has already done for the upcoming G20 Seoul Summit. As a host country of the G20 meeting, it seems that Korea has already had significant success in making the global financial safety net one of the main agenda items for G20 Seoul Summit.

NOTES

1. The original version of this chapter was published in the *Journal of Northeast Asia Development*, **12**, December 2010.
2. See Aizenman and Pasricha (2010) for the effect of the central bank swap.

REFERENCES

Aizenman, J. and G.K. Pasricha (2010), 'Selective Swap Arrangements and the Global Financial Crisis: Analysis and Interpretation', *International Review of Economics and Finance*, **19**, 353–65.

Goretti, Manuela and Bikas Joshi (2010), 'IMF's Crisis-Prevention Toolkit: A Step Closer to a Stronger Global Financial Safety Net', *IMF Survey Magazine: Policy*, 30 August, available at http://www.imf.org/external/pubs/ft/survey/so/2010/pol083010a.htm.

Henning, C. Randall (2008), 'Circumventing the IMF: International Principles Needed for Regional Financial Rescues', *Peterson Institute of International Economics*, 22 October, http://www.piie.com/blogs/?p=128.

IMF (2008), 'US Financial Crisis: IMF Head Urges Greater Regulation of Financial Sector', 29 September.

Kawai, M. (2009),'Reform of the International Financial Architecture: An Asian Perspective', ADBI Working Paper 167, Tokyo: Asian Development Bank Institute, http://www.adbi.org/files/2009.11.24.wp167.reform.international.financial.architecture.pdf.

Kawai, M. (2010), 'From the Chiang Mai Initiative to an Asian Monetary Fund', in Jeffrey D. Sachs, Majahivo Kawai, Jong-Wha Lee and Wing Thye Woo (eds), *The Future Global Reserve System – An Asian Perspective*, June, ADB, available at http://aric.adb.org/grs/papers/Kawai 5.pdf.

Moon, Woosik (2010), 'Whither economic integration in East Asia?' Paper presented at the seminar 'Korea and Europe at the Crossroad' organized by GSIS, Seoul Nation University and GEM, Sciences-Po, Paris, 18 October.

Moon, Woosik and Yeongseop Rhee (2009), 'Financial Integration and Exchange Rate Coordination in East Asia', in D.K. Chung and B. Eichengreen (eds), *Fostering Monetary and Financial Cooperation in East Asia*, Singapore: World Scientific, pp. 51–77.

Rothkopt, D. (2008), 'The Fund Faces up to Competition', *Financial Times*, 22 October.

Sachs, J. (2008), 'The Best Recipe for Avoiding a Global Recession', *Financial Times*, 27 October.

Siebert, H. (2008), 'Preventing Financial Instability and Currency Crises', Kiel Working Paper, 1401.

Woo, Wing Thye (2008), 'What the US and Asia Should Do: Establish a Global Financial Crisis Secretariat and an Asian Financial Facility', available at www.brookings.edu.

9. APEC: the future prospects for a bridge spanning the Pacific

Tomoyoshi Nakajima[1]

9.1 INTRODUCTION

The 20th anniversary of the formation of the Asia-Pacific Economic Cooperation (APEC) was in 2009. The steps taken by APEC – which espouses an 'Open Regionalism' aiming at the liberalization of trade and investment indicated by the Bogor Goals for the economic development of the Asia-Pacific region – have not been even, and the results have not always fulfilled the hopes of many members.

Today many of APEC's members have concluded bilateral or regional free trade agreements (FTAs) with countries and territories within and outside the region, and have realized the liberalization of trade and investment by means of exclusive frameworks. Moreover in East Asia, which is an important part of APEC, regional economic integration is being sought by means of frameworks such as ASEAN+3 and ASEAN+6 (see Section 9.3). Such moves have an impact on the United States, which faces the possibility of being excluded, and has induced major changes in its East Asian trade policy. Today, as a specific response thereto, the United States is proposing a Free Trade Area of the Asia-Pacific (FTAAP), with its area being APEC in its entirety.

In this chapter, on the premise of such changes in the environment, and in the area of the liberalization of trade and investment, I look to the future of APEC, which is a unique international organization linking East Asia and the United States.

9.2 OVERVIEW OF APEC

APEC, via a call from Australian Prime Minister Bob Hawke, was formed in 1989 as an organization for the Asia-Pacific region's economic development and regional cooperation. Initially it had 12 countries as its members, including Japan, the United States and Australia (Figure 9.1).

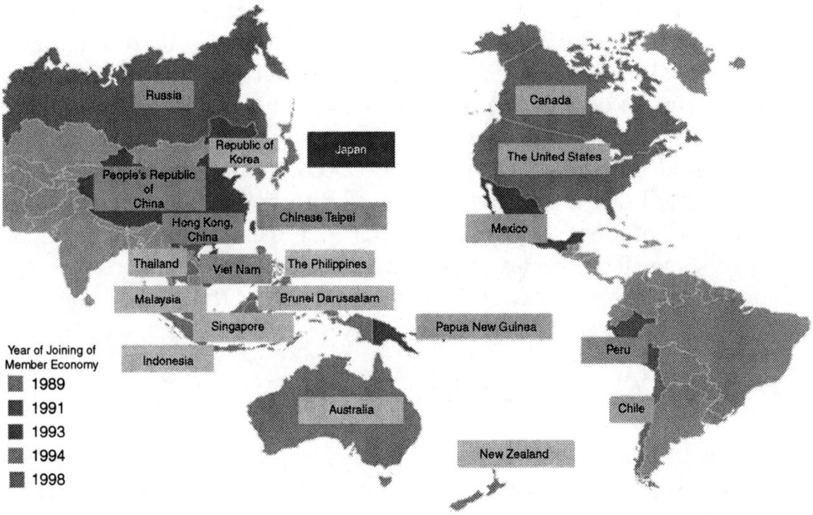

Source: Ministry of Economy, Trade and Industry (METI).

Figure 9.1 The member economies of APEC

Subsequently the membership increased, and currently it has expanded to 21 countries and territories, including China and Russia. In terms of economic scale, in 2008 it accounted for 53 per cent of global gross domestic product (GDP), and 43 per cent of total trade.[2]

APEC, at the summit held in Bogor in Indonesia in 1994, came to agreement on the Bogor Goals regarding the liberalization of trade and investment. The substance thereof was that: 'the industrialized economies will achieve the goal of free and open trade and investment no later than the year 2010 and the developing economies no later than the year 2020'. The members of APEC, towards the achievement of these goals, have been undertaking activities with the following three areas (the Three Pillars of APEC) as their basic philosophy:

- Trade and investment liberalization.
- Business facilitation.
- Economic and technical cooperation.

In addition APEC espouses an 'Open Regionalism', and the results which have been realized via the liberalization of intraregional trade and investment are, via the principle of most-favoured-nation status, that they have adopted the principle of this being applied even to nations outside the region.

APEC has created multilevel mechanisms to realize these objectives (Figure 9.2). The APEC summit which is held annually in autumn, and the ministerial meetings which are held as advanced preparation for the former, form the core of the organizational structure. In addition there are ministers' meetings for each sector, including trade, energy, small and medium-sized enterprises (SMEs) and telecommunications, and below these, meetings of experts have been set up to tackle policy issues for a large number of areas (Figure 9.2). Other than these, the APEC Business Advisory Council has been set up as an advisory body to make recommendations from the business world within the region to the APEC summit.

9.3 APEC AND US PARTICIPATION

The United States, as one of the founding members of APEC, has taken a position of leading its activities from the outset. When looking back at the first 20 years, however, the fruit in policy terms which has been yielded via APEC activities has not always satisfied the expectations of the United States. Amid such a reality it has become a matter that is coloured in accordance with the participation in APEC of the United States. Below I shall look back on US participation in APEC based on the summarization by Terada (2009) (see Table 9.1).

In the first period (1989–95) of the initial formation of APEC, the United States actively participated in its activities, including hosting the first summit for APEC in 1993 in Seattle. Amid this the United States aimed at creating some kind of legally binding force for APEC regarding agreement on the liberalization of trade and investment, yet was unable to obtain the approval of the other members. As a result, at the second summit in 1994 in Bogor, Indonesia, the Bogor Goals were established as an agreement without binding force.

In the second period (1996–2000) the United States, towards the realization of the Bogor Goals, aimed at the realization of Early Voluntary Sectoral Liberalization (EVSL) to come into force early in specific sectors, but the substantive results were poor owing to the passive positions of Japan and others.

It is thought that the United States therefore came to have doubts over the effectiveness of APEC as an arena for realizing the liberalization of trade and investment. Amid this the 11 September 2001 terrorist attacks occurred, and the United States selected an agenda to discuss security issues, including counter-terrorism measures, at the APEC forum (the third period, 2001–05). The effective results for counter-terrorism measures, however, were poor, and once more the US's position invoked the

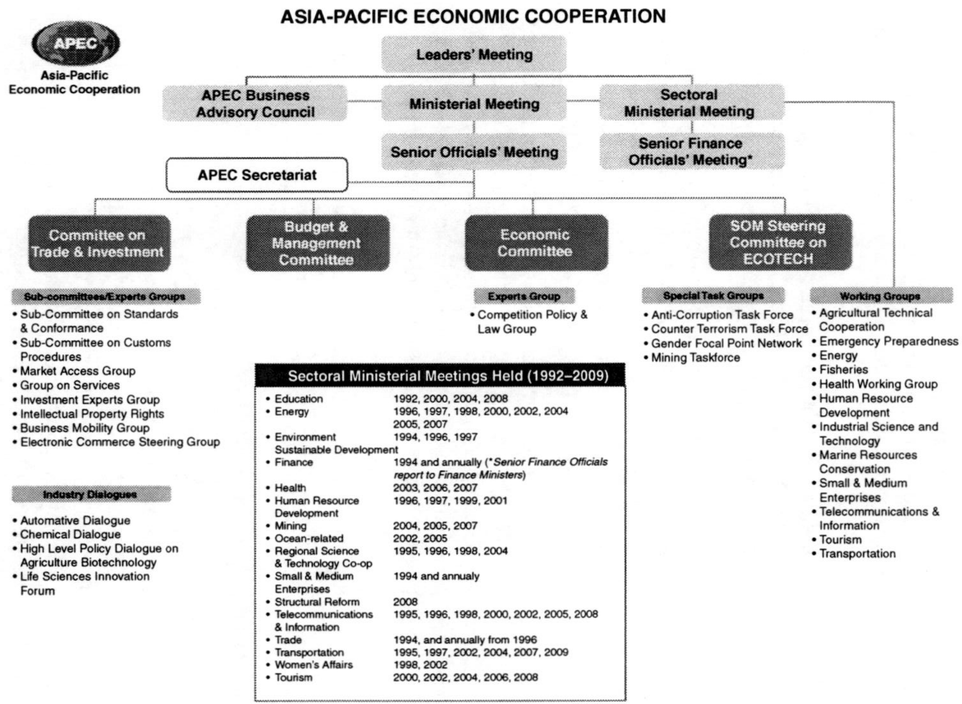

Source: APEC website.

Figure 9.2 APEC organizational structure

Table 9.1 The changes in the United States' involvement in APEC

Period	Major development(s)
First period (1989–1995)	As the host country for the first APEC summit in 1993, the United States heightened the international importance of APEC. At the subsequent summit in Bogor, Indonesia, however, it attempted to make the main topic the liberalization of trade and investment, but failed in making it have legally binding force. The non-binding Bogor Goals were adopted.
Second period (1996–2000)	Regarding the realization of the Bogor Goals, at the summit in Manila in 1996 the United States had to suffer the adoption of a method for the implementation of liberalization made up from Individual Action Plans (IAPs) and Collective Action Plans (CAPs). Regarding the content (marine and forestry products) of Early Voluntary Sectoral Liberalization (EVSL) to come into force early in specific sectors, however, it did not get the agreement of Japan, and the qualitative results of liberalization were poor.
Third period (2001–05)	Hit by the 11 September 2001 terrorist attacks, the United States established an agenda to handle security issues in the APEC arena also, yet no results appeared, and it invoked the opposition of Asian countries who regarded APEC's role as a place for discussion concerning economics.
Fourth period (from 2006)	The United States called for an FTAAP, having APEC as its area, and aimed toward a liberalization of trade and investment, having the legally binding force of an FTA.

Source: Compiled by the author with reference to Terada (2009).

opposition of Asian countries, which regarded APEC's role as being a forum for discussing economic matters.

Meanwhile in the third period, even within the APEC region which had espoused 'Open Regionalism', more bilateral FTAs[3] of an exclusive nature, and the like, were concluded. In addition the international environment surrounding APEC was being greatly transformed, including discussion on East Asian economic integration commencing within frameworks such as ASEAN+3 (Japan, China and the ROK)[4] and ASEAN+6 (Japan, China, the Republic of Korea, India, Australia and New Zealand).[5]

In the fourth period (from 2006), affected by these changes in environment the United States made the counterproposal of an FTAAP at APEC.

Here it became clear that the United States had bidden farewell to the concept of 'Open Regionalism'. In the following section I shall summarize in more detail the background surrounding the FTAAP, from this fourth period on.

9.4 FTAAP

At the 14th APEC summit held in Hanoi, Vietnam, in November 2006, the concept was raised of an FTAAP – an FTA covering APEC in its entirety – and the undertaking of an examination thereof as a 'long-term prospect' was incorporated in the declaration adopted (Table 9.2). According to Sugawara (2006), this was not the first occasion that the FTAAP concept had been raised in the APEC arena. ABAC (the APEC Business Advisory Council), an organization making proposals from the business world's standpoint to APEC, proposed it at the 12th APEC summit held in Santiago, Chile, in 2004. At that forum, however, many objections were voiced, and it was not taken as a subject for active discussion. Furthermore, at the 13th APEC summit also – in Busan, the Republic of Korea (ROK) – it got similar treatment.

Such a passive response to this concept is thought to be due to two big problems: the construction of an FTA covering all the territory of APEC, which constitutes half of global GDP, is difficult; and an FTA which has discriminatory workings towards those outside the region will be fundamentally in contradiction with the APEC stance which has until now espoused 'Open Regionalism'.

The reason for the FTAAP concept being raised abruptly in 2006 as a subject of discussion is because the United States shifted its policy in the direction of promoting this concept.[6] Below I shall analyse the background behind why this policy shift occurred.

C. Fred Bergsten[7] of the Peterson Institute for International Economics, a Washington, DC think-tank, is known as a proponent of the FTAAP concept. The expected aims of an FTAAP, indicated in Bergsten (2007), are given below. These items are not necessarily representative of the opinions of the then Bush administration, but their examination is considered useful as they summarize the benefits that an FTAAP brings the United States, and further decipher the reasons for the policy shift of the Bush administration:

1. A catalyst for the success of the Doha Round.
2. A contingency plan (Plan B) for trade liberalization in the event of the failure of the Doha Round or its becoming stymied.

Table 9.2 Moves concerning FTAAP and TPP

Year	Month	Particulars
2004	November	At the 12th APEC summit held in Santiago, Chile, ABAC proposed an FTAAP
2006	July	The coming into effect of the Trans-Pacific Strategic Economic Partnership Agreement (P4) (member states: Singapore, New Zealand, Chile and Brunei)
	November	At the 14th APEC summit held in Hanoi, Vietnam, an FTAAP was raised as a topic for discussion
2008	September	The Office of the United States Trade Representative officially announced participation in the P4
	November	Australia and Peru indicated their participation in the P4 (see note)
2009	November	US President Obama officially announced participation in the TPP in a speech in Tokyo
	November	At the 17th APEC summit held in Singapore, the continuation of examination of the concept of an FTAAP was incorporated in the declaration
	December	In the New Growth Strategy (Basic Policies) which the Hatoyama administration announced, it was specified that Japan would prepare a roadmap toward the establishment of an FTAAP, with 2020 as the target year
2010	March	The first negotiations began for the TPP adding the United States, Australia, Peru and Vietnam (initially participation as observers, formal participation from December)
	October	Prime Minister Naoto Kan indicated the examination of participation in TPP negotiations in a policy speech
	October	Malaysia participated in TPP negotiations
	November	At the 18th APEC summit held in Yokohama there was agreement on taking concrete steps toward the realization of an FTAAP, and there was the pointing out of: (1) ASEAN Plus Three; (2) ASEAN Plus Six; and (3) the TPP, respectively, as paths toward an FTAAP

Note: From that time on the expanded P4 came to be referred to as the Trans-Pacific Partnership (TPP) (Scollay, 2010).

Source: Compiled by the author from various materials.

3. Preventing the occurrence of discrimination or disharmony in new trade in the Asia-Pacific region, via the further proliferation of bilateral and regional FTAs.
4. Avoiding the risk of East Asia (or the Western Hemisphere) 'drawing a line down the middle of the Pacific', splitting the Asia-Pacific region.
5. Improvement of US–China economic friction.
6. The revitalizing of APEC itself.
7. Forcing a continuation in engagement in the US's trade problems in Asia and globally.

What is seen as important amongst these is the aim of 'avoiding splitting the Asia-Pacific region' in point 4. If we were to consider the point that support for an FTAAP from the Bush administration had been hammered out amid the heightening discussion of East Asian economic integration in the shape of ASEAN+3 and ASEAN+6, then it would be within reason to consider that such thinking was behind policy formation.

Concerning point 1, on the other hand, it could be called a way of thinking aimed at re-enacting the case where APEC's one-time moves towards the Bogor Goals stimulated the then European Community (EC), and pushed forward the Uruguay Round which had been making little headway. As for the practical problems, however, regarding the realization of an FTAAP, the difficulty overtaking consensus building at the Doha Round is something to be anticipated. In addition, by only creating a concept, as at the time of the Uruguay Round, it is doubtful that it would function as a draw for countries outside the region, such as Europe. It is thought that the current situation of APEC, with the virtual collapse of the Bogor Goals, will further reduce such an effect. Consequently, that the Bush administration attempted a policy shift with this as a major aim is something hard to contemplate.

Moreover point 2 may be called a way of thinking that complements point 1. Among the others, points 3, 5, 6 and 7 are not so much the principal objectives of the formation of an FTAAP; rather it may be said that it is apt to think of them as effects that are to be hoped for secondarily.

Considering these matters overall, behind the shift in policy of the Bush administration it can be seen, as shown by point 4, that there was an intention of curbing East Asian economic integration.

The Democrat Obama administration, which commenced in 2009, initially had its hands full with responding to the economic crisis following the Lehman shock, and the constructing of its own trade policy was delayed. Entering the second half of 2009, however, in similar fashion to the preceding administration, a position that stressed an FTAAP became clear. At the 17th APEC summit held in Singapore in November, the continuation of examination of the concept of an FTAAP was incorporated in the declaration, via a US initiative. Thereby it has been shown that the concept of an FTAAP has not been changed, even after going through a change of administration, and is the linchpin of US East Asia trade policy.

In Japan meanwhile the administration centred on the Democratic Party of Japan commenced in September 2009. In 'The New Growth Strategy (Basic Policies)' which the administration announced in December of the same year it was specified that: 'Japan will take advantage of its role as the host economy of the 2010 Asia-Pacific Economic Cooperation (APEC) meetings and utilize the APEC framework to prepare a roadmap towards the establishment of the Free Trade Area of the Asia-Pacific (FTAAP), with 2020 as a target year.'

At the 18th APEC summit held in Yokohama in November 2010 it was agreed to aim towards the realization of an 'APEC Community', having three elements of APEC as an 'economically integrated community', a 'robust community' and a 'secure community'. Of these, an 'economically integrated community' is the deepening of regional economic integration, and specifically has been taken to signify the realization of an FTAAP (Figure 9.3). Here it can be said that an FTAAP has been explicitly designated as a direction for APEC.

9.5 TRANS-PACIFIC PARTNERSHIP (TPP)

Based on the above, it would appear that throughout both the Bush and Obama administrations the position of the United States has been consistent, holding fast to an FTAAP as the core of its East Asia trade policy. On the other hand, however, it can be foreseen that the realization of an FTAAP which will include diverse countries and territories will take a long time. From the point of view of the United States, it appears that at the same time alternative proposals are also needed which can bring real economic results in a shorter period of time. Regarding these, Barfield (2007) has presented four scenarios which it is possible that the United States will subsequently adopt:

1. Promote bilateral FTAs with the countries of East Asia in the future as well.
2. Aim for voluntary FTAs among the member states and territories of APEC.
3. Aim for the realization of an FTAAP.

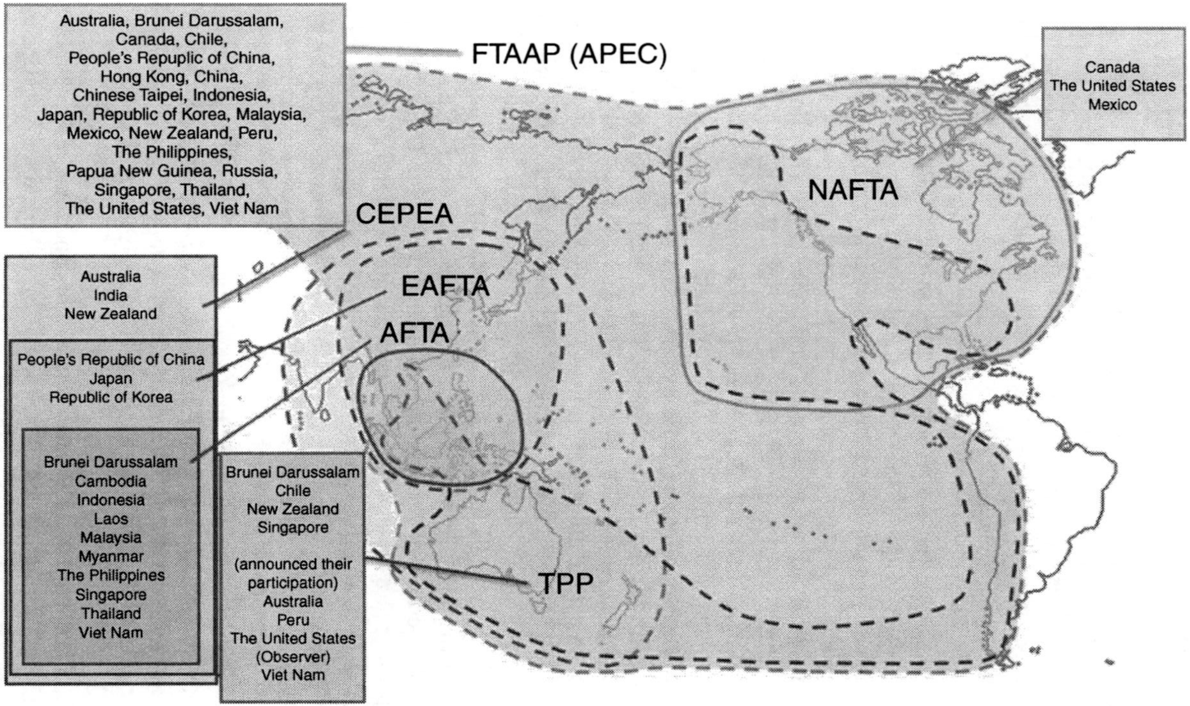

Source: Ministry of Economy, Trade and Industry (METI).

Figure 9.3 Major FTAs related to APEC member economies

4. Observe the situation for the foreseeable future, and in cooperation with allies such as Japan, the ROK and Singapore, respond in the event of some kind of move occurring.

Among the above, scenario 1 – being a matter which will continue the course of past bilateral FTAs which have progressed with the countries of ASEAN, the ROK, and so on – can, as an option, be called the most conservative. Meanwhile scenario 3, as introduced above, will be a long-term strategy.

Scenario 2 is a compromise proposal between 1 and 3, and offers the benefit of combining the two strong points of a presentation of a global vision, and a stepwise approach. On this point it has been considered that, in the sense of complementing scenario 3, the possibility is high of its being chosen as a policy option.

Indeed the Bush administration in September 2008 announced participation in the Trans-Pacific Strategic Economic Partnership (P4), an FTA by the four countries of Singapore, New Zealand, Chile and Brunei. Subsequently Australia and Peru also announced their participation in the same agreement, and it can certainly be rated a 'voluntary FTA' in the words of Barfield. Moreover, the expanded agreement is referred to as the Trans-Pacific Partnership (TPP) (Scollay, 2010).

Accompanying the changeover to the Obama administration, US participation in TPP deliberations has been delayed compared to the original plan. President Obama, however, in the speech he gave while visiting Tokyo ahead of the APEC summit in November 2009, announced the promotion of the TPP. In March 2010 the United States also took part, and official deliberations were commenced. In addition the United States called on Malaysia, with which it was negotiating a bilateral FTA, to participate in the TPP, and that country has also been taking part in negotiations since August 2010. Meanwhile, the Kan administration of Japan also announced examination of participation in TPP negotiations in October 2010.

At the 18th APEC summit held in Yokohama in November 2010, the TPP, along with ASEAN+3 (East Asia FTA – EAFTA) and ASEAN+6 (Comprehensive Economic Partnership in East Asia – CEPEA), was designated as one of the concrete paths towards the realization of an FTAAP[8] (Figure 9.3).

In terms of content the TPP has basically not sanctioned any items for exemption from the elimination of tariffs, and is heading in the direction of an advanced '21st century' FTA, aiming at comprehensive agreement even on sectors that are outside trade in goods, including services, investment and intellectual property rights.[9] If such a consensus building of high-level liberalization can be achieved via the TPP negotiations, it will form in advance the liberalization rules for a future FTAAP.

On the other hand, if the scope of the TPP were to stop at the nations currently participating in negotiations, it would inevitably be limited in terms of its actual economic effects. Regarding the nations currently participating in negotiations, there are many that have been relatively active on FTAs to date, and according to Scollay (2011), of the 36 pairings (dyads) among the nine nations, 25 were already covered by an existing FTA. Moreover, regarding the nations currently participating in negotiations, there are many whose economic scale is small, and the fact that the trade volumes between the various nations are small, except for trade with the United States, is also a factor that limits the economic effects.[10]

In order also to expand such direct economic effects for the TPP it is necessary to expand its scope. In addition, the expansion of participating nations is indispensible because of its aforementioned role as a path towards an FTAAP. From the scales of their economies and trade it can be said that it is particularly important that the Northeast Asian nations of Japan, China and the ROK participate in the future. Of these, at the present time, Japan's move in announcing examination of participation will be a variable having a great influence on the future of the TPP.

9.6 CONCLUSION

In this chapter I have looked back on the developments concerning APEC, centred on dealings with the United States. It can be said that the commencement of discussion concerning an FTAAP in 2006 has revealed – in the most important sphere of the liberalization of trade and investment – the reality that the concept of APEC's 'Open Regionalism' has become an empty phrase. The United States clearly aimed at utilizing APEC as a means to vie with the frameworks for East Asian economic integration of ASEAN+3 and ASEAN+6. The 'voluntary-FTA' TPP was designated to take on that complementary role.

Amid this, at the 2011 Yokohama APEC summit an FTAAP was designated as a means for deepening APEC regional economic integration. This marked the clear demise of 'Open Regionalism' for APEC. Furthermore, the TPP also, along with ASEAN+3 and ASEAN+6, was taken as one of the concrete paths towards the realization of an FTAAP, and was given a formal designation as such at APEC.

As stated above, present-day APEC has a multi-tier organization, and has become a forum for the discussion of a variety of economy-related areas. Consequently in the future it will also continue to hold a certain degree of significance in the Asia-Pacific region. Regarding the intra-regional liberalization of trade and investment which was the greatest objective for the establishment of APEC, however, the potential for realizing the Bogor Goals which raised 'Open Regionalism' has gone, and instead an approach with binding force via FTAs and having a long-term objective of the realization of an FTAAP has taken the lead role.

Turning now to Japan, in the early days of the Democratic Party of Japan's administration, it espoused active involvement in East Asian economic integration.[11] Meanwhile, using the opportunity of the Yokohama APEC summit, it aimed at the promotion of an FTAAP via the forum of APEC, and has put off the final decision regarding participation in the TPP. An FTAAP and the TPP were given the above-mentioned designation as a consequence of the summit. The subsequent path for Japan's trade policy, however, cannot be called clear. Aiming towards the long-term objective of the realization of an FTAAP, should they prioritize ASEAN+3 (EAFTA) and ASEAN+6 (CEPEA) which have been worked on with East Asian nations, or should they prioritize integration into the TPP, for which actual negotiations have been started?[12] Japan's trade policy can be said to be at a major crossroads.

NOTES

1. The original version of this chapter was published in the *Journal of Northeast Asia Development*, **12**, December 2010.
2. From Ministry of Economy, Trade and Industry website. http://www.meti.go.jp/policy/trade_policy/apec/data/data.html.
3. The Japanese government refers to a free trade agreement that includes varied matters – such as investment, labour movement, intellectual property rights and standards' certification, and not only trade in commodities and services – as an Economic Partnership Agreement (EPA). However, as shown by the North American Free Trade Agreement (NAFTA) for example, many FTAs in recent years deal with items other than trade in commodities and services under that appellation. Consequently in this chapter, other than for the proper names for individual agreements, the term FTA is used.
4. A framework for economic integration by a total of 13 countries: the ten ASEAN nations, Japan, China, and the ROK. The ASEAN+3 Summit Meeting has been held since 1997. It has realized several economic cooperation measures, such as the Chiang Mai Initiative, a currency swap arrangement to stave off a currency crisis. As for an FTA concept within the region, there is an EAFTA (East Asia Free Trade Agreement), and after joint research it was agreed at the 2009 summit to have intergovernmental discussion thereon.
5. A framework for economic integration by a total of 16 countries: the ten ASEAN nations, Japan, China, the ROK, India, Australia and New Zealand. The East Asia Summit (EAS) has been held from 2005. As for an FTA concept within the region, there is a CEPEA (Comprehensive Economic Partnership in East Asia), and after joint research it was agreed at the 2009 EAS to have intergovernmental discussion thereon. Regarding the EAS, however, it has been expanded, with the addition of the United States and Russia as new official members from 2011.

6. President Bush, in a speech at a university he visited in Singapore prior to the Hanoi summit, called an FTAAP a concept worthy of serious consideration.
7. According to Yamazawa (2010), already at the Eminent Persons Group stage of 1993, preceding the Bogor Declaration, Bergsten had advocated the necessity of trade liberalization having binding force by means of FTAs.
8. The fact that the three were included in the agreement enables a certain amount of consideration and interpretation for the positions of the countries of East Asia, and particularly for China. Meanwhile, Urata (2011) has pointed out the advantage of the TPP at the present point in time, as the other two have stopped at the concept stage.
9. At the TPP negotiations 24 working groups have been set up, and in addition to market access, place-of-origin regulations, trade facilitation, service trade, investment, the environment, and labour, and other sectors are included for which hitherto there have not been cases of handling within an FTA, such as small and medium-sized enterprises and regulatory cooperation (for more detail please see Barfield, 2011 and Kimura, 2011).
10. Scollay (2011) points out the mutual incompatibility of the expansion of participating nations with the high-quality targets for a TPP FTA.
11. The policy 'Strengthen Japan's foreign relations in Asia with the aim of building an East Asian Community' was included in the Democratic Party of Japan Manifesto for the general election of August 2009.
12. On this point Kimura (2011) has proposed a strategy of first designating participation in the TPP as a precondition, and subsequently consistently continuing to further other FTAs, including an EAFTA and a CEPEA, and making consideration of the special characteristics of each of them.

REFERENCES

In Japanese

Kimura, Fukunari (2011), 'Higashi Ajia no seichō to Nihon no gurōbaru senryaku' (East Asia's Growth and Japan's Global Strategy), in Keiichi Umada, Shujiro Urata and Fukunari Kimura (eds), *Nihon tsūshō seisaku-ron* (Japan's Trade Policy), Bunshodo, Tokyo: Bunshindo, pp. 249–67.

Scollay, Robert (2010), 'Kan-Taiheiyō pātonāshippu (TPP) kyōtei – Hajimari, igi oyobi mitooshi' (The Trans-Pacific Partnership: Origins, Significance and Outlook), *Ajiken World Trend*, **183**, 10–16.

Sugawara, Junichi (2006), 'Totsujo fujō shita Ajia Taiheiyō FTA (FTAAP) kōzō – Shinten suru Higashi Ajia keizai tōgō-e no Beikoku no kan'yo' (The Suddenly Emerged Structure of the Asia-Pacific FTA (FTAAP) – The United States Involvement in the Unfolding Economic Integration of East Asia), Mizuho Research Institute, Mizuho Seisaku Insight (Mizuho Strategic Insight), 8 December.

Terada, Takashi (2009), 'Beikoku to APEC no 20 nen' (The United States and Twenty Years of APEC), in Shujiro Urata and Japan Center for Economic Research (JCER) (eds), *Ajia Taiheiyō kyodai shijō senryaku* (Strategies for the Huge Asia-Pacific Market), Tokyo: Nikkei Publishing, pp. 25–41.

Urata, Shujiro (2011), 'APEC no arata-na tenkai to Nihon no taiō' (APEC's New Developments and Japan's Responses), in Keiichi Umada, Shujiro Urata and Fukunari Kimura (eds), *Nihon tsūshō seisaku-ron* (Japan's Trade Policy), Bunshodo, Tokyo: Bunshindo, pp. 101–19.

Yamazawa, Ippei (2010), Ajia Taiheiyō kyōryoku: 21 seiki no shin-kadai

(Asia-Pacific Cooperation: The New Challenges for the Twenty-first Century), JETRO.

In English

Barfield, Claude (2007), 'US Trade Policy: The Emergence of Regional and Bilateral Alternatives to Multilateralism', *Intereconomics Review of European Economic Policy*, **42**(5).

Barfield, Claude (2011), 'The Trans-Pacific Partnership: A Model for Twenty-First-Century Trade Agreements?' *International Economic Outlook*, **2**, American Enterprise Institute, Washington DC, June.

Bergsten, C. Fred (2007), 'A Free Trade Area of the Asia-Pacific in the Wake of the Faltering Doha Round: Trade Policy Alternatives for APEC', in Charles E. Morrison and Eduardo Pedrosa (eds), *An APEC Trade Agenda?* Singapore: Institute of Southeast Asian Studies (ISEAS), pp. 15–36.

Scollay, Robert (2011), 'Trans Pacific Partnership: Challenges and Potential', paper presented at the Japan Society of International Economics 60th Anniversary Symposium, Kyoto, 11 June.

10. The ASEAN economic community and East Asian economic integration

Taeyoon Kim

10.1 INTRODUCTION

Current economic conditions of East Asia countries have been more rapidly improved from a dramatic plunge caused by the global financial crisis of 2008 than other developed countries. Reasons for fast economic recovery in East Asia countries include government stimulus packages, recovering domestic demand and a revival in external demand, which have improved business expectations and consumer confidence in their economies (ADB, 2010). For instance, gross domestic product (GDP) growth rates for ASEAN-5 (see below), China, Korea and the world in 2010 are 6.92 percent, 10.33 percent, 6.16 percent and 5.11 percent, respectively, compared to 1.71 percent, 9.22 percent, 0.32 percent and −0.66 percent in 2009, respectively (see Table 10.1).

This shows that most East Asian countries, on average, have coped with the global financial crisis relatively well compared to the rest of the world, and these trends are continuing for the time being according to the GDP growth rate in 2010. Also, the number of free trade agreements (FTAs) in

Table 10.1 GDP growth rate in East Asian countries and world (% change)

Year	ASEAN-5	Singapore	China	Japan	Korea	World
2007	6.31	8.78	14.20	2.36	5.11	5.44
2008	4.81	1.49	9.60	−1.17	2.30	2.79
2009	1.71	−0.77	9.22	−6.28	0.32	−0.66
2010	6.92	14.47	10.33	3.96	6.16	5.11

Note: ASEAN-5 includes Indonesia, Malaysia, the Philippines, Thailand and Vietnam.

Source: World Economic Outlook Database, September 2011, IMF.

effect is 27 within East Asia countries and 51 if their FTAs with other countries are considered. Total number of FTAs for all countries is 90 as of July 2010 according to the Asia Regional Integration Center (ARIC). This means that East Asian economies have made many FTAs both within and beyond their regional area, so that their economies are more affected by not only regional economic conditions but also global economic trends. In addition, the degree of openness of East Asian economies, on average, is in the upper level compared to other world economies due to the high proportion of their exports compared to their domestic demand, which indicates that a high possibility of economic integration is also expected within this regional area.

The main question of this chapter is whether or not the Association of Southeast Asian Nations (ASEAN) makes a contribution toward East Asian economic integration. With regard to this question, this chapter attempts to find some implications on East Asian economic integration by reviewing the ASEAN Economic Community (AEC), focusing on: (1) key characteristics, strategies and action plans of the AEC blueprint; (2) ACE's meaning to ASEAN society; and (3) considering current regional economic frameworks such as the ASEAN–China FTA (ACFTA), the ASEAN–Japan Comprehensive Economic Partnership (AJCEP), the ASEAN–Korea FTA (AKFTA), ASEAN+3 and East Asia Summit (EAS). Section 10.2 gives an overview of AEC through its history, and several economic cooperation projects including a subregional cooperation, and examines AEC blueprints of strategies and specific action plans. Section 10.3 highlights current economic frameworks related to East Asian economic integration, which would demonstrate that many efforts have been made among member countries. Section 10.4 draws some insights and possible answers for how East Asian economic integration is being strengthened by focusing on existing frameworks. Section 10.5 concludes.

10.2 ASEAN ECONOMIC COMMUNITY: AN OVERVIEW

10.2.1 ASEAN's Brief History

ASEAN was officially established with five countries including Indonesia, Malaysia, Philippines, Singapore, and Thailand in August 1976. Brunei's joining ASEAN (1984) has been followed by Vietnam (1995), Laos and Cambodia (1997) and Myanmar (1998), so that ASEAN has now ten member countries.

The Declaration of ASEAN Concord II launched in October 2003 played an important role in making substantial progress on the ASEAN

Community. In November 2007, ASEAN members agreed on the acceleration of the ASEAN Community by 2015 with three pillars: the AEC, ASEAN Political-Security Community, and ASEAN Socio-Cultural Community. The Roadmap for ASEAN Community (2009–2015) consists of each pillar's blueprint, the Initiative for ASEAN Integration (IAI) Strategic Framework, and IAI Work Plan Phases II (2009–2015).

ASEAN's progress has encouraged neighboring countries like East Timor and Papua New Guinea to ask continually to become new members of ASEAN since the late 2000s after almost 12 years of Myanmar's joining ASEAN. This can explain one positive aspect of ASEAN's significance for neighboring countries. Moreover, ASEAN has recently started to discuss the next step for the ASEAN Community, such as a rules-based organization by 2022 (ASEAN, 2011), which seems far from 'powerless, slow moving and directionless' (Sakakibara and Yamakawa, 2003).

10.2.2 Economic Cooperation among Member Countries

The first economic cooperation plan among ASEAN member countries was the ASEAN Industrial Projects (AIP) in 1976, which established large-scale industrial projects. Its main strategy was to procure raw materials from regions, and produce final products for regions. It had limited success, however, due to delays in reaching consensus, difficulties in negotiating finance among members, and lack of national commitment to market sharing. The ASEAN Industrial Complementation (AIC) in 1981 was an improved version of the AIP with only one joint project approved, of sharing various auto parts among members. It had similar problems to the AIP, and thus each country later developed its own auto industry with multinational corporations (MNCs). The ASEAN Industrial Joint Venture (AIJV) in 1983 was a private sector version of AIP that opened to non-ASEAN nations as long as majority ownership was valid. However, members are unwilling to participate in the AIJV due to delays in bureaucratic processes and threats to their own industry. These early economic plans among ASEAN were considered extremely ineffective (Sakakibara and Yamakawa, 2003).

Preferential trading arrangements (PTAs) in 1977 were introduced for preferential tariff rates on basic commodities, even though many important products with high trade values were excluded. As a result, implementation was limited. Later in 1992, ASEAN created the ASEAN Free Trade Area (AFTA) in response to the outside environment of increasing regionalism, and made its framework of Common Effective Preferential Tariffs (CEPTs) mainly for reducing tariffs on goods traded within ASEAN. It is considered a significant achievement over PTA; however, amending

CEPT in line with the AEC framework is needed. The ASEAN Trade in Goods Agreement (ATIGA) replacing CEPT was signed in February 2009 and implemented on 17 May 2010. Its main goal is to achieve free flow of goods in ASEAN so that a single market and production base can be realized with deeper economic integration of the region by 2015.

10.2.3 A Subregional Cooperation

Several subregional programs developed by the Asian Development Bank (ADB) also play an important role in the AEC. The Greater Mekong Subregion program (GMS program) is the most active regional framework. It consists of five countries in ASEAN (Myanmar, Laos, Cambodia, Vietnam and Thailand) and two provinces in China (Yunnan province and Guangxi Zhuang Autonomous Region). With respect to reducing development gaps among ASEAN countries, the GMS program has contributed to this region in many ways. Especially, the development of several economic corridors such as the North–South Economic Corridor (NSEC), the East–West Economic Corridor (EWEC) and the Southern Economic Corridor (SEC) has been a core program which is strengthening physical infrastructure and streamlining both cross-border transactions and transportation costs. On 30 June 2011, GMS countries pay attention to the business environment, coordination between public and private partnership, and social and environmental concerns in order to both sustain and develop economic corridors (ASEAN, 2011).

Other countries are also interested in joining Mekong subregional development. The 3rd Mekong (except China) – Japan summit was held on 11 November 2011 in Bali, Republic of Indonesia, which mainly focused on comprehensive development in the Mekong region, construction of society valuing human dignity and expansion of human and cultural exchange. On 22 July 2011, the 4th Lower Mekong (except Myanmar and China) ministerial meeting with the United States of America (USA) was held in Indonesia, which made a contribution to health, education, infrastructure, environmental protection and water quality in Mekong region. Korea also had a ministerial meeting with Mekong countries (except China) on 27–28 October 2011, which resulted in six priorities for better cooperation: infrastructure, ICT, green growth, water resources development, agricultural and rural development, and human resources development.

10.2.4 ASEAN Economic Community (AEC)

The AEC was first introduced in the Bali Declaration of ASEAN Concord II in 2003, and is also stipulated in the ASEAN Charter of 2008 in the context of purposes and principles. Especially, it was well prepared for through the framework of the AEC Blueprint which was declared on the 40th Anniversary of ASEAN and at the 13th ASEAN summit held in 2007 in Singapore.

According to the ASEAN Charter (ASEAN, 2008a) which establishes the legal and institutional framework for ASEAN, major economic aspects are promoting economic cooperation, effective facilitation for trade and investment, and free movement of labor and capital. Fifteen economic principles emphasize ASEAN's efforts to abide by both multilateral trade rules and ASEAN's own rules. Also, this charter is regarded as a basic and essential framework by which many action plans for AEC are supported and exercised.

The four key characteristics of the AEC Blueprint are: (1) a single market and production base; (2) a highly competitive economic region; (3) a region of equitable economic development; and (4) a region fully integrated into the global economy. The Blueprint also includes a strategic schedule from 2008 to 2015 with four consecutive plans of two-year periods for implementing these four key areas.

For a single market and production base, seven strategies are included: free flows of goods, services, investment, and skilled labor, freer flows of capital, priority integration sectors, and food, agriculture and forestry. In the case of a highly competitive economic region, five strategies are added: a competition policy, intellectual property rights (IPRs), infrastructure development, taxation and e-commerce. Towards a region of equitable economic development, small and medium-sized enterprise (SME) development and initiatives for ASEAN integration (IAI) are included. For a region fully integrated into the global economy, two strategies are specified: a coherent approach towards external economic relations, and enhanced participation in global supply networks.

Each strategy has its specific action plans (see Table 10A.1). In the case of free flows of goods for a single market and production base, five plans are included: common effective preferential tariffs (CEPT), tariff reductions, eliminating non-tariff barriers (NTBs), rules of origin (ROO), and ASEAN single window.[1] Other action plans for a single market and production base are these: services liberalization, mutual recognition arrangements (MRAs), an ASEAN investment agreement (AIA), foreign direct investment (FDI), portfolio investment, and enhancing intra- and extra-ASEAN trade and the long-term competitiveness of ASEAN's agricultural commodities.

Overall, some important plans are these: tariff reductions for inclusion list (IL) products by 2010; elimination of NTBs by 2012 for the ASEAN-6;[2] at least 70 percent of foreign equity participation for all service industries such as air transport, e-ASEAN, healthcare, tourism and logistic sectors by 2013; full implementation of MRAs by 2015; continual liberalization plan of FDI and IPRs; various infrastructure plans; and an SME development plan.

The AEC blueprint has an effective implementation mechanism, including enhancing the implementation arrangements, streamlining the decision-making process of all ASEAN economic initiatives, and reviewing and monitoring compliance in implementing AEC. Resources and communications regarded as other major factors for AEC implementation are specified at the end of the AEC Blueprint, with seven actions for proper resources and four actions for better communications.

10.3 EAST ASIAN ECONOMIC INTEGRATION

10.3.1 ACFTA

The initial framework of the ASEAN–China FTA (ACFTA) was signed on 4 November 2002; the agreement on trade in goods was signed in November 2004; the agreement on trade in services was signed in January 2007; the agreement on trade in investments was signed in August 2009. The ACFTA finally came into effect in January 2010. This reduces tariffs on 7881 product categories, or 90 percent of imported goods, to zero in both China and the ASEAN-6. Cambodia, Laos, Myanmar and Vietnam (CLMV) will follow in 2015. The average tariff rate on Chinese goods sold in ASEAN countries fell to 0.6 percent, while that on ASEAN goods sold in China decreased to 0.1 percent. The trade volume of both was \$39.5 billion in 2000 and increased to \$192.5 billion in 2009.

China's initial purpose of an FTA with ASEAN focused not only on economic interests but also on political issues such as 'to eliminate suspicions over the so-called China threat' (Ye, 2010, p. 14). Thus, China not only allows ASEAN countries to have access to specific Chinese markets using the Early Harvest Program (EHP), which enables ASEAN firms to trade with China with zero tariffs, but also gives financial assistance in developing poor infrastructure in ASEAN. However, on 6 January 2010, Indonesia asked for a delay of the timeline for tariff reduction because of concerns over trade deficits and the weak competitiveness of ASEAN enterprises compared to China. Probably, China will need to maintain the present trade balance with ASEAN countries in order to obtain both initial objectives. ASEAN countries have been prepared by expanding their external economic relationship using various international frameworks, so that institutional challenges can be easily overcome as long as

ASEAN continues. It can also be expected that the ACFTA will help to increase intra-industrial trade volume especially in the manufacturing sector of both sides, which means their industry networks are getting closer.

10.3.2 AJCEP

Japan and ASEAN declared the ASEAN–Japan Comprehensive Economic Partnership (AJCEP) in November 2002, and it was signed in April 2008. It has five main objectives: (1) strengthening economic integration; (2) enhancing competitiveness; (3) liberalizing and facilitating trade in goods and services as well as creating a transparent investment regime; (4) developing appropriate measures for further cooperation; and (5) facilitating more effective economic integration and bridging the development gap among the ASEAN members (Sudo, 2009).

Japan's economic cooperation with ASEAN has been strengthened by two major areas of specialization, a special working program and an advanced version of the AJCEP. One is the Japan–ASEAN Integration Fund established in 2006 that supports ASEAN's effort to become the ASEAN Community by 2015. Its main interests are in Mekong Subregion development and the Human Resource Development Total Plan. The other is to bring joint efforts to achieve further development via the Initiative for Development in East Asia (IDEA). ASEAN agreed to establish the Economic Research Institute of ASEAN and East Asia (ERIA) in 2006, and asked Japan to develop the proposal for the Comprehensive Asia Development Plan (CADP), which is a revised version of the Comprehensive Economic Partnership for East Asia (Dent, 2008). This plan was approved among ASEAN member countries during the 17th ASEAN summit as well as the 5th EAS in October 2010. The Master Plan on ASEAN Connectivity (MPAC) which resulted from the 17th ASEAN summit shows that Japan made a very positive contribution to the high cooperation with ASEAN by integrating hardware development and software connectivity. This connectivity will be more developed in the CADP where India is another area being connected with ASEAN.

10.3.3 AKFTA

The ASEAN–Korea FTA (AKFTA) was discussed in October 2003, the agreement on trade in goods was signed in August 2006, the agreement on trade in services was signed in November 2007, and the agreement on trade in investments was signed in June 2009. Korea made a bilateral FTA with Singapore in 2004 and now is preparing for bilateral FTAs with

ASEAN member countries such as Vietnam, Malaysia and Indonesia even though these countries are affected by the AKFTA. Moreover, the AKFTA implementation committee examines market conditions for further market openness every year. According to research on the utilization rate of preferential tariffs for member countries, it is still low because of poor awareness among trading firms of both countries (Kim et al., 2009). Thus, Korea is now trying to make AKFTA more effective than before.

Being a new member of the Development Assistance Committee (DAC) since 2010, Korea wants to contribute to ASEAN's development plan in order to narrow the development gaps among ASEAN member countries. Since Japan, as an old member of the DAC, has been involved in regional development plans jointly with ASEAN and endorsed by neighboring countries, it provides good lessons for Korea in helping promote regional development. On the one hand, both Korea and ASEAN nations would benefit from AKFTA because it creates more trade, investment, labor cooperation and so on. On the other hand, Korea can participate in subregional programs such as the GMS program for creating regional development demand, which results in increasing relations between two parties. This is a concept of 'shared growth' adopted as the 'Seoul Development Consensus' in the G20 Seoul summit of 2010.

10.3.4 ASEAN+3

In December 1997, ASEAN invited the leaders of China, Japan and Korea to cope with the Asian financial crisis, which eventually established the ASEAN+3 framework as another important means of regional cooperation.

One of the most significant tasks that they agreed upon was to launch a regional liquidity support arrangement called the Chiang Mai Initiative (CMI) in 1999 and implement it with a partial sharing[3] of total $120 billion in 2010, which is called Chiang Mai Initiative Multilateralization (CMIM). In order to enlarge the CMIM scheme, ASEAN+3 launched the ASEAN+3 Macroeconomic Research Office (AMRO) in Singapore in 2011.

Another achievement was to make an agreement on establishing the East Asian Community (EAC) as a long-term objective, and to affirm the role of ASEAN+3 as the major framework for the EAC (Kawai and Wignaraja, 2007).

Since ASEAN has made bilateral FTAs with China, Japan and Korea, the East Asia FTA (EAFTA) can be regarded as the next step for ASEAN+3. As Kawai and Wignaraja (2007) and Lee et al. (2009)

mention, however, creating unified rules of origin (ROO) is the key factor in handling the 'spaghetti bowl effect' and minimizing transaction costs for intra-regional trade. Other important issues in making further bilateral FTAs among East Asia countries are utilization of the concession structure of existing FTAs, harmonization among countries, and facilitation measures directly linked to an appropriate funding mechanism (Lee et al., 2009).

10.3.5 EAS

Another regional forum among East Asia countries is the East Asia Summit (EAS), agreed in November 2004; its first meeting was held in December 2005. This is an expansion of ASEAN+3 by including India, Australia and New Zealand. Japan mainly regarded the EAS as an appropriate group for East Asia's trade and investment cooperation (Kawai and Wignaraja, 2007).

In September 2010, ASEAN leaders had a second meeting with a US leader which resulted in welcoming the US President's intention to participate in the EAS, and Secretary Clinton's attendance as an observer at the 5th EAS (ASEAN, 2010a). ASEAN leaders unofficially welcomed Russia to participate in the EAS at the beginning of 2010. As a result of the 5th EAS meeting in 2010, the US and Russia joined the EAS, so that it has now eight member countries. In 2011, Indonesia held the 6th EAS meeting, which mainly discussed an economic and security agenda including connectivity, energy and food security, maritime issues, terrorism, piracy and the Korean Peninsula.

10.4 ASEAN'S STRATEGIES TOWARD REGIONAL INTEGRATION

10.4.1 Competition between Centrifugal and Centripetal Force

There are economic development gaps among ASEAN member countries, such that regional economic integration might not be an easy task. In Table 10.2, for instance, per capita income ranges from US$702 in Myanmar to US$43 117 in Singapore in 2010. Trade dependency using the ratio of total trade to gross domestic product (GDP) ranges from 39.0 percent in Indonesia to 282.2 percent in Singapore in 2009. These differences indicate that centrifugal force among member countries continues as long as development gaps are not narrowing. On the other hand, the IAI was launched to narrow development gaps within ASEAN as well

Table 10.2 Economic indicators for ASEAN member countries in 2010

ASEAN member countries	Growth rate of GDP (%)	Inflation rate (%)	Per capita income USD	Ratio of total trade to GDP[1] (%)
Brunei	2.0	1.3	31 239	88.9
Cambodia	5.8	4.0	814	85.8
Indonesia	6.1	7.0	3015	39.0
Lao PDR	8.4	6.0	984	53.1
Malaysia	7.2	1.7	8423	145.1
Myanmar	3.3	9.4	702	40.8
The Philippines	7.3	3.8	2007	52.0
Singapore	14.5	2.8	43 117	282.2
Thailand	7.8	3.3	9221	108.3
Vietnam	6.8	8.9	1 174	130.7

Note: [1] 2009 data from ASEAN Secretariat.

Source: Global Insight, IMF, ASEAN Secretariat.

as between ASEAN and other parts of the world. The IAI work plan for CLMV countries focuses on infrastructure development, human resource development, information and communication technology and promoting regional economic integration so that centripetal force can be maintained within ASEAN member countries.

Also, there is a regional organization other than ASEAN for economic cooperation. The Ayeyawady–Chao Phraya–Mekong Economic Cooperation Strategy (ACMECS) is aiming at economic development through trade and investment among Mekong river countries such as Myanmar (Ayeyawad), Thailand (Chao Phraya), Cambodia, Laos and Vietnam. However, it has not yet been recognized an ASEAN subregional economic zone even though ACMECS consists of five ASEAN member countries (Yamakage, 2010). The GMS program which was developed by the ADB and is well recognized within ASEAN's framework has been focusing on infrastructure development for CLMV countries. Both regional programs indicate that a competition between centrifugal and centripetal force is continuing, along with their improvement of the AEC.

10.4.2 Changes in Constructive Engagement

ASEAN's approach, especially in 2004, to the ruling junta in Myanmar is known as constructive engagement because on the one hand ASEAN embraces Myanmar even though the Prime Minister was ousted by military force, while on the other hand ASEAN encourages Myanmar to engage in democracy and open up its market. In February 2011, Myanmar launched a new government called the Republic of the Union of Myanmar by its national election and it is described as 'a multiparty democratic system' under its 2008 constitution.

In February 2011, Indonesia as a chairman of ASEAN mediated upon border conflicts between Thailand and Cambodia. Later, the two countries eventually made an agreement for avoiding further clashes, an event labelled 'a victory of ASEAN' regarding regional integration. These two events suggest that ASEAN's non-interference policy is changing, and its role is strengthening toward regional integration by opening dialogs within ASEAN and enhancing regional cooperation under ASEAN's framework.

10.4.3 Acceleration in Economic Issues

ASEAN is trying to be a hub of FTAs within East Asia. It has AFTA, so that tariffs in all general products which are categorized in the AFTA framework have already been removed within the ASEAN-6 in 2010 and will be eliminated within ASEAN by 2015. ACFTA, AKFTA and AJCEP were also implemented in 2005, 2007 and 2008, respectively. India, Australia and New Zealand also made FTA agreements with ASEAN, which were implemented in 2010.

Moreover, each ASEAN member country is considering participating in bilateral FTAs. For instance, Vietnam, Malaysia and Indonesia are doing a feasibility study of a bilateral FTA with Korea. Other regional economic agreements are also under negotiation. Vietnam, Brunei, Singapore and Malaysia are joining Trans-Pacific Partnership Agreement (TPP) negotiations with Chile, Peru, Japan and the United States. The TPP requires all participants to open their markets, including for sensitive products such as agricultural products, so it is described as a high-level economic cooperation.

In terms of foreign direct investment (FDI) according to ASEAN statistics, ASEAN's total net inflow was expected to be about $75 757.7 million in 2010 compared to $37 881.3 million in 2009. In 2010, 16 percent of net FDI came from ASEAN while 84 percent of net FDI flowed from other countries. The European Union (EU), Japan, USA, China, Korea, Australia and India were the largest investors, in descending order, between 2008 and 2010.

Since ASEAN has made many FTAs with other nations, ASEAN can benefit from development projects with the help of foreign companies which receive many investment incentives based on those FTAs. Also, ASEAN's activities toward both fast economic development and regional stability using official development assistance (ODA) contributes to accelerating regional integration by widening economic cooperation with foreign countries.

10.4.4 Evolution and Adaptation

ASEAN has agreed to be a single market and production base by 2015, according to the AEC Blueprint (see Table 10A.1). ASEAN adopted the AEC Blueprint in 2007 in order to achieve this goal. The AEC scoreboard mechanism was developed in 2008 to monitor the implementation of each measure in the AEC Blueprint. In 2010, ASEAN measured the status of the AEC for the first two-year period (2008–2009) as 73.6 percent achieved (ASEAN, 2010b). This informs not only member countries, but also other nations, that ASEAN has evolved into the AEC in terms of free flow of goods, services, investment, capital and skilled labor.

The score of a competitive economic region is 50 percent, which is lower than the AEC average of 73.6 percent. A competition policy, consumer protection and strengthening IPRs are the main issues for creating a competitive regional market. ASEAN studied competition policies and laws in the East Asia Summit countries and eventually created ASEAN-wide Guidelines on Competition Policy and the Handbook on Competition Policy and Law for Business (see ASEAN, 2010b). These will help ASEAN to be a more competitive regional market. Also, a coordinating committee on consumer protection has been established to give a high level of consumer protection. Moreover, ASEAN has launched an online directory of IPR-related resources and services for businesses and other interested parties. These efforts will help ASEAN become a single market, production base and a competitive regional market, as scheduled in the AEC framework, by 2015.

10.5 CONCLUSION

A global financial and economic crisis has given some lessons to East Asian countries especially on the importance of both strong domestic demand and economic cooperation with world economies. In the process of overcoming recent global financial crisis, ASEAN's recovery, along with that of other East Asian countries such as Korea, Taiwan and Japan, resulted from stable exports mainly to China. In addition, bilateral FTAs among East Asian countries have been helping them to increase intra-industrial trade with confidence. These understandings are also supported and developed by Lee et al. (2009)'s finding that the current global crisis has made East Asian countries grow their intra-regional market. This is because the United States and the European Union could not increase their domestic markets, so that absorbing exports from East Asian countries was difficult for them.

The AEC has developed well compared to East Asian economic integration, because the former has good frameworks and specific schedules while the latter has not. Even though income per capita of each ASEAN member country is relatively low and its variations among member countries are quite large, ASEAN's influence has increased as a whole by actively participating not only in economic cooperation but also in security cooperation with international organizations. Recently, because of both China's growing influences and the US's continuous interest in the East Asia region, ASEAN invited the US and Russia to participate in the EAS as guests of the chair at the 5th EAS meeting in 2010. This event resulted in approving the two countries as members at the 6th EAS meeting in 2011. This is another major step in strengthening regional economic cooperation as well as security cooperation.

ASEAN's centrality in East Asian economic integration is regarded as an important factor because ASEAN is involved in most regional cooperation, sitting in the 'driver's seat' (Yamazawa, 2011). Regarding future economic cooperation in East Asia, three expressions can be borrowed from Kawai and Wignaraja (2007): ASEAN as the driving force because it has already made bilateral FTAs with other East Asian countries; ASEAN+3 as the main vehicle for the realization of an eventual East Asian economic community once some challenges are solved such as unifying rules of origin, harmonizing the concession structure, and facilitation measures directly linked to appropriate funding mechanisms; and 'EAS as an integral part of the overall evolving regional architecture' even though it has a long way to go.

It is also important to evaluate the creation of the AEC by 2015 as a factor for East Asian economic integration. Creating the AEC by 2015 is not an easy task for member countries, because of many centrifugal forces including development gaps. However, the creation of the AEC as a single market, production base and regional competitive market is in progress, through competition between centrifugal and centripetal forces, changes in constructive engagement, acceleration on economic issues, and evolution and adaptation.

NOTES

1. ASEAN single window means a system which enables ASEAN member countries to have a single submission and processing of data and information, a single decision-making for customs release and clearance.
2. ASEAN-6 includes Indonesia, Malaysia, Philippines, Thailand, Singapore and Brunei.
3. China and Japan will share 32 percent each, Korea 16 percent and ASEAN 20 percent.

REFERENCES

ADB (2010), 'Asia Economic Monitor: July 2010', Asia Development Bank.
ASEAN (2008a), 'The ASEAN Charter', ASEAN Secretariat.
ASEAN (2008b), 'ASEAN Economic Community Blueprint', ASEAN Secretariat.
ASEAN (2010a), 'Joint Statement of the 2nd ASEAN–US Leaders' Meeting', ASEAN Secretariat.
ASEAN (2010b), 'ASEAN Economic Community Scorecard', ASEAN Secretariat.
ASEAN (2011), 'ASEAN Leader's Joint Statement on the ASEAN Community in a Global Community of Nations', ASEAN Secretariat.
Dent, Christopher (2008), 'The Asian Development Bank and Developmental Regionalism in East Asia', *Third World Quarterly*, **29**(4), 767–86.
Kawai, Masahiro and Ganeshan Wignaraja (2007), 'ASEAN+3 or ASEAN+6: Which Way Forward?' ADB Institute Discussion Paper No. 77, Tokyo: Asian Development Bank Institute.
Kim, H.S., M.J. Cho, J.W. Jeong and M.S. Kim (2009), 'Effective Implementation of Korea-ASEAN FTA: Trade in Goods', Korea Institute for International Economic Policy.
Lee, C.J., H.S. Kim, H.K. Bang and Y.Y. Noh (2009), 'From ASEAN+1 FTAs to an East Asia FTA', Korea Institute for International Economic Policy.
Sakakibara, Eisuke and Sharon Yamakawa (2003), 'Regional Integration in East Asia', Policy Research Working Paper 3078, World Bank.
Sudo, Sueo (2009), 'Japan's ASEAN Policy: Reactive or Proactive in the Face of a Rising China in East Asia?' *Asian Perspective*, **33**(1), 137–58.
Yamakage, Susumu (2010), 'ASEAN, Old and New: An Overview', in Japan Institute of International Affairs (ed.), *ASEAN Study Group Report*, Tokyo: Japan Institute of International Affairs, pp. 1–10.
Yamazawa, Ippei (2011), 'New IAP Peer Review Process toward FTAAP', paper presented at APEC Study Center Consortium Conference, San Francisco, CA, 22–23 September.
Ye, Shulan (2010), 'China's Regional Policy in East Asia and Its Characteristics', Discussion Paper 66, China Policy Institute.

APPENDIX

Table 10A.1 Main strategic schedule for ASEAN economic community

Strategic approach	Priority Actions			
	2008–09	2010–11	2012–13	2014–15
A. Towards a Single Market and Production Base				
A1. Free Flows of Goods				
• CEPT-AFTA	• Enhance CEPT agreement (2008)			
• Tariffs Reduction	• Complete the tariff reduction to 0–5% for all IL[1] products for Laos and Myanmar	• Complete the tariff reduction to 0–5% for all IL products for Cambodia (2010)		
• Elimination of NTBs	• Abide by the commitment of a standstill and roll-back on NTBs, effective immediately	• Eliminate NTBs for ASEAN-5 (2010)	• Eliminate NTB for the Philippines (2012)	• Eliminate NTB for CLMV (2015) with flexibility to 2018 for some sensitive products
• Rules of Origin (ROO)	• Continually reform and enhance the CEPT ROO to respond to changes in global production processes			

Table 10A.1 (continued)

Strategic approach	Priority Actions			
	2008–09	2010–11	2012–13	2014–15
A1. Free Flows of Goods				
• ASEAN Single Window	• ASEAN-6 operationalize their national single windows by 2008		• CLMV operationalize their national single windows no later than 2012	
A2. Free Flows of Services				
• Services Liberalization under AFAS	• At least 51% foreign equity participation for the 4 priority[2] services sectors (2008)	• At least 70% foreign equity participation for the 4 priority services sectors (2010)		
	• At least 49% foreign equity participation for logistics and other services (2008)	• At least 51% foreign equity participation for logistics and other services (2010)	• At least 70% foreign equity participation for logistics services (2013)	• At least 70% foreign equity participation for all services (2013)

• Mutual Recognition Arrangement (MRAs)	• Complete MRAs currently under negotiation, i.e, architectural accountancy services, surveying qualifications, medical practitioners and dental practitioners (2008)	• Identify and develop MRAs for other professional services by 2012		• Full implementation of completed MRAs (2015)
A3. Free Flows of Investment				
• ASEAN Investment Agreement (AIA)	• The new ASEAN Comprehensive Investment Agreement (ACIA)			
A4. Free Flows of Capital				
• Foreign Direct Investment	• Assess and identify rules for liberalization for freer flows of foreign direct investments	• Progressively liberalize, where appropriate and possible, the pre-identified list of rules for freer flow of foreign direct investments		• Continue to liberalize, where appropriate and possible, any other items related to FDI, portfolio investments, other types of capital flows
• Portfolio Investment	• Assess and identify rules for liberalization for freer flows of portfolio Investments, particularly in debts and equity	• Progressively liberalize, where appropriate and possible, the rules identified for freer flow of portfolio investments		

Table 10A.1 (continued)

Strategic approach	Priority Actions			
	2008–09	2010–11	2012–13	2014–15
A5. Free Flows of Skilled Labor				
	• Develop core competencies for job skills required in the priority services sectors by 2009			• Develop core competencies for job skills required in all services sectors by 2015
A6. Priority Integration Sectors				
	• Conduct a bi-annual review to monitor the status, progress and effectiveness of PIS roadmaps	• Complete most of the measures identified under the roadmap of original 11 priority integration sectors	• Complete most of the measures identified under the roadmap for integration of logistics services	
A7. Food, Agri, and Forestry				
• Enhance intra- and extra-ASEAN trade and long-term competitiveness of ASEAN's commodities	• HACCP (2009)		• Good Agriculture Practices by 2012	• SPS by 2015
	• Harmonize the MRLs by 2010			

B. Towards a Highly Competitive Economic Region				
B1. Competition Policy				
• Building capacity and introduction of best practices for competition policy	• Carrying out a foundation-laying study, review of study findings and recommendations, and convening a regional meeting on study findings and recommendations	• Drawing up a regional work plan on competition policy and law		
		• Exploring funding opportunities for the implementation of selected elements of the work plan		
B3. Intellectual Property Rights				
• Action Plan	• Studies on contribution and implications of copyright system to the economic development, the best utilization by various countries of flexibilities, collective management societies and copyright tribunals	• To set a common goal to be attained so as to facilitate the development of copyright-based industry	• To enhance the competitiveness of copyright industries	• Establishment of collective management societies in all ASEAN countries
			• To develop online access to copyright notifications	

Table 10A.1 (continued)

Strategic approach	Priority Actions			
	2008–09	2010–11	2012–13	2014–15
B4. Infrastructure Development				
• Transport Action Plan Singapore–Kunming Rail Link Road Safety Requirements	• Completion of Poipet–Sisophone Rail Link (2009)	• Implementation of the ASEAN five-year Regional Road Safety Action Plan	• Member countries to develop ASEAN standard measures for road safety	
• ASEAN Framework Agreement on Multimodal Transport	• Have enacted necessary domestic legislations to put into effect this agreement	• At least two countries implementing this agreement	• ASEAN-wide implementation of this framework	
• ASEAN Framework Agreement on the Facilitation of Goods in Transit (AFAFGIT)	• Implement AFAFGIT	• Conclude protocol 6 (railway borders and interchange stations) of the ASEAN FAGIT		• Full implementation of AFAFGIT
• ASEAN Framework Agreement on the Facilitation of Inter-State Transport (FAIST)	• Conclude FAIST	• Start implementation of FAIST (2010)		• Full implementation of FAIST

• Information Infrastructure	• Implement the ASEAN Telecommunications Regulators Council MRA on conformity assessment for telecommunication equipment • Develop a general framework for coordinated ASEAN e-gov. programs	• ASEAN-wide implementation of ASEAN MRA		
• Energy Cooperation	• Ratify MOU on ASEAN Power grid			• Firm up the institutional and implementing arrangements to realize the APG (starting 2015)
• Trans-ASEAN Gas Pipeline	• Adopt the updated TAGP conceptual master plan	• Formation of model ASEAN Joint Venture (JV) Gas Pipeline Company	• Adopt business model for ASEAN gas pipeline owner-ship and operation	• Optimize TAGP
B5. Taxation				
		• Complete the network of bilateral agreements on avoidance of double taxation by 2010		

Table 10A.1 (continued)

Strategic approach	Priority Actions			
	2008–09	2010–11	2012–13	2014–15
B5. E-Commerce				
	• Member countries to enact their e-commerce laws	• Update relevant legislations		• Harmonize legal infrastructure for e-commerce fully in ASEAN
		• Adopt the best practices on other cyber-law issues		
C. Towards a Region of Equitable Economic Development				
C1. SME Development				
	• Establish a common curriculum for entrepreneurship	• Establish a comprehensive SME service centre	• Establish a regional program for the promotion of internship scheme for staff exchanges and visits for skills training	• Establish a regional SME development fund
C2. Initiatives for ASEAN Integration (IAI)				
	• Conduct periodic socio-economic studies to monitor/evaluate the impact of economic integration			

	• Build/strengthen capacity of government officials			
D. Towards Full Integration Into the Global Economy				
D1. Coherent approach towards External Economic Relations and enhance participation in global supply networks	• Review FTA/CEPT/ ASEAN internal integration commitments	• Publish a handbook on international best practices and standards in production and distribution	• Adoption of production and distribution in ASEAN with international best practices and standards	• Achieved consistency in ASEAN's FTA commitments vis-à-vis ASEAN's AEC commitments 2015
	• Establish a system for enhanced coordination in ASEAN's external economic relations and in regional and multilateral fora	• Implementation of projects to upgrade the less developed ASEAN member countries' industrial capabilities and productivity		
	• Identification of technical assistance needs for the less developed ASEAN member countries			

Notes:
1. IL stands for Inclusion List.
2. 4 priority services sectors include air transport, e-ASEAN, healthcare and tournament.

Source: ASEAN (2008b).

11. Global financial regulation: G2 or G20?

T.J. Pempel[1]

11.1 INTRODUCTION

July 1997 saw the beginnings of a massive run on the Thai baht. Despite a strenuous bailout effort costing $26 billion, the Thai government was not able to stem the attack, following which a financial panic was unleashed across much of East Asia. In quick succession the governments of Indonesia, Malaysia, the Philippines and South Korea faced similar challenges, and by the end of 1998, what had once been dubbed the 'East Asian Miracle' appeared to be in serious jeopardy as growth rates staggered, unemployment soared and political turmoil spread.

Eleven years later, in March 2008, Bear Stearns, a major US global investment bank and securities brokerage and a heavy investor in subprime mortgages, found itself on the verge of bankruptcy. In a move pressed by the US Federal Reserve, Bear Stearns was absorbed by other financial institutions at a fraction of its value a bare month earlier. The Bear Stearns debacle proved to be but a precursor to the chaos that was to follow. On 15 September Lehman Brothers, a global financial services firm facing $60 billion in bad investments and unable to secure US government assistance, declared what was then the largest bankruptcy in American history, triggering a global financial panic and the largest recession in the United States since the Great Depression of 1929–33.

In the wake of the Asian financial crisis, the G20 was established. Its first meeting took place in Berlin on 15–16 December 1999, hosted by German and Canadian finance ministers. The G20 brings together the finance ministers and central bank governors from 20 of the systemically most important countries in both the industrialized and the developing worlds. The central purpose of the G20 is to provide opportunities for dialog on national policies, international cooperation and international financial institutions, with the ultimate goal of strengthening the global financial architecture, supporting global growth, and minimizing the chances for future crises.

The 1999 inauguration came too late for the G20 to do much for the countries damaged by the crisis in Asia. However, following the Lehman meltdown the G20 put into place the largest single stimulus package ever designed, committing to unprecedented and coordinated macroeconomic policies that involved US$5 trillion in fiscal expansion along with a series of unconventional monetary measures. Also significantly enhanced were the G20's structural capabilities, notably by the establishment of the Financial Stability Board (FSB) as well as the strengthening of various international financial institutions and their lending facilities (Republic of Korea, 2010).

The recent actions of the G20 make it appropriate to ask about the extent to which the G20 can serve as an effective coordinating mechanism for the global financial system. More specifically, given the complexities of orchestrating the actions of 20 quite different countries, as well as the fact that the United States (US) and the People's Republic of China (PRC) are now the two largest economies in the world, and particularly since China represents such a strong presence in Asia, is the G20 a better vehicle for global financial leadership or would a G2 be better?

This chapter begins in section 11.2 by assessing the increasing importance, interdependence and mobility of global capital. It then moves on to show how the two major crises noted above arose from inadequate financial controls, poor coordination of exchange rates, the downsides to esoteric financial instruments that circulate globally, and the dangers of unregulated capital movements. Section 11.3 examines the changes in the governing leadership of global finance, followed in section 11.4 by an examination of why a G2 is neither appropriate nor feasible. Finally, section 11.5 asks what the prospects are for coordinated leadership by the G20.

11.2 UNGOVERNED AND INTERCONNECTED GLOBAL FINANCE

According to the Bank for International Settlements (2010), average daily turnover in global foreign exchange markets is estimated at $4 trillion, as of April 2010, a growth of approximately 20 percent over the $3.21 trillion daily volume three years earlier. Such rapid turnover is but one striking indicator of the split-second mobility of global capital (see Figure 11.1). In addition, global capital markets are linked through an extensive web of long- and short-term borrowings, cross-border investments, derivatives and security sales, to mention only a few of the key components of the now interdependent global financial system. The impact of such 'hot money' was conspicuously at play in the Asian financial crisis of 1997–98.

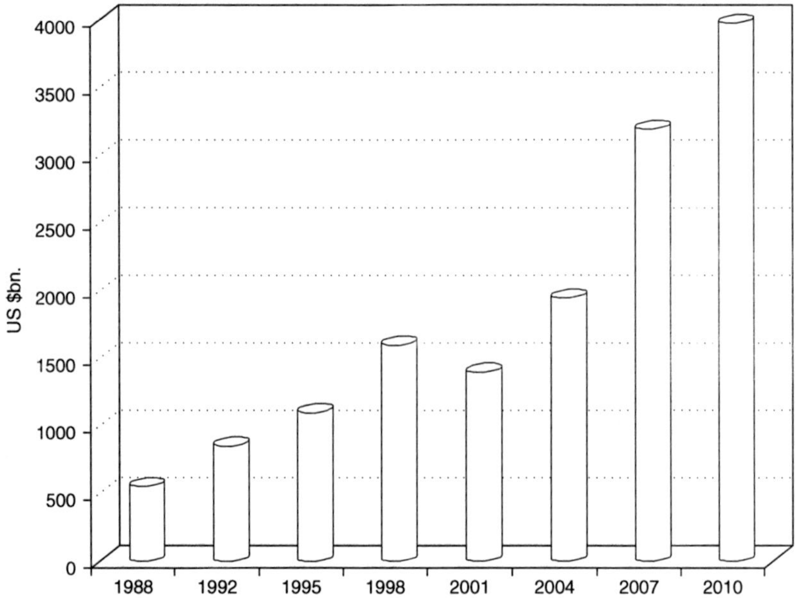

Figure 11.1 *Average daily turnover (1988–2007)*

The Asian countries most deeply affected by that crisis had been unable to finance their massive investment booms in the 1980s by relying solely on domestic savings mediated through domestic financial institutions, as they had done in the past. Instead private capital began to supplant official capital as the consequence of high levels of foreign borrowing. In 1990 nearly 80 percent of total global foreign direct investment (FDI) went to the developed world, while FDI into Asia totaled just about 11 percent. That Asian figure rose rapidly to 15.6 percent in 1995 and to 17.2 percent in 1997 (United Nations, 1998: 7).

Within Asia, external capital inflows jumped from an average of 1.4 percent of gross domestic product (GDP) during 1986–90 to 6.7 percent during 1990–96, with even greater increases immediately prior to the onset of the crisis. These foreign funds constituted the equivalent of about 15 percent of GDP in Thailand and the Philippines, 8 percent for Malaysia, and 5 percent for both Indonesia and the Republic of Korea (ROK). The vast bulk of this inflow came in the form of short-term overseas borrowing by Asian financial institutions and domestic corporations, and the borrowed money was then often loaned out on a long-term basis locally, thus creating a mismatch that would prove critical to the speed and depth of the crisis. Exchange rates pegged to the dollar posed an additional difficulty once the previously falling dollar began to rise in value. National treasuries were quickly depleted in unsuccessful efforts to hold the peg.

Furthermore, between 15 and 40 percent of this incoming investment was injected, not into long-term infrastructural projects, but rather into far more speculative investments such as property and stocks. The result was a Vesuvius of 'hot money' during the period when Asia seemed unstoppably dynamic. But then once the crisis materialized, that money was moved out of Asia as mercurially as it had been moved in (Winters, 1999). The five most severely affected economies (Indonesia, Korea, the Philippines, Malaysia and Thailand) saw a massive reversal in capital flows: from an inflow of $54 billion in the 12 months from the fourth quarter of 1996 to the third quarter of 1997, to an outflow of $68 billion in the fourth quarter of 1997 and the first quarter of 1998.

The turnaround in bank lending between 1996 and 1997 was equivalent to 9.5 percent of the combined GDPs of the five crisis countries (MacIntyre et al., 2008: 4–5). Output losses ranged from perhaps 17.6 percent to nearly 98 percent in the most severely affected countries (Sheng, 2009: 98), and some 15–17 million Asians who were not there already fell below their nations' poverty lines (Sheng, 2009: 309; see also MacIntyre et al., 2008: 4–13). The result was a cascading downward of asset values and growth, a leap in unemployment, and extensive social dislocation.

The sources of the 2008–09 crisis trace to at least two different sets of problems. At the global macroeconomic level, in the run-up to the crisis the world faced an unsteady balance between an overconsuming and undersaving US economy on the one hand, and an underconsuming and overcapitalized rest of the world (Rajan, 2010: 6; Chinn and Frieden, 2011). At the heart of this imbalance was the huge public and private sector borrowing by the United States, that fluctuated between $500 billion and $1 trillion per year from 2000 to 2007, and the conversely limited consumption and high savings elsewhere, particularly in Asia. Escalating global sales plus low spending at home allowed foreign economies to move huge quantities of unspent foreign capital into the US, thus bolstering the seemingly insatiable demands of US consumers.

Such global macroeconomic imbalances dovetailed with an emerging set of risky developments within the US domestic economy: the disastrous interplay of the previously lauded amalgam of free-flowing and highly leveraged capital in the unmonitored pursuit of maximum profits, and the unregulated sale of esoteric financial instruments, many of which were linked to a vastly inflated housing market and the unexamined optimism that housing prices would always move up (Lewis, 2010; Rajan, 2010; Reinhart and Rogoff, 2009; Sheng, 2009, *inter alia*).

In the run-up to the crisis, low interest rates fueled a surging housing

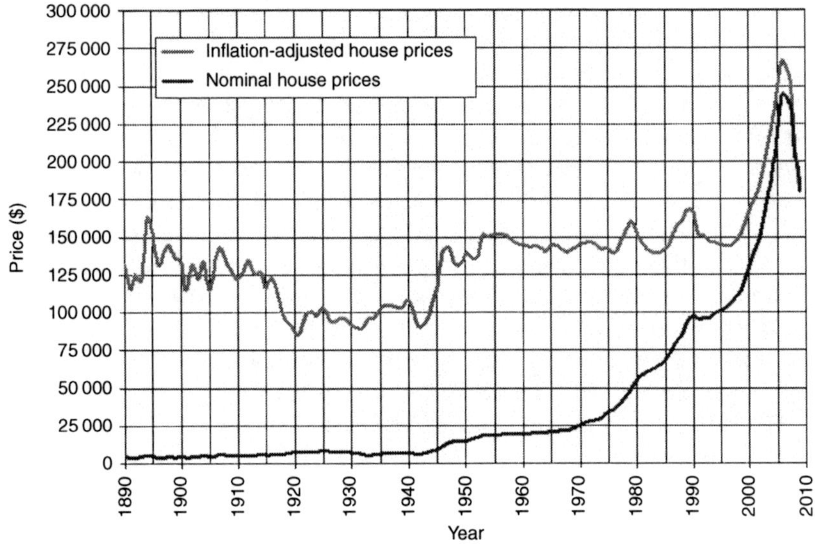

Figure 11.2 *US house prices (1890–2008)*

market that seemed to be a goose laying golden eggs for both home owners and financial institutions. Housing demand soared in conjunction with rapidly rising housing prices, thus fueling an upward spiral that to many appeared unending (see Figure 11.2).

With housing prices soaring parabolically from the early 1970s and accelerating astronomically in the 2000s, banks and other financial institutions became ever more anxious to lend to ever more dubious borrowers. Homeowners, even those with the most pockmarked credit ratings and little prospect of actually being able to sustain payments on their mortgages once they had moved into their new homes, became eligible for mortgages based on the low teaser rate monthly payments that were typically guaranteed only for short periods (usually two years). After that the borrowers became eligible to refinance their (now more valuable – at least on paper) homes with newer mortgages. Financial institutions made huge profits through the issuance and then reissuance of these mortgages, and all players had a strong interest in perpetuating the highly profitable system on the implausible presumption that housing prices would move ever upward.

Integral to the rising housing market and its funding was an increasingly potent element in the eventual American financial collapse, namely the newly created financial product known as 'credit default swaps', and its variant, 'collateralized debt obligations'. Credit default swaps were not really 'swaps' at all, but rather insurance policies, typically on a corporate bond, with semi-annual premiums and a fixed term (Lewis, 2010: 29). Essentially such instruments constituted low-cost bets that particular assets (including such things as securitized mortgages) would not go into default. In the rapidly expanding housing market such credit default swaps seemed immune to any worries about potential default. As a result billions of dollars worth of such credit default swaps were issued with great profitability by financial institutions such as the American Insurance Group's now infamous Financial Products unit (AIGFP), with little apparent concern about either the quality of the underlying mortgages and the borrowers who held them, or the fact that such securitized mortgages were in fact poorly diversified across geographical areas or dates for refinancing. So long as housing prices continued to soar, there would be no significant defaults, and hence the credit default swaps would never require pay-outs by the issues. Few of those involved in the system anticipated that housing prices might go down, let alone collapse.

Meanwhile, securitization of mortgages meant that virtually all of these new mortgages would be quickly disposed of by the issuing banks, unlike in past decades when issuing banks typically held mortgages until maturity. Instead they were woven into a new financial instrumentality by being bundled together, 'securitized', and sold as the equivalent of AAA bonds; a fiction made possible by the collusion of allegedly independent ratings agencies which were paid fat fees by Wall Street firms for each deal they rated. Some 80 percent of this rising tower of mortgage-based debt was rated AAA (in sharp contrast to the roughly 1 percent of corporate bonds that received such a high rating). Michael Lewis correctly observes that these new credit default obligations were in effect 'a credit laundering service for the residents of Lower Middle Class America. For Wall Street [they were] a machine that turned lead into gold' (Lewis, 2010: 73). The increasingly complex and interconnected nature of these credit default obligations and the rising number of arcane derivative products eventually created a mixture that was beyond the ability of many financial regulators to comprehend (Sheng, 2009: 356; Lewis, 2010: 218).

Complicating this situation, many of the world's (and especially the US's) financial institutions and hedge funds had become ever more highly leveraged in their 'search for yield', while incentives for financial institutions and their managers became ever more tied to short-term, as opposed to longer-term, profits. The result was the creation of a manic explosion of what Susan Strange (1986) more than two decades ago labeled 'casino capitalism'.

At least two political elements contributed substantially to the suddenness and depth of the 2008–09 crisis. Firstly, the wave of financial deregulation that had begun in the Reagan years meant limited-to-zero political oversight of the increasingly complicated, interlinked and risky financial practices and instruments described above. And secondly, the Federal Reserve had essentially committed to putting a floor under asset prices by refusing to raise interest rates even when they had reached dangerous levels approaching 'irrational exuberance'. In criticizing Fed chairman Alan Greenspan on this matter, Raghuram Rajan (2010: 113) puts it bluntly: Greenspan recognized the possibility of asset bubbles; however, he essentially 'told traders and bankers that if they gambled, the Fed would not limit their gains, but if their bets turned sour, the Fed would limit the consequences. All they had to ensure was that they bet on the same thing, for if they bet alone, they would not pose a systematic threat'. That government floor on capital losses became self-evident when the housing bubble burst and the credit default swaps and related high-risk bets had to be settled. The US, reversing its ideological proclivity for limited market intervention, quickly jettisoned its ideological predispositions at the prospect of a capital market freeze-up. US Secretary of the Treasury Henry Paulson, a long-time advocate of markets unfettered by government actions, abandoned his prior neoliberal commitments and moved quickly to mobilize massive government monies to bail out the troubled financial institutions, because they were collectively deemed 'too big to fail'. The result was a massive injection of public money through the Troubled Asset Relief Program (for example Rajan, 2010: 149). Within weeks over $1 trillion in public funds was allocated to the relief effort.

11.3 GLOBAL CAPITAL CONTROL

These two crises reveal different facets of the downsides of unregulated global capital movements. The Asian crisis reveals the problems that can arise from mismatched exchange rates and rapidly moving 'hot money'. The US crisis demonstrates how easily poorly regulated financial markets in any powerful country can destabilize the entire global network of now deeply interdependent financial institutions.

How, then, is global finance to be regulated? For many laissez-faire zealots the answer is a variant of 'not at all'. But in the postwar period at least two major coordinative efforts must be noted even in traditionally laissez-faire countries. From the earliest days following the Second World War, the US and Britain agreed that some mechanism was needed to prevent the kinds of national currency manipulations that had been so conducive to the outbreak of the war. The result was the Bretton Woods system, in which the US agreed to make the dollar the 'currency of last resort' and to guarantee that it would redeem dollars for gold at the rate of $35 an ounce. This system worked to smooth financial and trade expansion until the US broke all rules for fiscal responsibility by simultaneously attempting a massive expansion in its welfare programs (The Great Society) and a costly and unpopular war in Vietnam. By refusing to raise US taxes to pay for either, but instead borrowing massively from abroad, the US triggered a widespread outflow of gold during the Nixon administration, and Nixon's eventual decision to scrap the world's monetary structures by abdicating US commitments under Bretton Woods and allowing the dollar to depreciate.

Following a variety of vaguely coordinated and largely unsuccessful efforts at ensuring exchange rate stability, the leaders of Germany, France and Britain met with President Nixon in a May 1973 effort to bring about currency stability. The 23–29 June 1995 edition of *The European* quoted a German participant as saying: 'We agreed there was a need for someone to be in control again on an international scale. We hardly knew each other prior to the meeting. But mutual appreciation and sympathy developed as we talked, laying the ground for successful cooperation'. From that meeting evolved the idea of the Group of Seven (G7) which was officially born in 1976 with Japan, Italy and Canada added to the countries at the 1973 meeting. At their 1976 meeting in San Juan they declared their *raison d'être*: 'The interdependence of our destinies makes it necessary for us to approach common economic problems with a sense of common purpose and to work toward mutually consistent economic strategies through better cooperation'. At the time, the G7 nations dominated the global financial and banking system and their currencies had reserve status in the rest of the world. Additionally, they were linked into a number of international bodies including the Organisation for Economic Co-operation and Development (OECD) in Europe; they held close to 40 percent of the votes at the International Monetary Fund (IMF) and the World Bank; and were all members of the United Nations Security Council (Women's International Media Group, n.d.). The group has met several times a year since, in an effort to deal with emerging and evolving economic and financial problems including in the wake of the 2008–2009 crisis. But it was really the G20 that proved critical during this latest meltdown.

11.4 WHY NOT A G2?

The most pervasive economic story of the 2000s has been the 'rise of China'. Staggering double-digit growth rates in annual GDP have captured the world's attention, as has the fact that in 2010 China's GDP surpassed that of Japan, moving it into the number two spot globally behind the US. Asia and the Asia-Pacific have become the most economically dynamic regions in the world, and China is at the hub of the region's production networks. China is the world's largest holder of foreign reserves and has become a central player in petitions for financial aid from countries like Mongolia and Pakistan. And the US and Chinese economies have become increasingly linked in recent years, with US multinationals deeply invested in China, with the two countries as the other's major trading partner, and with much of America's overconsumption being funded by Chinese oversavings and consequent purchases of US treasuries. Meanwhile Japan has been in a 20-year slump and Europe faces colossal internal economic challenges. Why not allow the Big Two to run the global financial show, as they seem to be doing anyhow?

Clearly the G7 is on the wane. A recent examination (Adam and Kolet, 2010) based on IMF data showed that the share of world GDP held by the G7 was likely to fall below 7 percent in 2012, a dramatic decline from the 70 percent it held in the mid-1980s. But importantly, the US share of world GDP has also been in rather steady decline since the beginning of the 2000s, falling from roughly 30 percent to about 22 percent today. China indeed is rising, likely to hold a 10 percent share of world GDP in 2012, a fivefold jump from 1987. Yet it is clear that the putative G2 would still account for only about 34–35 percent of the global market. The real story of global wealth is not just the decline of the G7 and the rise of China but, equally importantly, the dynamism of emerging markets beyond China such as those of Brazil, India, Russia, Indonesia and Turkey.

In addition to simple economics, there are other reasons for not transferring global financial power to a G2. Following the Lehman crisis with its roots deep in the poorly supervised housing, capital and derivatives markets in the US, it is far from clear that the US any longer enjoys the kind of global respect that would allow its future decisions about capital regulation to be widely accepted. China has proven an equally prickly partner in Asia's rise at times, leaving much of Southeast Asia, certainly Japan, and increasingly South Korea, dubious about China's possible exploitation of its growing economic power to press its national interests in everything from sovereignty claims within the South China and East China Seas, to support for the Democratic People's Republic of Korea (DPRK), along with slow movement toward currency reform, massive intellectual property theft, and politically driven restrictions on both exports and imports of rare earth minerals. Furthermore, China has yet to show much willingness to surrender any significant measure of national control in order to be the generous provider of public goods that would be intrinsic to its taking a leadership role as part of a G2. Clearly few outside the US and China would be enthusiastic about a G2.

11.5 CAN THE G20 COORDINATE GLOBAL FINANCE?

Prior to the creation of the G20, at the initiative of the G7, similar groupings were organized to promote dialog and analysis. The G22 met at Washington DC in April and October 1998 in an effort to involve non-G7 countries in the resolution of global aspects of the Asian financial crisis. Two subsequent meetings comprising a larger group of participants (G33) were held in March and April 1999 to explore reforms of the global economy and the international financial system. The proposals made by the G22 and the G33 to reduce the world economy's susceptibility to crises showed the potential benefits of a regular international consultative forum embracing the emerging-market countries. Such a regular dialogue with a constant set of partners was institutionalized by the creation of the G20 in 1999 (Republic of Korea, 2010).

Together, member countries of the G20 represent around 90 percent of global gross national product, 80 percent of world trade (including European Union intra-trade) as well as two-thirds of the world's population. The G20's economic weight and broad membership gives it a critical degree of legitimacy and influence over the management of the global economy and financial system (Republic of Korea, 2010). The G20 also engages closely with the IMF and the World Bank by including their top executives in G20 meetings.

As noted in the introduction above, it was the G20 that played the largest global role in responding to the crisis of 2008–09 with its coordinated effort at expansionary macroeconomic policies, including the fiscal expansion of US$5 trillion. Additionally, it agreed to enhance global financial regulations by, among other things, establishing the Financial Stability Board (FSB), and strengthening international financial institutions. It has since attempted to coordinate economic and interest rate policies to spur growth and forge stricter regulation of banks and other financial institutions seen as responsible for the meltdown.

At its 2010 Seoul meeting, the G20 appeared likely to head off a currency and trade war centered on demands from the US and other rich countries for a revaluation of the Chinese yuan and the currencies of other major developing countries, so as to curtail their trade surpluses with the West. Even more surprisingly, on 23 October of that year the G20 reached an agreement to restructure membership in the International Monetary Fund so as to give a larger voice to the developing world.

Under the agreement, the European countries will give up two of their eight seats on the 24-member board, thereby enhancing the voting weight of emerging powers such as China and India. More than 6 percent of IMF voting power will be transferred to under-represented countries at the fund, and China will become the third-biggest member of the 187-strong institution. In a separate deal, the G20 also agreed to double the IMF's $340 billion quota, which will put it in a better position to cope with future financial crises. 'It is a very historic agreement,' Dominique Strauss-Kahn, then managing director of the fund, said after the G20 meeting. 'This makes for the biggest reform ever in the governance of the institution' (Song, 2010).

Since the changes took effect in late 2011, Brazil, Russia, India and China are all included among the fund's ten biggest shareholders. The US, with a 17.67 percent share of IMF quotas, will however still retain its veto power over the fund's key decisions, as these decisions will continue to require a super-majority of 85 percent.

From the most recent perspective, the G20 appears to be doing tolerably well in its coordination efforts. And because the body's collective economic muscle is so great, its actions are likely to have a considerable impact on global finance. At the same time, over the longer haul it remains to be seen whether the G20 can deal with two serious problems.

Firstly, will it be able to reach and implement coordinated agreements once the immediate crisis has passed? That it agreed to a restructuring of the IMF is a good sign that G20 actions are as much structural as tactical, and that they go beyond short-term efforts simply to staunch the threatened global capital market seizure.

Secondly, will the now most powerful members, most particularly the US but also China, be prepared to surrender elements of their national autonomy to such a global body? The US for example has shown a penchant for unilateralism in an extensive legacy tracing back at least to Nixon and Bretton Woods. And in the case of China, it remains to be seen whether the country, as its economic power increases, will remain satisfied to be a multilaterally responsible partner in a 20-member body.

Such questions are of course unanswerable at present. But clearly, the institutions of global coordination have changed drastically over the post-war period, and future adjustments are by no means precluded as power positions change. A G2 seems implausible but the G20 may well have a significant future as the key coordinating body for global finance.

NOTE

1. The original version of this chapter was published in the *Journal of Northeast Asia Development*, **12**, December 2010.

REFERENCES

Adam, Shamin and Ilan Kolet (2010), 'G-7 Shares of World GDP Seen Below 10% by 2012', Bloomberg.com, available at http://www.bloomberg.com/news/print/2010-10-21/g-7-share-of-world-gdp-seen-below-50-by-2012-chart-of-the-day.html.

Bank for International Settlements (2010), 'Triennial Central Bank Survey of Foreign Exchange and Derivatives Market Activity in April 2010 – Preliminary Global Results – Turnover', available at http://www.bis.org/publ/rpfx10.htm.

Chinn, Menzie D. and Jeffry A. Frieden (2011), *Lost Decades: The Making of America's Debt Crisis and the Long Recovery*, New York: Norton.

Lewis, Michael (2010), *The Big Short: Inside the Doomsday Machine*, New York: Norton.

MacIntyre, Andrew, T.J. Pempel and John Ravenhill (2008), 'East Asia in the Wake of the Financial Crisis', in Andrew MacIntyre, T.J. Pempel and John Ravenhill (eds), *East Asia: Coping With the Crisis*, Ithaca: Cornell University Press, pp. 1–22.

Rajan, Raghuram G. (2010), *Fault Lines: How Hidden Fractures Still Threaten the World Economy*, Princeton, NJ: Princeton University Press.

Reinhart, Carmen M. and Kenneth S. Rogoff (2009), *This Time is Different: Eight Centuries of Financial Folly*, Princeton, NJ: Princeton University Press.

Republic of Korea (2010), 'What is the G-20?' available at http://www.g20.org/about_what_is_g20.aspx (accessed 22 October 2010).

Sheng, Andrew (2009), *From Asian to Global Financial Crisis: An Asian Regulator's View of Unfettered Finance in the 1990s and 2000s*, Cambridge: Cambridge University Press.

Song, Jung-a (2010), 'G20 Reaches Deal on Reform of IMF', *Financial Times*, 23 October, available at http://www.ft.com/cms/s/0/816ee036-dea2-11df-9b4a-00144feabdc0.html (accessed 23 October 2010).

Strange, Susan (1986), *Casino Capitalism*, Oxford: Basil Blackwell.

United Nations (1998), *World Investment Report, 1998*, New York: United Nations.

Winters, Jeffrey A. (1999), 'The Determinants of Financial Crisis in Asia', in T.J. Pempel (ed.), *The Politics of the Asian Economic Crisis in Asia*, Ithaca, NY: Cornell University Press, pp. 79–97.

Women's International Media Group (n.d.), 'Who are the Group of Seven?' available at http://www.womensgroup.org/G-7REPOR.html (accessed 23 October 2010).

12. East Asian community building

Wei Pan[1]

12.1 INTRODUCTION

In this chapter I intend to address three related issues: (1) explaining obstacles to the progress of building the East Asian community; (2) presenting a new theory of international relations in the 21st century; (3) following the new theory, suggesting solutions to overcome the obstacles.

12.2 OBSTACLES TO BUILDING THE EAST ASIAN COMMUNITY

At a time of globalization, to build an East Asian 'economic' community is not difficult. In the first decade of the 21st century, East Asia has already become a closely linked community in the economic sense. China, Japan, Korea and the Association of Southeast Asian Nations (ASEAN) countries have already built and institutionalized close economic linkages. Bilateral free trade agreements (FTAs) in the region are expanding; and the East Asian countries have become major trading partners with each other. We should be quite satisfied with this economic community. Furthermore, East Asia is a major economic partner with the United States (US) and the European Union (EU), and China has become the number one trading partner with Africa and South Asia, and the number two trading partner with Latin America. A four-engined picture of the world economy is foreseeable. The engines might be the US, EU, East Asia and China.

I exclude China from East Asia, however. China is certainly part of East Asia, and it is the engine for the East Asian economic community. Yet, China is also a problem for community building. I exclude China from East Asia for the following reasons:

1. Although the Chinese economy is geographically a part of the East Asian economy, its influence is far beyond the region – like how the US economy is hardly just a part of the North American economy.

2. Because of China's strength, which is still rapidly increasing, most other East Asian countries worry about their security whenever there is a dispute with China.
3. Because of these security concerns, the East Asian countries would welcome outsiders to join them: the US, EU and India are invited to join the East Asian community in one way or another, so as to balance China's influence.
4. Because of these strong third parties, ideological and military factors are involved, and differences in socio-political settings are exaggerated. The progress of regional integration through the effort to build the economic community often suffers major difficulties.

China is both an East Asian country and an isolated world power. Ideological and military factors often lead to the claim that the Chinese socio-political settings prevent further cooperation by East Asians. There are even attempts to build Cold War-like ideological blocs to balance China. Because of the existence of China, building a regional community suffers ups and downs.

This year (2010), China seems to be falling into diplomatic trouble with nearly all the other East Asian countries; and the US as the third party looms large in those troubles. That is a situation very different from 2009, when the US and China seemed to be in a honeymoon period, joining hands in solving the world financial crisis. The US obviously has independent strategic targets in the region, and stronger bonds among the regional countries may not serve US strategy.

In short, China is the engine of regional economic cooperation, and is also a problem to it. When the US–China relationship is good, the East Asian community becomes solid. When the US–China relationship becomes bad, the East Asian community becomes vulnerable. Moreover, many East Asian countries reasonably expect that the China–US relationship will be neither very good nor very bad. A very good relationship would free China's hands; and a very bad relationship would force them to take sides, in which case the costs would exceed the benefits. That is the obstacle to further community building.

12.3 A NEW THEORY OF INTERNATIONAL RELATIONS

The above obstacle to regional integration leads to my second point: a new theory of international relations. I discuss this to provide a theoretical basis for the solutions which I will propose in the next section.

In the 19th and 20th centuries, the sovereign nations' instinct for survival created four core tasks which shaped most countries' behavior:

1. Preparing for a major war among major powers.
2. Gaining or maintaining military supremacy.
3. Forming alliances to contain a potential enemy.
4. Designing a comprehensive grand strategy for the expansion of national interests.

In the 21st century, however, those clear tasks no longer seem as natural as they were:

1. A major war is impossible in the foreseeable future; and peace among major powers may reasonably be expected.
2. The role of military supremacy seems obsolete, as is shown in both Iraq and Afghanistan, and in the US's 'decline' despite its overwhelming military power.
3. Alliances of a military nature have been effectively undermined by global economic and social ties, and by the lack of a clear enemy.
4. The search and deep respect for grand strategy designs seems to be a phenomenon of the last century. Few could meaningfully have foreseen and prepared for the sudden rise of new hot topics such as climate change, terrorism and financial crises.

We could well be 'realists'; but the reality has changed. The reality in the 21st century is different from the realities in the 19th and 20th centuries. College students today do not buy our lectures on the old international relations (IR) logic. They suffer from the extreme uncertainties generated by globalization. They need to find jobs in international job markets, not just in their own countries; they are interested in other cultures and life styles; and they are much less ideological or nationalistic than those of our time. They understand that we need to solve our problems together, because we have made the problems together.

The world is entering a new stage, a stage of uncertainty and post-polarity. The collapse of the Soviet Union was followed by waves of 'globalization' in terms of technology, commodities, capital, ideas and human beings, which created uncertainty throughout the world. The power of globalization is much stronger than that of any superpower. No single power is as effective as before in deciding world affairs. The US global military involvement has not reduced but only increased uncertainties. All world affairs are intertwined; and conflicts in one issue area are likely to be neutralized by cooperation in another issue area, and turned into 'competition'. The era of superpower dominance seems to be ending. Moreover, in the 20th century, we have seen first-world countries turned into third-world countries, such as Argentina, Brazil and Russia. In the 21st century, even the underdeveloped countries in Asia, Latin America and Africa have good chances for development.

What has created this new logic of the 21st century? The answer is simple: nuclear weapons and globalization. Nuclear weapons prevent a major war among major powers; and globalization further reduces the incentives to go into such a war. Due to globalization's uncertain impacts on different localities, the world of certainty has turned into one of extreme uncertainty. No one predicted the 'Arab Spring'; and no one knows where it is going, or whether it will incite a 'European Spring'. How possible is it that we could meaningfully predict what will be the most important agenda ten years from now?

Military and ideological factors in East Asia will continue to make our community vulnerable. However, the 21st century IR logic denies the effectiveness of war, of military supremacy, of military alliances, and of a grand strategy by a superpower. The 21st century is the century for peace and development.

In the recent months of this year (2010), for whatever reason, a US aircraft carrier has undertaken intensive joint exercises around China, in the Japan Sea, Yellow Sea, East China Sea, and all the way to the South China Sea. If we indulge in the old IR logic, that could be perceived as an effective way of the US making a 'return' to East Asia. However, it has achieved nothing but burning dollars. And it might give the Chinese navy a good excuse for requesting a larger budget to accelerate its modernization. 'Sufficient defense' against the US military is the purpose of the Chinese military.

The old IR logic is becoming obsolete. The military means is no longer as effective as before. The radical differences of socio-political settings may not prevent community building, as is shown in the ASEAN case. Despite major disputes, economic cooperation between China and Japan, China and the US, and China and the EU has been expanding rapidly. Our peoples' welfare hinges on just that. In the 19th and 20th centuries, peoples' welfare used to depend on military solutions and racial or ideological bias. In the 21st century those are no longer viable solutions.

Then how could we improve our community building?

12.4 FROM ECONOMIC COMMUNITY TO SOCIO-CULTURAL COMMUNITY

East Asia has already built an economic community. It is doing well. By the standard of the EU, however, it is less of a community. Is it a failure? Few in East Asia really want an Asian copy of the EU. It is less integrated than the EU for sure, but much more tolerant and open than the EU. Like ASEAN, East Asians have more tolerance to different religions and socio-political settings; and East Asians are more open – to the US, South Asia, Oceania, Russia and even North Korea, when it is ready to open itself.

Because of China's size and rapid growth, material conflicts are less of a problem for East Asian community building. The problem mainly lies in distrust among one another, doubt and suspicion about China's military intentions, and prevailing bias against China's socio-political setting. Therefore, the problem is less economic than socio-cultural.

Therefore, here I make a few suggestions for further community building. East Asia still needs to continue doing the easy things, namely deepening its economic cooperation. For this it could consider:

1. Pushing for FTAs among Japan, China, Korea, ASEAN and the US.
2. Further financial cooperation, such as building an exchange rate regime.

However, I am more interested in the confidence-building measures of a military and social-cultural nature:

3. Freezing territorial disputes, and making treaties to regulate behaviors in disputed territories.
4. Regular joint military exercises to build security confidence.
5. Multiple-entry short-term tourist visas, valid for multiple years, as in Singapore, to encourage the exchange of people.
6. Exchange of high school students during summer vacations, as in France and Germany, to allow the people to build friendships.
7. Exchange of university credits to allow intensive exchange of higher education.
8. Building research centers of regional collaboration to facilitate exchange of scholars.
9. Building intergovernmental institutions to solve routine problems, such as a standing executive commission at the ministerial level.
10. Granting a joint security guarantee to North Korea, to settle the last hot spot of war in the region, and help North Korea to join the East Asian community.

Community is based on trust. Community building tends to progress when trust is being built up, and it fails when distrust prevails.

Through our intensive economic, social and cultural exchanges, East Asian countries may understand each other better, which may allow them to consolidate their community and better prepare for the uncertain world of post-polarity in a time of globalization.

NOTE

1. This is a revised version of the special speech delivered at the second conference of the Asia Economic Community Forum which was held on 9 November 2010 in Incheon, Korea.

13. Sino–US relations: possible trends and implications for the East Asia community

Liu Yongtao[1]

13.1 INTRODUCTION

With China's steady economic growth and social development, and profound changes in the United States in the post-9/11 era, the first decade of the 21st century has witnessed dramatic and dynamic interactions between China and the United States (US), whose relationship has been claimed as one of the most crucial and complicated interstate relationships in world politics.

Much research has been done on the nature of this complicated Sino–US relationship in the 21st century from various perspectives regarding aspects of cooperation, competition, disagreements and even contests (Foot and Walter, 2010; Friedberg, 2011; Rosecrance and Gu, 2010; Sun, 2011; Sutter, 2010; Zhao, 2007; Zhu, 2006). Instead of accumulating, or adding more comments on, existing data, this chapter focuses on possible trends of the Sino–US relationship in security politics and their implications for the East Asia community. What are the possible scenarios of security politics that the early 21st century may witness in East Asia? How will Sino–US relations look in those possible scenarios? And which scenario, among them, is most likely to emerge as the dominant one in East Asia? To answer these questions, the chapter takes an approach that combines material and normative perspectives, aiming at sketching several imaginary pictures in which possible trends of the Sino–US relationship in security politics are examined in the hope that refining and filtering these pictures rationally may help provide a meaningful sense for the (re)-construction of a political and security relationship that is of great benefit to China and the US as well as to the East Asia community as a whole.

I am fully aware that there are dangers in understanding such a complicated bilateral relationship of two large countries like China and the United States by putting it in imaginative and highly reductive contexts, because these contexts may not correspond to factual developments in future, or may appear to overlap one another. I am also aware that a given structure, while restraining the unfolding Sino–US relationship, is in turn constituted by that relationship. That said, the chapter attempts to draw some structural pictures of the Sino–US relationship, aiming to help delineate that relationship clearly in the early 21st century.

The chapter is organized into four subsequent sections. Section 13.2 takes account of basic claims of both material and normative perspectives in international relations (IR) theories regarding the explanation and understanding of international systems, and then highlights conceptual and methodological merits of incorporating these two perspectives into an integral material–normative approach to IR studies. In section 13.3 the chapter imagines five possible scenarios that may emerge in East Asia, assuming that unfolding international relations in the region are a process of political and social (re)construction. Section 13.4 foresees the possible Sino–US relationship in security politics by embedding that relationship into those imaginary scenarios, predicting that different scenarios may help to shape different social constructions of both Chinese and US identities, which may in turn determine the way the two countries perceive each other's changing distribution of material capabilities and understand the meanings given by those changes. Different social identities of the two countries make their bilateral relationship in security politics different in those scenarios. Finally, in section 13.5 the chapter attempts to figure out which scenario, among them, is most likely to emerge as the dominant one in East Asia.

13.2 TWO STRANDS OF PERSPECTIVES COMBINED

One way to look at possible trends of security politics between two countries like China and the United States is to put them in a given international system, in hopes that it may reveal basic aspects of future Sino–US relations in security politics in a broad sense.

In terms of systemic studies, there have been two major perspectives in IR theories. One is a materialist perspective that puts emphasis on the distribution of material capabilities among nation-states, arguing that the nature of interstate relationships in security politics is shaped largely by the positions of those states' physical power in the international system.[2] It has been regarded as a 'mainstream' perspective to look at international politics through a material lens. Despite different strands within this perspective, and even heated debates among them, those who advocate this perspective share basic claims about their understanding of the nature of international politics.

Firstly, nation-states in international politics are the most important actors, and possess the right to use violent force legitimately within a certain scope of their territories. Sovereignty implies that a state actor has the ultimate authority to formulate and enforce domestic laws. Only by guaranteeing national security can society, arts and culture within the nation in question survive, be preserved and evolve. The realization of national security depends on the physical might of the state; therefore the top priority of a nation-state is to organize, arrange and manage its physical strength. In principle, each nation is taken as a power state defined by its material capabilities. International relations are understood as material ones among nation-states in the international system.

Secondly, due to a lack of common political culture or authority, anarchy is a constant and featured phenomenon in international politics. Each state must rely on its own means to protect its own national security and interest. In other words, each state believes in, and pursues, a self-help principle. In an anarchical world social relations between nation-states tend to be competitive and even antagonistic. A state usually prefers to achieve its goals in international politics by threatening to use, or actually using, military force. This means that there is always the possibility of resorting to violence in international politics.

Thirdly, the distribution of material capabilities among states, especially major powers, is a crucial determinant that may affect the stability of or change in the international system. Although factors on the national level such as types of polity, the nature of the social system or the (in)-competence of political leaders matter much, the material structure of the international system determines states' behaviors and the nature of their interactions within that structure (Morgenthau, 1960; Waltz, 1979; Mearsheimer, 2001).

However, there are two major divergent views within the material perspective as to what kind of distribution of material capability is most desirable for the stability of a given international system. A neorealist view argues that an arrangement of bipolar powers is the most ideal condition of distribution of material capabilities in the international system. The rest of the states in the system choose which power bandwagon they will jump on. The bipolarity creates a balance of power for the sake of the distribution of material capabilities. Any state that is taking advantage of its power over others will be counterbalanced collectively by those that are less powerful, so as to make all powers balanced. The emergence of unipolar or multipolar power indicates the end of the bipolar balance of power (Mearsheimer, 1990; Waltz, 2000). In contrast, the view of hegemonic stability emphasizes the leading role played by a single hegemonic state in dealing with global economic and political affairs, and thus creating and managing the stability of a given political and economic order through the hegemonic state's superior strengths and long-term self-serving interests (Gilpin, 1987).

Another major perspective in the study of systemic levels, in contrast, puts its focus more on social aspects of a given international system. It is a normative one, that is concerned with social and cultural elements in international politics. According to this perspective, social identities and distributions of ideas in international systems matter to the extent that they affect states' interests and behaviors. In other words, the normative perspective focuses more on how the nature of the security relationship between two nation-states is conditioned by their social relations in the international system.

Three basic assumptions are claimed by the normative perspective about the ontological nature of international systems. Firstly, the international system is not only materially and but also conceptually constituted. Social and cultural factors shape and fundamentally determine the meaning of the material structure in a given international system. In other words, the meaning of a state's material capability and its distribution can be figured out only in the social context of that system in which the state itself is situated. For instance, to other states, the meaning of a state's military capability depends on the perceived social identity of that state as a rival, competitor or friend in the eyes of those other states. Secondly, a given social structure helps to shape a state's national interests and identity. In other words, the social structure of a given international system determines what a state wants, and its social relations with other states as competitors, rivals or friends. Thirdly, states and the system in which they are situated are mutually constitutive, rather than the system simply restraining the state (Finnemore, 1996; Wendt, 1999).

The two perspectives mentioned above address, respectively, international physical and ideational structures as two critical determinants – material capabilities and social identities – which help to shape the interstate relationships of security politics. International politics is an arena where not only material capabilities are distributed among nation-states, but ideas and values are distributed among them as well. The material perspective, however, has limitations in its explanatory power when it overstates narrow physical power in the international system while downplaying and even ignoring the social contexts in which international politics is working. The normative perspective, in contrast, throws more light on social and cultural aspects of the international system, but offers less insight on the conception of physical power.

Therefore, it is an inviting effort to marry the two perspectives in IR studies in the hope that they may be incorporated into a more sophisticated material–normative approach to the analysis of interstate relations in a given international system. The new approach may facilitate getting epistemologically closer to 'realities' in understanding and explaining interstate relations. Moreover, it offers methodologically the possibility to examine international politics through the means of both causal analysis and interpretive narrations.

The possible trends of early 21st century China–US relations in the field of security politics can be approached by taking this combined perspective, with which several scenarios in East Asia are materially and socially imagined.

13.3 FIVE POSSIBLE SCENARIOS IN EAST ASIA

East Asia is one of the most important and dynamic regions in world politics today. The description of the post-Cold War era as 'one superpower and multiple great powers' is reflected in East Asia, where are located the United States as a sole superpower; a cluster of major powers – Russia, Japan and China; and such power blocs as the Association of Southeast Asian Nations (ASEAN) and the US–Japan alliance. Of seven officially recognized nuclear states in the world, three (the United States, Russia and China) are in the region, and there are other states that seek to develop nuclear weapons. These states and power blocs are in different positions in terms of their distributions of material capabilities, and have complicated social relations with one another in the international system of the region. Within this system the Sino–US relationship constitutes an integral part of the politics of the security in the early 21st century in East Asia.

Drawing on insights from previous research on patterns of the international system, this chapter imagines five possible scenarios of the international system in East Asia, and delineates them in order from the most disadvantageous to the most advantageous in terms of Sino–US relations in security politics.[3]

The first scenario is a bipolar one. It is a type of regional order that is achieved through the balance of two polar powers. Within this scenario, because of the emergence of two superpowers once again in the region, East Asia is likely to become the location of a new round of bipolar rivalry. The United States is assumed to maintain its superpower status. There are several candidates for another superpower status, including Russia, Japan and China.

Historically, Russia suffered occasions of setbacks and even defeat in international politics, but each time it recovered and came back. As a strong candidate, Russia today still retains basic features that a superpower needs to possess, such as large territory, abundant resources, nuclear weapons and (space) technology, potential in science and technology, energy resources and permanent status in the Security Council at the United Nations. Therefore, it is possible that Russia may seek to restore the same status of military and political power enjoyed by the former Soviet Union during the Cold War. The problem is, however, that its current economic condition prevents the realization of this ambition in the short run. Japan, in contrast, is a global economic power, but its insular geography and limited resources, especially its narrow-minded mentality on historical issues, severely limit the country from acquiring the natural resources and political temperament that are required conditions as a superpower status. So, to some commentators, given its rapid and continuous economic growth, China seems to have better qualities to meet the conditions of superpower status and bring about a significant impact on the security environment in East Asia (Roy, 1994: 149–62; Ross, 1999: 81–118; Wilkinson, 1999: 141–72; Buzan, 2004: 71, 113–16).

Similar to the Cold War era, the new bipolar scenario helps to maintain, to some extent, regional order through the rivalry of the two superpowers. In the unfolding process, the two superpowers will develop a set of rules and norms that are intended to regulate and restrain their behaviors as well as the behaviors of their respective allies. Also in this scenario, states and power blocs in the region have to make a choice once again as to which superpower they will follow.

The second is a scenario of hegemony. It is a regional order that is achieved through the hegemonic arrangement of a sole superpower. In this scenario, the extent of the stability of security in East Asia depends chiefly on the competence and performance of that superpower. The US is supposed to retain its predominant position in this scenario on the ground that it continues, in a foreseeable future, to possess greater material capabilities and more valuable resources than any other states and power blocs in the region. By actively involving itself with various affairs in the region, the US intends to prevent other regional states and power blocs from challenging the status quo of the hegemonic order that is claimed and maintained by the US, or prevent them from making any attempt to compete with the US's superpower status. Within this scenario, other states or power blocs have to take, willingly or unwillingly, the position of obedience and submission to the superpower's governance.

The third is the scenario of balance of power. It is a regional order that is arranged through the balance of multiple powers. In this scenario, the international system in East Asia is no longer dominated by superpower(s) in a bipolar or hegemonic form. The emergency of this scenario requires at least two preconditions. One is that the comprehensive strength of the United States declines gradually, and finally it gives up or loses its status as the sole superpower in the world. Another precondition is that no other state in the region is willing to become a superpower or replace the US's superpower status, rather they are content to retain themselves as regional or global powers.[4] Hence, given the circumstances of no superpower, power relations among states in the region tend to act more as mutual checks and balances toward each other. In this scenario, the major regional powers are roughly as follows: a still powerful United States with its physical and normative capabilities irreversibly declining; an economically recovered Russia; a politically redefined Japan; a culturally re-emerging China; and the increasingly important role of power blocs like ASEAN in regional economics and geopolitics. The scenario of balance of power is more or less that of so-called 'multipolarity' represented at the regional level.

The fourth scenario is a security community, a regional order that is obtained through multilateral security efforts. As a mechanism guaranteeing regional security, the security community transcends both conceptually and pragmatically the traditional ideas of balance of power or hegemonic stability. In an imaginary East Asia security community, states share strategic goals of security and the arrangements of interests, norms, values and discourses of security politics, making the idea and act of resolving disputes among them by violent means least desirable.[5] In this scenario, what is Europe today, in terms of security politics, is supposed to be East Asia tomorrow. The regional security in East Asia is maintained by established rules and legal mechanisms achieved through dialogic efforts within the community.

The fifth is a scenario of a Sino–US strategic alliance. It is a regional order that is achieved through the formation of a Sino–US strategic partnership. In this scenario the United States upgrades its ties with China by redefining its strategic partner(s) in East Asia. The sole predominant role of the US shifts into a political rearrangement of 'common governance' by both the US and China; some commentators have suggested a concept of ideally a Group of Two (G2), describing a special relationship between the United States and China which play predominant roles collectively in regional as well as global economic, financial and security affairs. Following this concept, the East Asian order is maintained by the arrangement of shared responsibilities of the United States and China. Regional peace and stability is dependent on the extent of the consensus reached by the two states on their regional goals, and the means to reach those goals.

13.4 SINO–US RELATIONS IN DIFFERENT SCENARIOS

This section attempts to figure out trends of the Sino–US relationship in security politics by embedding that relationship into the five possible scenarios, examining how the bilateral relationship may look from the material–normative perspective.

In the first scenario, a bipolar condition reappears in East Asia. If the supposition that the Soviet Union's status during the Cold War will be replaced by a rising China in the post-Cold War era is accepted, then according to the material perspective the United States and China will confront each other in terms of their material capabilities, and constitute a rival or at least competitive relationship. Other states and power blocs have to make a choice between China and the US as to which ideology and political system they will follow. A renewed arms race may emerge in East Asia within the context of the renewed bipolar structure. This scenario may produce either of two situations: a 'Cold War' or a 'Hot War' between China and the United States, whose social relationship turns out to be antagonistic.

According to the normative perspective, however, it is questionable whether this scenario will be bound to drag East Asia back into a Cold War era again. On the one hand, a rising China will not be the same as the Soviet Union in the past. Ideologically, China no longer advocates a communist utopia as the direction of human society in the world; it does not support anti-government groups in neighboring countries or the region, nor is it selling revolutionary ideas such as those of 'guerrilla wars'. On the other hand, China is embracing the process of globalization by encouraging a market economy at home, and promoting conceptions of free and fair trade abroad. The proportion of shared values is expanding between China and the US in economic and social aspects as well as in international affairs, while the two countries retain important differences between them. Therefore, if China and the US could find more common ground in their understanding and ideas, their social relations may turn to be competitive rather than antagonistic. In this sense, the meaning of their respective material capabilities will not be understood in the same way as what the US and the Soviet Union did to each other during the Cold War.

In the second scenario, the United States as a sole superpower plays a hegemonic role in East Asia. The post-Cold War international system in East Asia has mirrored some features related to this type of scenario. Perceiving such a scenario, the material perspective argues that other states and power blocs in the region will counterbalance the US's predominant power in order to guarantee a relative balance in the distributions of material capabilities in the region. So states like Russia, Japan and China, as major counterbalancers, will express their unwillingness, in words and deeds, to accept certain regional arrangements made by and centered upon the US. In this sense, China and the US are in a competitive relationship in their struggle for markets, capital, natural resources, labor force and investments. It can be argued that within this scenario, diplomatic tensions between China and the US may arise at any moment. The competition is constant and sometimes cruel.

While accepting that within this scenario there exist both hegemonic force and the force of counterbalance, I contend, by taking the normative perspective that introduces the variable of social identity, that states like Japan and other US allies in East Asia may arguably be followers and dependents, rather than counterbalancers, of US hegemonic presence in the region – partly because they share democratic values and political beliefs with the US. Moreover, they may even invite and embrace US leadership in the region, in order to check and counterbalance a militarily as well as economically rising China that may adhere to different social values and political beliefs. According to this perspective, Sino–US relations within this scenario depend on how the two sides treat each other in their social identities. Provided that China and the US share more values and ideas in dealing with global affairs, and provided that China articulates clearly that it will not challenge US security interests in East Asia, the two states' social relationship can be one of competitiveness and friendliness.

In the third scenario, China, the US and other states have their material capabilities more or less equally distributed in East Asia, constituting a regional arrangement in the form of a balance of power. According to materialist views, there are only lasting interests, no lasting friends in interstate relations, so both China and the US in a scenario of balance of power may seek cooperation in security and diplomatic affairs, but the cooperation is selective and contingent, restrained by time and specific issues rather than institutionalized or regulated arrangements.

In addition, China and the US in this scenario may pursue and perform mutually parallel policies, paying more meaningful (rather than symbolic) attention to constant consultation and coordination through multilateral channels such as international or regional forums. Both sides will make use of communication and dialog so as to reduce disagreements existing between them. Social relations between China and the US in this scenario are critical, but since the two states have roughly equal distribution of their material capabilities, the meanings given to their material capabilities are not as sensitive or decisive as seen in the first and second scenarios.

In the fourth scenario, the social and political construction of the multilateral security community in East Asia will reshape regional interstate relations, including Sino–US relations. The material perspective has long been downplaying and marginalizing the subject of the security community, contending that the nature of interstate relationships is determined ultimately and decisively by national interests and physical power, not by collective ideas or any shared norms and values.

According to the normative perspective, however, the multilateral security community is believed to be a mechanism that is conducive to the construction of a peaceful and stable East Asia. One assumption is that member states in a security community, thanks to their mutually shared values and norms, tend to solve their disputes and conflicts through peaceful means and make their interests and behaviors more predictable and transparent. The social relations of the states in the security community are defined as friendliness, not hostility. Their respective material capabilities constitute part of the collective goods of the security community. However, two situations may occur. One is that both China and the US join the East Asia security community and become its members. That contributes to the sound development of the Sino–US relationship. Another, but less possible, situation is that the regional security community is initiated by the US but China is excluded from it, or vice versa. In that case the regional security community may produce negative effects on the Sino–US relationship.

In the fifth scenario, both China and the US form a strategic partnership and alliance, maintaining a coalition attitude in all (not partial) aspects and taking highly consistent defensive or offensive efforts to reduce commonly perceived threats. From both material and normative perspectives, this scenario helps create a forum of formal or informal communications in a wide range of fields. The Sino–US relations in this scenario are sound, intimate and lasting. One major feature of this relationship is that both sides have high mutual trust in the perceived change of their material capabilities and the understanding of the intentions and purposes as to how to use their respective power, since the social relations of the two states are identified as 'strategic partners' and 'allies'.

It must be pointed out that whatever the scenario, if China's economy and society keep developing, and if both China and the United States continue to maintain their close relationship in a wide range of fields including trade and economics, the dynamic social and economic interactions between China and the US will produce effects on their relations in security politics. On the one hand, Chinese economic growth and social development will contribute to promoting the country's comprehensive strength, and may bring about a redistribution of material capabilities and change the US's role in the region. On the other hand, closer interdependence of

China and the US in many fields may function as a crucial driving force in pushing forward the improvement of the East Asia community, as well as a staple pillar in stabilizing their bilateral relations in security politics. I argue that changed social relations between China and the US will directly and indirectly affect the meaning of changes in the material capabilities between them.

13.5 WHICH SCENARIO IS MOST LIKELY TO EMERGE?

So, what is the most likely scenario that will emerge in the unfolding 21st century East Asia? Or, among those five scenarios mentioned above, which will Sino–US relations in security politics most likely be affected and conditioned by? In this section I attempt to answer these questions, following the order from the most unlikely scenario to the most likely one in East Asia.

As already stated above, in terms of Sino–US relations in security politics, the ideal scenario is the formation of a strategic alliance between China and the United States. The recently coined buzzword 'Chimerica', that blends the words 'China' and 'America' into one, has somewhat expressed this wishful sentiment. Yet the possibility of this type of scenario emerging in East Asia is practically the least likely. International history has so far illustrated that it is uncommon to see two major powers ally with each other in the absence of common enemies. All alliances have the motivation of confronting commonly shared external threats, either material or ideological, or both. In the foreseeable future, China and the US will not encounter in East Asia a common antagonistic actor that is hard to deal with alone. Without a defining external threat, the drive to forge a China–US alliance is strategically weak, or even does not actually exist. Of course, both China and the US will (and do) confront common threats such as epidemic diseases, global warming, international terrorism, financial crisis and energy shortages, but all these threats are not adequate to make the two countries form an alliance in the conventional sense. In addition, one cardinal principle guiding Chinese foreign policy is to form no alliance with any country, nor to seek a hegemonic position in world politics.

The security community is another desirable scenario. Yet in the foreseeable future, its emergence in East Asia is not very likely either. In Northeast Asia, for example, due to its recent historical experience replete with wars, conquests, resistance, divisions, victims and other suffering, most countries in the region have entrenched themselves in disputes and even conflicts over issues of territorial borders, sovereignty, political cultures as well as historical narratives and collective memories. These emotional issues constitute obstacles that often prevent the states in question from sharing ideas, values, knowledge, beliefs and discourses in security politics.

In addition, if the US retains itself as a superpower, then the bilateral, not multilateral, security arrangement that has been dominant in East Asia since the end of the Second World War is very likely to persist and discourage the desire to restructure a security community in the region. However, with the increase of regional economic interdependence and closer social interactions, a theoretically optimistic assumption is that economic cooperation and social mobilization in the region may spill over to the field of regional security politics. Yet pragmatically it is not an optimistic situation when most actors – especially those in Northeast Asia – tend to transform their increased economic wealth into the build-up of their military might, thus making the regional security locked notoriously into a 'security dilemma'. With these problems, the realization of a security community in East Asia has a long way to go.

The scenario of balance of power, similar to the one of 'multipolarity', is anticipated. But the emergence of that scenario is preconditioned by the exclusion of a hegemonic superpower in the region. This involves at least two aspects. Firstly, the US would no longer enjoy its sole superpower status. Since the late 1980s there indeed have been continual debates within (and outside) the United States over the question of whether the US is declining. Since 9/11 and the global financial crisis, the US has encountered attacks and setbacks.[6] Despite the view that the world is entering a 'post-American era', with more economic and cultural centers emerging around the world (Zakaria, 2008), the United States retains its military, economic and technological advantages, and will be superior to most other states or power blocs unless the US itself decides to give up its superpower status. Secondly, even if the US lost its superpower status, willingly or unwillingly, no state would be willing to come out and replace it as the next superpower. As long as there is a superpower in the region, the emergence of a scenario of balance of power will prove to be difficult.

There are possibilities of a bipolar structure coming back in East Asia. But the chances are few. As one commentator has smartly observed, the number of superpowers is historically and gradually diminishing, not increasing: from several superpowers during the 19th century and the first half of the 20th, to the two superpowers during the Cold War, and to only one superpower after the end of the Cold War (Buzan, 2004: 31–45). In a pragmatic sense, even though China is regarded as a major candidate for the next superpower in the eyes of some, the question is whether China is willing to become a superpower, or would be more content with its status quo as a major (but not super) power. Having its national interests so closely related to the unprecedented process of globalization, China favors constructing a harmonious world that addresses equality, fairness and justice. China has not designed for itself 'a strategy and theory of establishing regional or global hegemony' (Guo, 2004: 157).

In the coming decades, the most likely scenario in East Asia is one similar to the scenario of hegemonic arrangement. As the predominant power, the early 21st century US is not willing to give up its leadership in East Asia and hopes to maintain a regional order that is consistent with its core values and interests there. In East Asia, the US guards against the emergence of any state or power bloc that may challenge and unsettle its status quo position in the region, making and preserving somewhat unbalanced distributions of material capabilities in the region as long as possible. It is argued that in the short run US power is not likely to decline, and its status in world politics is not likely to change (Wang, 2005: 40). As mentioned above, one prominent feature of post-war US East Asia security policy has been inclining to bilateral rather than multilateral arrangements, which are represented in the US forming security alliance relationships with its East Asian allies in a 'hub and spokes' pattern. The US guarantees that these allies' material capabilities will not surpass those of the US, and makes use of the alliance relationships to check and even contain those states that are supposed to pose potential threats to US national interests in the region.

That said, this hegemonic management is not perfect.[7] While there is no single state or power bloc in the region that has the political will or physical capacity to challenge it, this regional arrangement is not static or unchanged. Firstly, the rising of certain states in the region may partly counteract the US's material and economic might. Secondly, these newly ascendant states may not indefinitely tolerate the US's hegemonic power in the region, and will vent their resentment through both rhetoric and action, expressing willingness to undertake multilateral efforts rather than bilateral alliances in dealing with regional security politics. Therefore, the (re)rising of regional powers 'seems not to be beneficial to this hegemonic order' (Yang, 2000: 283). Thirdly, as a dynamic and crucial area in international politics, East Asia confronts a series of major (non)-traditional security problems, including North Korea, nuclear issues and environment degradation. No state can deal with them alone; collective efforts are needed. If that is true, then there is no such US hegemonic governance in the pure sense. And this may become more clear with the passage of time.

13.6 CONCLUDING REMARKS

This chapter has taken a combined material–normative approach to the study of the international system in East Asia, and imagined the possible trends of Sino–US relations in security politics by embedding the relationship into five imaginary scenarios in the region. Some concluding remarks are as follows.

Firstly, the international system in East Asia is both physically and socially constructed. In the five imaginary scenarios, the meanings of material capabilities vary with the different nature of the social relations among the states in the region. As for Sino–US relations in security politics, the ideal scenario is that both China and the US form a strategic alliance, while the least desirable scenario is that a bipolar structure emerges once again in the region, where the two countries are located at opposite poles. The other scenarios between these two provide contexts for competition and cooperation of the two states in their relationship of security politics, to different extents.

Secondly, both material capabilities and social identities are equally important, because they are the units of analysis in understanding Sino–US relations in security politics. Since the end of the Cold War, the material capabilities and social identities of both China and the US have been in constant change, and their relations are in frequent (re)adjustment. That is probably one of the major reasons why this bilateral relationship is full of twists and turns in the post-Cold War era. As the changes are still under way, the vicissitudes will continue accordingly.

If the social relations of all major powers can be roughly categorized as friends, competitors or adversaries, then the category that the Sino–US relations in security politics fall into will depend to a great extent on how the two states perceive each other's changing identities. These changing identities will in turn affect how they perceive each other's changing material capabilities. If one shares and accepts the identity of the other and they form the feeling of a collective identity, then the relationship of the two states will move towards the direction of the category of friends. If the two states have differences in their identities of ideology and political beliefs, they will treat each other as a threat to their own ideological or political system, thus forming a competitive and even rival relationship. China and the US are gradually expanding the scope of their shared values, ideas and knowledge. The US is more willing to mobilize major powers including China to deal with what it defines as 'major threats', rather than (re)-construct major powers as threats to US national security as it did during the Cold War era.

Thirdly, the possible scenario of an international system in East Asia is very likely to be one similar to a hegemonic arrangement by a predominant power, as seen now. However, this hegemonic governance is incomplete, because the evolution and change of other powers in the region are bound to weaken US power relatively in the region. If China and the US maintain their current social systems and political cultures with no fundamental changes, the disputes and conflicts in their relationship are structural. If they can expand their shared values, ideas and knowledge in other aspects (say, dealing with common global problems, and reaching consensus on global strategic goals of security politics), then this will be conducive to reducing their disputes and conflicts derived from political and social differences, making a competitive relationship move to a friendly relationship. Within this broad context, the material capabilities of the two sides may be partially transformed into collective goods needed in tackling common global problems so as to reach common strategic goals in East Asia.

NOTES

1. The original version of this chapter was published in the *Journal of Northeast Asia Development*, **12**, December 2010.
2. In the field of IR theories, political realism – especially neorealist ideology – takes this perspective.
3. The literature that the chapter refers to on the subject of the assumptions of patterns of international system in future include: Koehn and Cheng (1999), Mastanduno (2003) and Buzan (2004).
4. Some scholars have done interesting analysis on the mentality of major powers in this scenario. See Buzan (2004), pp. 132–46.
5. For the systemic studies of conception of security community and empirical analysis, see Adler and Barnett (1998).
6. For instance, the US possesses the most up-to-date military technology and capabilities in the world, yet it is unable to end the two wars it has launched in Afghanistan and Iraq, respectively. It is labeled as the strongest power in the world economy, yet it has not launched in Iraq a reconstruction project similar to the Marshall Plan after the Second World War aiming at European reconstruction; it advocates democracy and freedom in global scope, yet it faces moral and ethical setbacks in the world because of its invasion of Iraq. Also see Pape (2009).
7. Some argue that US dominance in the post-Cold War Asia-Pacific region has not followed other hegemonic paths in history, rather it has taken a benign form with 'a clearly national style'. See Ikenberry and Mastanduno (2003), pp. 7–8.

REFERENCES

Adler, Emanuel and Michael Barnett (eds) (1998), *Security Communities*, Cambridge: Cambridge University Press.

Buzan, Barry (2004), *The United States and the Great Powers: World Politics in the Twenty-first century*, Cambridge: Polity Press.

Finnemore, Martha (1996), *National Interests in International Society*, Ithaca, NY: Cornell University Press.

Foot, Rosemary and Andrew Walter (2010), *China, the United States, and Global Order*, Cambridge: Cambridge University Press.

Friedberg, Aaron (2011), *A Contest for Supremacy: China, America, and Struggle for Mastery in Asia*, New York: Norton & Company.

Gilpin, Robert (1987), *The Political Economy of International Relations*, Princeton, NJ: Princeton University Press.

Guo, Wanchao (2004), *Zhognguo jueqi: yige dongfang daguo de chengzhang daolu* (China Rising: Road for Growth of an Oriental Power), Nanchang: Jiangxi Renmin chubanshe.

Ikenberry, G. John and Michael Mastanduno (eds) (2003), *International Relations Theory and the Asia-Pacific*, New York: Columbia University Press.

Koehn, Peter H. and Joseph Y.S. Cheng (1999), 'The Outlook for US–China Relations in the 21st Century: Regional Security, Trade and Information, and Cultural Exchange', in Peter H. Koehn and Joseph Y.S. Cheng (eds), *The Outlook for US–China Relations Following the 1997–1998 Summits*, Hong Kong: Chinese University Press, pp. 1–26.

Mastanduno, Michael (2003), 'The US–Japan Alliance and Models of Regional Security Order', in G. John Ikenberry and Takashi Inoguchi (eds), *Reinventing the Alliance: US–Japan Security Partnership in an Era of Change*, New York: Palgrave, Macmillan, pp. 21–42.

Mearsheimer, John J. (1990), 'Back to the Future: Instability in Europe after the Cold War', *International Security*, **15**(4), 5–56.

Mearsheimer, John J. (2001), *The Tragedy of Great Power Politics*, New York: Norton.

Morgenthau, Hans J. (1960), *Politics among Nations: The Struggle for Power and Peace*, 3rd edn, New York: Knopf.

Pape, Robert A. (2009), 'Empire Falls', *National Interest*, January/February, pp. 21–34.

Rosecrance, Richard and Guoliang Gu (eds) (2010), *Quanli yu kezhi: zhongmei guanxi de gongtong yuanwang* (Power and Restraint: A Shared Vision for the US China Relationship), Beijing: Shehui kexue wenxian chubanshe.

Ross, Robert S. (1999), 'The Geography of the Peace: East Asia in the Twenty-first Century', *International Security*, **23**(4), 81–118.

Roy, Denny (1994), 'Hegemon on the Horizon? China's Threat to East Asian Security', *International Security*, **19**(1), 149–62.

Sun, Zhe (ed.) (2011), *Hou weiji shijie yu zhongmei zhanlue jingzhu* (Post-crisis World and China–US Strategic Competition), Beijing: Shishi Chubanshe.

Sutter, Robert G. (2010), *US–Chinese Relations: Perilous Past, Pragmatic Present*, Lanham, MD: Rowman & Littlefield Publishers.

Waltz, Kenneth N. (1979), *Theory of International Politics*, New York: McGraw-Hill.

Waltz, Kenneth N. (2000), 'Structural Realism after the Cold War', *International Security*, **25**(1), 5–41.

Wang, Jisi (2005), 'China's Search for Stability with America', *Foreign Affairs*, **84**(5), 39–48.

Wendt, Alexander (1999), *Social Theory of International Politics*, Cambridge: Cambridge University Press.

Wilkinson, David (1999), 'Unipolarity without Hegemony', *International Studies Review*, **1**(2), 141–72.

Yang, Jiemian (2000), *Hou lengzhan shiqi de zhongmei guanxi: waijiao zhengce bijiao* (Post-Cold War Sino–US Relations: Comparing Diplomatic Policies), Shanghai: Shanghai People's Publishing House.

Zakaria, Fareed (2008), *The Post American World*, New York: W.W. Norton Company.

Zhao, Suisheng (ed.) (2007), *China–US Relations Transformed: Perspectives and Strategic Interactions*, London: Routledge.

Zhu, Zhiqun (2006), *US–China Relations in the 21st Century: Power Transition and Peace*, London: Routledge.

14. Middle powers and the building of regional order: Australia and South Korea compared

David Hundt[1]

14.1 INTRODUCTION

This chapter compares two middle powers, Australia and the Republic of Korea (ROK), during the transition to a new regional order in the Asia-Pacific. These two states have been allies of the United States (US) since the early phases of the Cold War, during which a US-led series of alliances, known euphemistically as the 'hubs and spokes' or 'San Francisco' system (Tow, 2001), was ranged against a less cohesive Chinese-led bloc of communist states. Since the early 1990s, the division between these two blocs has blurred. The collapse of the Soviet Union and the fall of its satellites in Eastern Europe are generally accepted as markers for the end of the global Cold War (Dockrill and Hopkins, 2006). China's turn to capitalism and its subsequent 'rise', the growing economic integration of East Asia since the financial crisis of 1997–98, and the emergence of multilateral security institutions such as the Association of Southeast Asian Nations (ASEAN) Regional Forum (ARF), add further weight to the claim that the Cold War-era dualism is passing in the Asia-Pacific region.

This chapter examines how Australia and South Korea have contributed to the building of a new regional order. In doing so, it distinguishes between the purposeful building of formal institutions which are designed to govern regional security issues, and other policies which indirectly enhance a sense of 'regionness' (Hettne and Söderbaum, 2000). First, section 14.2 reviews the concept of order and the variant of order which ASEAN – the self-appointed vanguard of regionalism in the Asia-Pacific – has proposed. Notably, given the status of Australia and the ROK as formal alliance partners of the US, the vision of regional order which ASEAN has proposed does not oppose the ongoing presence of the United States in the region. Indeed, even some states who are not formal allies of the US have indicated that they believe the US alliance system helps to stabilize the region. Another set of policy decisions which indirectly influence the formation of regional order involves free trade agreements (FTAs). Section 14.3 focuses on the role of FTAs in solidifying military alliances amid the intensification of economic interdependence in the region. As the economies of Australia and the ROK become increasingly dependent upon that of China, they have sought to enhance their links to the United States.

Sections 14.4 and 14.5 examine specific initiatives by South Korea and Australia to influence the building of a new regional order. The chapter focuses on Korean collaboration with ASEAN, which plays host to groupings such as the ARF and the Chiang Mai Initiative (CMI). It also examines the Australian proposal for an Asia-Pacific community. In the building of institutions intended to govern the security affairs of a region, an unavoidable issue arises as to the membership, scope and purpose of institutions, and thus the identity of the region. Finally, section 14.6 considers the implications of the transition between orders for middle powers, including how they have defined their identities and interests since the dissolution of the Cold War order.

14.2 ORDER AND THE ROLE OF MIDDLE POWERS

What is order? When considered in terms of outputs, order is the means by which states within a region address security issues of common interest (Lake, 2009). The assumption here is that geographic proximity – and thus perhaps cultural affinity – elicits similar responses to security concerns, locking states into a regional security complex. Order may be equated with security architecture, or what William Tow and Brendan Taylor (2010: 96) define as 'an overarching, coherent and comprehensive security structure for a geographically-defined area, which facilitates the resolution of that region's policy concerns and achieves its security objectives'. Security architecture is the sum total of 'broader multilateral efforts to promote the common security concerns of the participants' (Bisley, 2010).

If the output of order is a mechanism for resolving and preventing disputes within a given region, what inputs make order possible? A defining feature of order is stability: 'Regional order . . . means the existence of a stable structure of regional inter-governmental relationships informed by common assumptions about the bases of inter-state conduct' (Leifer, cited in Khong, 2005). If order is to be a '*viable* instrument for the management of regional security' (Tow and Taylor, 2010), it must have sufficient stability to withstand the vicissitudes of international politics. It should require renewal or replacement only in the wake of epochal shifts in power between states. In the interim, '[p]rudence, a rudimentary code of interstate conduct, gives a measure of stability' (Leifer, cited in Khong, 2005).

A second factor which determines the structure of an order is the type of security practices in a region. Order may be either equitable or hierarchical: the variation in its form resembles a spectrum, on which the balance of power, concerts and collective security arrangements are located at one end, and security communities and pan-national integration are located at the other (Lake, 2009). It is also possible that inter-hegemonic settlements can be reached. Security practices vary widely: whereas limited war is considered 'an order-sustaining or creating tool' in the balance of power, 'neither the expectation of nor the preparation for organized violence as a means to settle interstate disputes' exists in a security community (Adler and Greve, 2009). Subsequently, for order to be durable, the states of a region must subscribe to 'a set of shared assumptions about the interrelationships among resident and external states', strive for 'common goals' or share 'a common strategic perspective' (Leifer, cited in Khong, 2005).

In terms of the spectrum of orders, the Asia-Pacific region approximated a balance of power during the Cold War. Both the US and China supported smaller states in the region within a sometimes conflictual balance of competing powers. Korea and Vietnam endured civil wars which were partially internationalized, and Southeast Asia experienced a variety of limited war (*konfrontasi*) as well as numerous communist insurgencies. The founding of ASEAN in 1967 represented a significant development in the passing of the Cold War. After being founded as an anti-communist league, ASEAN's expansion and encompassing of all ten states in Southeast Asia by the late 1990s represented a symbolic transition away from the divisions of the Cold War. The Southeast Asian subregion has, consequently, been far more stable and consultative than other regions (Khong, 2005).

What type of order replaces that of the Cold War remains an open question. It is tempting to address the question in terms of binary outcomes. One possibility is that the US alliance system will remain the central organizing principle of the region as the 'American century' is extended. Adherents of this scenario would take heart from statements by US Secretary of State Hillary Clinton (2009, 2010) that the Obama administration has no intention of forsaking American interests and its perceived responsibilities in the Asia-Pacific region. There are also suggestions, for instance, that the United States should create 'new institutional entities organised around common democratic values, or more crudely, a China containment rationale' (Tow, 2007). Another possibility is that the seemingly inexorable rise of China will reprise the Sino-centric order which existed until the 19th century (Kang, 2007), perhaps in conjunction with the formation of a Eurasian version of the North Atlantic Treaty Organization (NATO). Some authors foresee a region in which Chinese power supersedes that of the United States, resulting in hegemonic transition – and possibly conflict (Zakaria, 2008; Zhao and Liu, 2008).

Rather than either of these outcomes, some hybrid form of order, in which increasingly prosperous and militarily self-sufficient states interact and cooperate via an intricate web of institutions and regional bodies (Bisley, 2010), seems more likely to emerge. Indeed, ASEAN envisions 'omni-enmeshment' of the major powers to regional security affairs, facilitating the emergence of 'a hierarchical regional order that approximates the following preferred power distribution: (1) superpower overlay: United States; (2) regional great power: China; (3) major regional powers: Japan and India; and (4) major regional players: ASEAN, Australia, and South Korea' (Goh, 2007). In a speech to the Asia Society in 2010, ASEAN's Secretary-General, Surin Pitsuwan, confirmed this conditional acceptance of the American presence by comparing the US to an umbrella: 'The umbrella is not straight overhead, it has to be symbolically behind, not direct, not overwhelming, not imposing, but there to provide that sense of security, trust and confidence to the region' (Pitsuwan, 2010).

These comments imply that ASEAN wishes to see the US's role in the region change from that of leader to that of partner; it also implies that ASEAN views itself as the gatekeeper to regional security affairs, one capable of endorsing the presence of the US – an Asia-Pacific state – in East Asian affairs. For Zhu Liqun of the China Foreign Affairs University, such a transition away from a balance-of-power structure is well under way: 'I use the term "balance of engagement" in order to grasp the essence of the current structure of East Asia [because] the main feature of today's situation in East Asia is not a play of power politics, but mainly cooperative, sometimes competitive, interaction among multi-players' (Milner et al., 2010).

Perspectives on the optimal shape of order architecture differ greatly, and depend in part on how states define their identities and thus their region. Self-identifying Asia-Pacific states such as the US tend to share the view that the new order should retain the hubs and spokes alliance system. Bilateral ties should be supplemented by multilateral forums which are capable of producing concrete solutions to specific problems rather than focusing merely or predominantly on processes. In contrast, Asian states such as Japan tend to take a longer-term perspective and are less concerned about the immediacy of outcomes. ASEAN in particular focuses on formal institutions, especially those centred on itself (Tow and Taylor, 2010).

Despite the differences which cultural identity exerts on definitions of region, a commonality between Australia and South Korea is their status as activist middle powers. The middle power concept envisages states with moderate degrees of power using their influence in ways which benefit the development of international society. These states are identified as 'good international citizens' (Lightfoot, 2006) which promote respect for 'the rules of the game' on the part of both great and small powers, especially in terms of the norms governing institutions such as the United Nations. Middle powers can act as catalysts of new initiatives, facilitators of coalitions in support of existing initiatives and agenda-setting, and as managers of extant institutions (Cooper, 1997).

What is underplayed, however, is the relationship between middle powers and their more powerful counterparts. Middle powers may be 'team players', but they are rarely leaders. Nor are they neutral in their political allegiances or in their preferred visions of global and regional order. A certain subset of middle powers, such as Australia and South Korea, demonstrate relatively strong faith in the value of US leadership, especially in the Asia-Pacific region, and indeed have premised their national security strategies on the maintenance of alliance relations with the US. In addition to acting as security partners to the US, the ROK and Australia have also been prime movers in the G20 process, a new form of global governance. The ROK, for instance, has emphasized its potential to be a 'creative and mature global state' due to its successful transition from underdevelopment and authoritarianism to prosperity and democracy (Jeong and Lee, 2010). This chapter proceeds to explore the ways in which Australia and the ROK have contributed to the shaping of a new regional order in the Asia-Pacific.

14.3 THE UNDERPINNINGS OF ORDER: ECONOMIC INTERDEPENDENCE

One of the main drivers of efforts to demarcate a specific region and an order to govern relations within it is economic interdependence. A sense of regional identity and purposeful action (regionalism) may result from the intensification of economic relations within a geographical space (regionalization). Regionalism connotes 'a programme and strategy and may lead to formal institution-building', whereas regionalization 'denotes the (empirical) process that leads to patterns of cooperation, integration, complementarity and convergence within a particular cross-national geographical space' (Hettne and Söderbaum, 2000).

In partnership with Japan, the United States has succeeded in incorporating China into the regional and global political–economic systems during the past three decades. Given its status as the leader of the capitalist world, this can be considered an ideological victory for the US. China has tacitly admitted to the shortcomings of socialism, but a new battle is under way to decide which variety of capitalism – the liberal democratic model suggested by the United States, or the Chinese state-led alternative – will prevail in the 21st century (Beeson, 2009). In the transition from an American and Japanese-centred political economy to a Sino-centric one, smaller states such as Australia and South Korea are forced to calculate economic and political interests simultaneously. The politics of FTAs, which further intensify interdependence, sheds light on those calculations.

Neither South Korea nor Australia is a stranger to FTA negotiations. By one estimate, the ROK has been the world's most active negotiator of FTAs; more than 40 agreements are at various stages of completion (Lie and Kim, 2008). Since 2004, the ROK has ratified FTAs with Chile, Singapore, the European Free Trade Area and ASEAN (ROK, 2008), and is negotiating with Canada, India, Mexico, New Zealand and the Gulf Cooperation Council. An agreement with the European Union signed in September 2010 that came into effect in mid-2011 secured access to what is collectively South Korea's second-biggest market (Miller and Dalton, 2010). Australia, meanwhile, has ratified FTAs with New Zealand, Thailand, Singapore and the United States, and is negotiating with states including China, Malaysia and Indonesia (Ravenhill, 2009). Furthermore, the Closer Economic Relations agreement, which unites Australia and New Zealand, was formally linked to the ASEAN FTA in 2010 (Walters, 2009).

To date, Australia and South Korea have mainly sought agreements with economies of similar scale and with complementarity. However, when FTAs link economies of different scale and complexity, there are implications for the sovereignty of smaller states. Consequently, FTAs have great symbolic meaning in international politics. FTAs may evolve within a security alliance (Snyder, 2009), as in the case of the Australia–United States FTA (AUS FTA), so long as the externalities resulting from increasing economic interdependence are not detrimental to military ties. Preferential trade agreements may also evolve between states whose political and security relations are divergent but which enjoy economic interdependence, as in the case of Korea's proposed FTA with China.

In the context of the 'war on terror', the Bush administration intensified the use of 'security-embedded' or securitized FTAs. That is, the US expanded its FTAs with its most loyal allies, viewing such agreements as a reward in the form of preferential access to American markets and technology (Higgott, 2004; Koo, 2009). The US views economic interdependence as a way of reinforcing its military alliances, a pattern which is evident in its choice of FTA partners (USTR, 2010a). The prioritization of economic ties has outlived the Bush era: in late 2009 the Obama administration announced its intention to form a Trans-Pacific Partnership, which would combine existing bilateral agreements in a 'high-standard, broad-based regional pact', and help achieve the administration's goal of increasing American exports by 50 per cent (USTR, 2010b).

In the case of the AUS FTA, political leaders on both sides were predisposed to the norm of free trade, reducing the difficulties in negotiating the agreement. Critics argued that the FTA would damage Australian interests. For instance Australia would have to accept delayed access to American agricultural markets; it would need to weaken the Pharmaceutical Benefits Scheme, whereby an independent public assessment was made of the value of new drugs; and the capacity of the Foreign Investment Review Board to scrutinize the impact of foreign investments on the national interest would be circumscribed (Weiss et al., 2004). Nonetheless the agreement was ratified and came into effect in 2005. The value of the agreement from Australia's perspective appeared to lie in the intensified linkage of Australia to the US, and the security benefits which that implies.

South Korea was another target for America's securitized FTA strategy, despite tensions between the Bush and Roh governments. Indeed, President Roh Moo-hyun seemed to view an FTA as a way of overcoming the difficulties which the two allies had experienced during the early years of his term in office. Subsequently, negotiations for the South Korea–US (KORUS) FTA proceeded quickly, and an agreement was signed in 2007. In early 2008, President Lee Myung-bak's government announced that it would lift restrictions on the importation of American beef, seemingly the final impediment to the ratification of the FTA. Beef imports had halted in 2003 after the detection of 'mad cow disease' in the US. US officials argued that the problem had been addressed sufficiently, and that US beef was safe to consume. Ratification thus hinged on the lifting of the ban. The announcement that beef imports would resume, with some limits on the types of meat which would be allowed, sparked a wave of protests in Korea during mid-2008.

The economic slowdown, especially in the industrial heartland of the Midwest, encouraged American leaders to push harder for concessions from trade partners such as South Korea for a deal which would help the car industry recover. The ROK wanted the deal to remain in its original format, but US carmakers sought greater access to the Korean market (Reuters, 2010). According to American researcher Troy Stangarone, 'The United States is facing a potentially much more critical crisis (than Korea) and Korea could strengthen the alliance by showing . . . flexibility in the United States' time of need' (cited in Hwang, 2008). When visiting Washington in April 2010, President Lee emphasized the strategic importance of the agreement, arguing: 'The United States should always keep in mind China, which is growing fast, militarily and economically. The ratification of the KORUS FTA has a *much more important meaning* than simple economic cooperation between two allies' (cited in Stangarone, 2010). The agreement was eventually signed soon after President Obama's visit to Seoul in November 2010.

Lee's comments signal that FTAs can appeal to smaller states as long as the enmeshment of interests between alliance partners is seen to have a net benefit in terms of security. There are high 'sunk costs' for states such as the ROK, Japan and Australia, whose entire national security strategy is premised on the continuation of their alliances with the US. North Korea remains at the center of the ROK's security concerns, but in the long term China also looms large. Of the surrounding powers in Northeast Asia, the United States is the only one never to hold territorial ambitions on the Korean Peninsula. This suggests that, like Australia, the ROK is willing to compromise on political autonomy in order to maximize security through the US alliance system.

As Lee hinted in Washington, a key motivation for South Korea's FTA strategy is to mitigate any adverse effects of economic interdependence with China, and also a growing relative dependence. South Korea's degree of dependence on China for overall trade rose from 2 per cent in 1985 to 19 per cent in 2006 (Chung, 2008, 2009). China accounts for about 80 per cent of South Korea's overall trade surplus: the surplus with China hit a record $38 billion in 2009, almost double the level of the previous year (Kim, J.W., 2010). Despite the ROK being a beneficiary of the China boom, some concern has emerged about the ability of Korean firms to compete with a rising China. In this view, South Korea is a 'sandwich' between its two large neighbours, at risk of being crushed by low-cost China on one side and technologically advanced Japan on the other (Seong et al., 2005). The Roh and Lee governments envisaged the KORUS FTA as a means for Korean firms to benefit from the economies of scale which access to the US market would provide.

Many of the concerns expressed in Korea about the effects of integration with China also pertain in Australia. With the AUS FTA finalized, Australia has shifted its focus to China. A particular issue of concern for Australia is the extent of Chinese investment in strategic sectors such as natural resources. The issue came to a head in 2009, when the government signaled its unease about a bid by state-owned Chinalco to increase its share in Rio Tinto, one of the largest Australian mining houses. The bid was withdrawn, but not without repercussions. After the rejection of what would have been China's single biggest foreign investment, Rio's chief iron ore negotiator, Stern Hu, was arrested for stealing commercial secrets in July 2009. In April 2010, Hu was sentenced to ten years' imprisonment. Subsequently, there has been greater scrutiny of investment by state-owned enterprises in a wide range of sectors, including sugar refining (Frith, 2010).

Surveys detect unease among investors and the general public. According to the 2010 Lowy Institute for International Policy poll, 57 per cent of Australians (compared to 50 per cent in 2009) thought that 'the government is allowing too much investment from China' (Hanson, 2010). Despite these concerns, '170–180 deals with Chinese businesses have been approved since [the current government] took office in November 2007, with 60–70 having been processed [in 2010] alone. So far, none have been turned down, despite Australia having one of the most restrictive foreign investment regimes in the world' (Barry, 2010).

14.4 THE NEW ASIAN DIPLOMACY: WORKING WITH ASEAN

The evolution of South Korea's regional diplomacy mirrors the gradual passing of the Cold War. As a state created at the outset of the Cold War – and as host to one of its 'hot' episodes – the ROK became one of the most loyal adherents to US foreign policy prerogatives. Park Chung-hee committed thousands of Korean troops to the Vietnam War, for instance, at the behest of the US. Under Roh Tae-woo, however, the ROK normalized relations with erstwhile enemies such as the Soviet Union, and also began to pursue economic opportunities in China. Perhaps the most notable achievement in South Korea's regional diplomacy was the Sunshine Policy, which prioritized engagement over confrontation and containment in inter-Korean relations. South Korea can also take credit for founding the East Asian Vision Group, the East Asian Study Group and the Northeast Asia Security Dialogue (Shim, 2009), all of which have contributed to a sense of regional identity.

A more recent initiative from the ROK has come in the form of its 'new Asian diplomacy', announced by Lee Myung-bak in March 2009. This initiative represents an ambitious bid to compete with China and Japan for regional influence. ASEAN, as the host of forums relating to security and economic matters, has become a special target for influence by the Northeast Asian 'plus three' states (China, Japan and South Korea). These states have expanded their levels of development assistance, proposed intensified economic cooperation including the finalization of

FTAs, and strengthened cooperation about global issues (Choi, 2009). For instance, China gave $14.8 billion in aid to ASEAN from 2002 to 2007, and Japan provided $20 billion in official aid and $5 billion in 'green' projects during the same period. South Korean aid disbursements, by way of comparison, were minimal to a region which is collectively the ROK's third-biggest trading partner and the second-largest destination of South Korean investment. However the New Asia Initiative will see a substantial increase in South Korean aid to ASEAN: the ROK will provide $400 million per year until 2015 (Ahn, 2009).

From South Korea's perspective, ASEAN is also valuable in that it offers an opportunity to influence North Korea indirectly. The ARF is the only security forum of which North Korea is a member, and given the stalemate in the Six Party Talks, one of the few venues in which the North can be socialized (Choi, 2009). There is evidence that the ROK is using ASEAN's model of 'quiet diplomacy' to improve the effectiveness of its own regional initiatives. For instance in 2005, the Roh government projected itself as the 'hub of Northeast Asia', but aroused some hostility and suspicion from Japan and China, whose economic transactions would presumably be diverted to South Korea in the process. Similarly, a proposal that the ROK could act as a 'balancer' between North Korea and the United States raised questions in Washington about Seoul's commitment to the bilateral alliance. In 2008, the ROK tried to have the issue of North Korean provocations added to the agenda of the ARF, but ASEAN refused to countenance discussion of such a divisive issue. Confronting North Korea so openly in a public forum, at which Pyongyang's benefactor Beijing would also be present and forced to openly side with the North, was not in keeping with the 'ASEAN way' (Kim, 2009).

A high point of South Korea's relations with ASEAN came in the form of a 'special summit' which the ROK hosted in May 2009. The summit commemorated the 20th anniversary of the ROK's formal ties to ASEAN, and Lee Myung-bak hosted bilateral summits with the leaders of all ten ASEAN states. The summit, which carried the slogan of 'Partnership for real, friendship for good', represented a rare occurrence of ASEAN holding a formal gathering outside Southeast Asia; the only other occasions when ASEAN has played the role of guest rather than host were when similar summits were held with China and Japan. The regular Japan–ASEAN summits began in 1997 (Hamanaka, 2009), endowing Japan with a significance that was later extended to China. The 2009 Jeju summit thus elevated the ROK to a status broadly commensurate with its two large Northeast Asian neighbors (Choi, 2009).

There is a strategic logic to the mutual courting of ASEAN and South Korea. Unlike Japan, China and the US, South Korea lacks the capacity to threaten ASEAN. The ROK shares a common history with Southeast Asian states insofar as both suffered under the Japanese colonial yoke in the first half of the 20th century, and both have at times been treated as 'barbarian' societies by China. South Korea and ASEAN are thus kindred spirits of a sort in the region, seeking to protect their interests while avoiding subjugation at the hands of the great powers (Kim, 2009).

This sense of commonality also applies to the Asian financial crisis, when states such as Indonesia, Thailand and South Korea were the most spectacular victims of the crisis. To prevent a repetition of the speculative attacks against their currencies and stock markets, the ASEAN+3 states launched the Chiang Mai Initiative (CMI) in 1999. The Initiative in part resembles the stillborn 'Asian Monetary Fund' which Japan proposed in the midst of the financial crisis: pooled funds which could be disbursed to member states with insufficient foreign exchange reserves to prevent capital outflows. Member states pledge to set aside contingency funds which can be called upon in a crisis situation. In May 2009, the CMI was transformed from a series of bilateral swap agreements to a fully fledged multilateral pool totalling $120 billion. China and Japan each provide 32 per cent of the funds; ASEAN members collectively supply 20 per cent; and South Korea is responsible for 16 per cent (Kim, 2009). The allocation of the quotas means that ASEAN and the ROK have a larger combined share of the funds than either China or Japan.

The ASEAN+3 states now have a proven stock of 'pooled resources, national commitments, policy agendas' and, in the form of the CMI, they have 'a record of concrete results including measures to protect members against future financial crises' (Emmerson, 2010). In the decade following the founding of the CMI, the capacity of the pooled fund to operate during a crisis was not tested. For instance, the CMI was not used to respond to the financial instability which afflicted the region following the subprime crisis in the United States. It is also unclear what conditions, if any, would apply to loans. Nonetheless, the CMI represents a new stage in the evolution of mechanisms for crisis management in the region. The ROK has added an element of democracy to the decision-making process by strategically cooperating with ASEAN, thus lending greater legitimacy to the ASEAN+3 architecture.

14.5 THE ASIA-PACIFIC COMMUNITY: CONTESTING REGIONAL IDENTITY

Given his expertise in the Chinese language and politics, his years in the diplomatic corps, and his holding the shadow portfolio for foreign affairs and trade, it was only to be expected that Kevin Rudd would propose a significant foreign policy initiative during his Australian prime ministership. Rudd proposed, in July 2008, a 'regional institution that spans the entire Asia-Pacific region' which was capable of engaging in 'the full spectrum of dialogue, cooperation and action on economic, political and security issues' (Rudd, cited in Milner et al., 2010). Rudd, who became Foreign Minister after being deposed as Prime Minister by his own party, was continuing a tradition among Labor governments in Australia of attempting to contribute, albeit with limited success, to 'the building of multilateral institutions, including the United Nations. In [the Asia-Pacific] region, Australia tried without success to promote the Asia and Pacific Council in the 1960s, and then played a key role in the founding of APEC [Asia-Pacific Economic Cooperation]' (Milner et al., 2010). Rudd's call for a new institution implied that extant bodies in the region, such as APEC, had failed to advance dialogue on security, political and economic issues. The new institution, which was envisaged as necessary for a region which is home to the United States, China, Japan, India and Indonesia, would assist in the peaceful resolution of disputes which inevitably emerge when such powerful states coexist (Woolcott, 2009). The mooted 'Asia-Pacific Union' thus implied that a regional community needed to include the US. Indeed, Rudd's vision appeared to assume that the United States would continue to exercise leadership in the region (Sheridan, 2009).

Having proposed a new institution, the Rudd government sought to attract the support of other states in the region. Richard Woolcott, a former Australian diplomat and a mentor of Rudd's during his time in the Foreign Service, was given the task of gauging the opinions of other governments. Australia was criticized for its 'failure to consult' Singapore and Malaysia prior to Rudd's announcement of his intention to form a new body. India, Indonesia and Singapore also criticized the proposed body out of concern it implied the building of a European Union (EU)-like structure (Kerin, 2009). Woolcott's consultations confirmed that other states had little or no interest in building new institutions; instead they preferred to strengthen extant bodies. One commentator (Heseltine, 2009) suggested that if the attraction of a new body was that it would include the US, the United States could be invited to join the East Asia Summit (EAS).

The proposed body was relabelled an 'Asia-Pacific Community' – thereby implying less formality than union – but 'Rudd's suggestion was so coolly received in Asia that its profile had to be reduced . . . the "C" in "Community" was lower-cased' (Emmerson, 2010), and Australia tried to assuage the concerns of other states in the region and attract support. For instance, during President Lee Myung-bak's visit to Australia in

March 2009, the two states promised to 'consult closely on the Asia Pacific Community initiative' (DFAT, 2009). After almost one year of consultations, 'most governments in the region [were] at least open to' the concept (Kerin, 2009), and Australia invited 21 nations to Sydney for a '1.5-track' conference in December 2009 to discuss the Asia-Pacific community (APc) initiative in more detail.

At the Sydney meeting, Rudd sought to dispel any perception that Australia was critical of institutions such as ASEAN and APEC. Instead, he argued that some new form of regional architecture would be required in future, and he claimed that his government was merely seeking to sketch an agenda for such a body (Rudd, 2009). Han Seung-soo, a former South Korean Prime Minister and diplomat, reminded his audience of Australia's support for APEC and other regional groupings. Given the 'growing consensus' about the necessity of a body capable of addressing issues such as the global financial crisis, climate change and non-traditional security issues, Han suggested an eminent persons' group be formed to devise a 'concrete action plan for the eventual creation of an Asia Pacific community' (Han, 2009).

Despite this show of support, 'the Australian host had to acknowledge Asian distaste for complicating the regional architecture . . . the Singapore delegation was particularly upset at the prospect that the centrality of ASEAN in East Asian regionalism might be jeopardized' (Emmerson, 2010). Singaporean academic Seng Chye Tan, for instance, argued that: 'The idea of a supranational organisation would not be acceptable to the regional countries, due to the likely dominance in such an organisation of the larger powers in the region . . . The APc would not be acceptable to ASEAN' (Milner et al., 2010). Tan defended ASEAN's legacy by arguing that since its founding in 1967, 'there has been no war or any major conflict in the region. The existing institutions and ASEAN's dialogue relationships have contributed to its political, economic and social progress and a peaceful and stable environment in the region' (Milner et al., 2010). An even more robust defence of ASEAN came from Singaporean academic and 'ambassador at large' Tommy Koh (2009a), who emphasized 'ASEAN's centrality' to the region. Following the meeting, Koh (2009b) was even blunter in his assessment of ASEAN and his dismissal of the APc.

Defenders of ASEAN also emphasized the complementarity of existing institutions. Tan, for instance, argued: 'The existing institutions or dialogue relationships –ASEAN+1, the ASEAN+3 relationships, the EAS and the ARF, as well as the ASEAN Dialogue Partnerships – enable ASEAN to play a central role as a driving force in region building' (Milner et al., 2010). In this view, no new institutions are required, given the existence of these 'complementary concentric circles – ASEAN inside APT [ASEAN+3] inside EAS' (Emmerson, 2010). Thepchatree Prapat, from Thammasat University in Bangkok, defended ASEAN by comparing it to actual and proposed functional rivals, including the APc. When criteria such as membership and geographic scope, the capacity to elicit cooperation, a shared sense of community and identity, and support from regional states are considered, Prapat argued, ASEAN and the ASEAN-centric forums outperformed the APc and other alternatives. Thus, Prapat concluded, it was ASEAN which was the ideal entity via which to 'develop ASEAN+3 into an East Asian Community' (Milner et al., 2010).

The controversy over the APc also highlights how definitions of 'region' differ markedly and in seemingly incompatible ways. Whereas states such as Australia subscribe to 'Pacificism', with its emphases on an inclusive pan-Pacific notion of region and a belief that the San Francisco system provides geopolitical stability, other states are more influenced by 'Asianism', which proposes an exclusionary form of regionalism and emphasizes Asian solidarity (Wesley, 2009). Another interpretation of these divergent forms of regionalism is that Asianism represents a 'primordial' form of identity formation that emphasizes ethnicity, whereas Pacificism represents a 'pragmatic' logic of grouping (J.S. Kim, 2010). The APc debate resembles the APEC versus East Asian Economic Caucus (proposed by Malaysia's Mahathir Mohammed) controversy of the early 1990s. According to Anthony Milner, 'The "East Asian" vision which [Mahathir] advocated – a narrower regionalism that would be driven by Asian states – had many supporters, and gained strong momentum with the creation of the ASEAN+3' (Milner et al., 2010). It remains to be seen whether the perceptual distance evident between Australia and ASEAN over the APc will affect Australia's future engagements in order-building.

14.6 CONCLUSIONS

ASEAN's preferred model for order-building seems to be a hierarchical and yet consultative security community hosted by various processes centred on ASEAN. Crucially, from the perspective of middle powers allied to the US, the projected new order does not reject an ongoing role for the United States. Notably, the ROK, Japan and Australia signed ASEAN's Treaty of Amity and Cooperation and thus acceded to the East Asia Summit, on the proviso that it did not compromise their security alliances with the US (Ravenhill, 2009). In this sense, the proposed regional order does not categorically damage the interests of the US's allies. Just as the US alliances need not prevent states such as Australia and the ROK from participating in order-building, so the growing interdependence of the Asia-Pacific region, or regionalization, is compatible with both the Asianist form of regional order suggested by ASEAN, and also the broader, Pacificist form of order preferred by non-Asian states such as Australia.

South Korea's strategic interaction with ASEAN, especially in terms of the Chiang Mai Initiative, contributes directly to ASEAN's preferred form of regional order. Due to the sense of victimhood which these smaller players within the East Asian and Asia-Pacific region share, they have emerged as natural allies, even if the ROK has been less willing than ASEAN to promote a narrower East Asian identity. In its perceived criticisms of the performance and role of ASEAN in the region, and its promotion of a new pan-regional institution based on an Asia-Pacific rather than East Asian logic, Australia found itself somewhat isolated from the most active promoters of a new regional order. Nonetheless, Australia's Foreign Minister claimed that the government is committed 'to the strongest possible relations with our Asian neighbours' and said that Australia's admission to the Asia–Europe Meeting from 2010 would complement its 'engagement in other regional groupings such as the East Asia Summit and APEC' (Smith, 2009).

The form of the future regional order has not yet been decided, and ASEAN's claims that it is indispensable to the region are not beyond challenge. ASEAN is internally divided along numerous lines, not least of which are levels of economic development and political organization. Despite the grouping's aspirations to be the gatekeeper of regionalist projects, and its self-asserted centrality, it seems more likely that the region's most powerful states will ultimately prove to be the most influential in shaping the security practices which determine the coming regional order. Other candidates in the region, such as Japan, also appear incapable of offering leadership. Even after six decades, Japan has yet to overcome the legacy of its wartime aggression and is heavily reliant on the American alliance for its security. China's leadership aspirations have grown since the Asian financial crisis, and received another fillip in the wake of the ongoing global economic slowdown which emanated from the subprime crisis in the United States. Overt displays of Chinese nationalism, evident in the 2010 dispute with Japan over the arrest of the crew of a Chinese fishing boat (Garnaut, 2010), however, have raised fears about how China might act if and when it attains regional dominance. China's embargo on shipments of rare earth minerals to Japan – and the threatened use of this tactic against the United States – only solidifies such fears (*AFP*, 2010). Leadership implies the existence of followers, and the conservative instinct of middle powers such as Australia and the ROK to retain their close ties with the United States may contribute to the preservation of American leadership for much longer than is sometimes predicted.

Identities need not be treated as immutable to change, as this chapter has noted in its allusion to the primordial and pragmatic variants of regionalism. Australia's proposal for an APc attracted criticism as much for its style of presentation as its substance, especially for the threat it posed to ASEAN's leadership. As the Cold War order continues to pass and the shape of the new order emerges, even some core Asian states may come to define their interests in broader terms than the Asianist framework predicts.

NOTE

1. This chapter was originally published in the spring 2011 issue of *Korea Observer*, **42**(1), 69–94. I am grateful to the journal's editor for granting me permission to reproduce the article in this edited collection.

REFERENCES

Adler, Emanuel and Patricia Greve (2009), 'When Security Community meets Balance of Power: Overlapping Regional Mechanisms of Security Governance', *Review of International Studies*, **35**(S1), 59–84.

AFP (2010), 'China halting Key Minerals to US', *Korea Herald*, 19 October, 9.

Ahn, Chung-yeong (2009), 'Dae-ASEAN Soft Gyeongje Oegyo-ui Sae Jipyeong' (New Horizons for Soft Economic Diplomacy towards ASEAN), *Munhwa Ilbo*, 4 June, http://www.munhwa.com/news/view.html?no=2009060401033137191002.

Barry, Paul (2010), 'China's Quarry', *Monthly*, August, 36–40.

Beeson, Mark (2009), 'Hegemonic Transition in East Asia? The Dynamics of Chinese and American Power', *Review of International Studies*, **35**(1), 95–112.

Bisley, Nick (2010), 'China's Rise and the Making of East Asia's Security Architecture', paper presented at Workshop on the Rise of China and Its Impact on the Asia-Pacific, Melbourne, 5 July.

Choi, Jong-mun (2009), 'Han–ASEAN Jeongsangdeul ui Teukbyeolhan Mannam eul Junbihamyeo' (Preparing for the Special Meetings between the Leaders of Korea and ASEAN), available at http://korea.kr/newsWeb/pages/brief/hotIssue3/view.do?issueNewsId=71516508&newsDataId=148670333&packageId=49500458&currPage=3 (accessed 27 July 2009).

Chung, Jae Ho (2008), 'Geodae Jungguk kwa deobuleo Saneun Beop' (How to Live Together with a Giant China), *Dong-A Ilbo*, 27 August.

Chung, Jae Ho (2009), 'China's "Soft" Clash with South Korea: The History War and Beyond', *Asian Survey*, **49**(3), 468–83.

Clinton, Hillary Rodham (2009), '"We are Ready to Listen" to Asia', available at http://asiasociety.org/policy-politics/international-relations/us-asia/hillary-clinton-we-are-ready-listen-asia (accessed 2 August 2010).

Clinton, Hillary Rodham (2010), 'Remarks on Regional Architecture in Asia: Principles and Priorities', available at http://www.state.gov/secretary/rm/2010/01/135090.htm (accessed 1 August 2010).

Cooper, Andrew F. (1997), 'Niche Diplomacy: A Conceptual Overview', in Andrew F. Cooper (ed.), *Niche Diplomacy: Middle Powers after the Cold War*, London: Palgrave Macmillan, pp. 1–24.

Department of Foreign Affairs and Trade (DFAT) (2009), 'Joint Statement on Enhanced Global and Security Cooperation between Australia and the Republic of Korea', available at http://www.dfat.gov.au/geo/rok/fta/090305_joint_statement.html (accessed 31 March 2010).

Dockrill, Michael L. and Michael F. Hopkins (2006), *The Cold War, 1945–1991*, 2nd edn, New York: Palgrave Macmillan.

Emmerson, Donald K. (2010), 'Asian Regionalism and US Policy: The Case for Creative Adaptation', S. Rajaratnam School of International Studies Working Paper, March.

Frith, Bryan (2010), 'Chinese State Group Misses a Sweet Deal', *Australian*, 6 July, 24.

Garnaut, John (2010), 'China Detonates Regional Goodwill', *Sydney Morning Herald*, 23 October, 20.

Goh, Evelyn (2007), 'Great Powers and Hierarchical Order in Southeast Asia: Analyzing Regional Security Strategies', *International Security*, **32**(3), 113–57.

Hamanaka, Shintaro (2009), *Asian Regionalism and Japan: The Politics of Membership in Regional Diplomatic, Financial and Trade Groups*, London: Routledge.

Han, Seung-soo (2009), 'The Asia Pacific's Growing Global Profile: What Can the Region Offer the World?' paper presented at Asia-Pacific: A Community for the 21st Century, Sydney, 5–6 December.

Hanson, Fergus (2010), *The Lowy Institute Poll 2010: Australia and the World: Public Opinion and Foreign Policy*, Sydney: Lowy Institute for International Policy.

Heseltine, Colin (2009), 'Asia Pacific Community: Reinventing the Wheel?' *Asialink Essays*, September, 1–8.

Hettne, Björn and Fredrik Söderbaum (2000), 'Theorising the Rise of Regionness', *New Political Economy*, **5**(3), 457–72.

Higgott, Richard (2004), 'After Neoliberal Globalization', *Critical Asian Studies*, **36**(3), 425–44.

Hwang, Doo-hyong (2008), 'US Scholar urges Korea to be Flexible in FTA Auto Provisions', available at http://english.yonhapnews.co.kr/news/2008/12/09/0200000000AEN20081209000600315.HTML (accessed 6 March 2009).

Jeong, Keewong and Jeong Hee Lee (2010), 'G20-wa Junggyeon Gukka Yeokhallyeon: Hanguk Woegyo Jeollyak ui Mosaek kwa Two-face Game' (The G20 and the Theory of Role of Middle Powers: The Search for a Korean Diplomatic Strategy and Two-face Games), in *International Conference Celebrating the G20 Seoul Summit*, Jinju: Center for Area Studies, Gyeongsang National University, pp. 36–54.

Kang, David C. (2007), *China Rising: Peace, Power and Order in East Asia*, New York: Columbia University Press.

Kerin, John (2009), 'Rudd to Host Asia Community Meeting', *Australian Financial Review*, 14 October, 5.

Khong, Yuen Foong (2005), 'The Elusiveness of Regional Order: Leifer, the English School and Southeast Asia', *Pacific Review*, **18**(1), 23–41.

Kim, Jae-won (2010), 'Current Account Surplus with China Hits Record High', *Korea Times*, 18 June, 2.

Kim, Jun-seok (2010), 'From "Primordial" to '"Pragmatic" Identity: A Search for Regional Identity in East Asia', East Asia Institute Issue Briefing, 7 July.

Kim, Yeong-ho (2009), 'Han–ASEAN "Eobu Dongmaeng" Hara' (Korea and ASEAN Should Form a "Fishermen's Alliance"), *Kyeonghang Sinmun*, 1 June, https://news.khan.co.kr/kh_news/khan_art_view.html?artid=200906011807495 fcode=990000.

Koh, Tommy (2009a), 'Australia's Asia Pacific Community Proposal: Some Issues for Discussion', paper presented at Asia-Pacific: A Community for the 21st Century, Sydney, 5–6 December.

Koh, Tommy (2009b), 'Rudd's Reckless Regional Rush', *Australian*, 18 December, 14.

Koo, Min Gyo (2009), 'Embracing Asia, South Korean Style: Preferential Trading Arrangements as Instruments of Foreign Policy', East Asia Institute Issue Briefing, 11 November.

Lake, David A. (2009), 'Regional Hierarchy: Authority and Local International Order', *Review of International Studies*, **35**(S1), 35–58.

Lie, John and Andrew Eungi Kim (2008), 'South Korea in 2007: Scandals and Summits', *Asian Survey*, **48**(1), 116–23.

Lightfoot, Simon (2006), 'A Good International Citizen? Australia at the World Summit on Sustainable Development', *Australian Journal of International Affairs*, **60**(3), 457–71.

Miller, John W. and Matthew Dalton (2010), 'EU Nations approve Free Trade Pact with South Korea', *Wall Street Journal*, 17 September, 15.

Milner, Anthony, Liqun Zhu, Seng Chye Tan and Thepchatree Prapat (2010), 'Regionalism – An Asian Conversation: Three Viewpoints', *Asialink Essays*, June, 1–13.

Pitsuwan, Surin (2010), 'A New Landscape in Southeast Asia', available at http://asiasociety.org/policy-politics/international-relations/us-asia/new-landscape-southeast-asia (accessed 1 August 2010).

Ravenhill, John (2009), 'East Asian Regionalism: Much Ado about Nothing?' *Review of International Studies*, **35**(S1), 215–35.

Republic of Korea (ROK) (2008), *Trade Policy Review: Report by the Republic of Korea*, Geneva: World Trade Organization.

Reuters (2010), 'S. Korea Wants US to Stick to Original Trade Deal', *Korea Herald*, 21 October, 6.

Rudd, Kevin (2009), 'Conference Summary Record', *Proceedings of Asia-Pacific: A Community for the 21st Century*, Sydney, 5–6 December.

Seong, Somi, Steven W. Popper and Kungang Zheng (2005), *Strategic Choices in Science and Technology: Korea in the Era of a Rising China*, Santa Monica, CA: RAND Center for Asia-Pacific Policy.

Sheridan, Greg (2009), 'A Vision Splendid for Asia-Pacific Alliance', *Weekend Australian*, 12–13 September, 23.

Shim, David (2009), 'A Shrimp amongst Whales? Assessing South Korea's Regional-Power Status', available at http://www.giga-hamburg.de/workingpapers (accessed 23 May 2010).

Smith, Stephen (2009), 'Australia to join the Asia–Europe Meeting (ASEM)

Process', available at http://www.foreignminister.gov.au/releases/2009/fa-s090528_asem.html (accessed 6 August 2010).

Snyder, Scott (2009), *China's Rise and the Two Koreas: Politics, Economics, Security*, Boulder, CO: Lynne Rienner.

Stangarone, Troy (2010), 'President Lee pushes for KORUS FTA, China could be Korea's Next FTA Partner', available at http://newsmanager.commpartners.com/kei/issues/2010-05-03/1.html (accessed 24 May 2010).

Tow, William T. (2001), *Asia-Pacific Strategic Relations: Seeking Convergent Security*, Melbourne: Cambridge University Press.

Tow, William T. (2007), 'America's Asia-Pacific Strategy is Out of Kilter', *Current History*, September, 281–7.

Tow, William T. and Brendan Taylor (2010), 'What is Asian Security Architecture?' *Review of International Studies*, **36**(1), 95–116.

United States Trade Representative (USTR) (2010a), 'Free Trade Agreements', available at http://www.ustr.gov/trade-agreements/free-trade-agreements (accessed 4 August 2010).

United States Trade Representative (USTR) (2010b), 'Trans-Pacific Partnership', available at http://www.ustr.gov/tpp (accessed 4 August 2010).

Walters, Patrick (2009), 'Rudd Vision for Region Evolves', *Australian*, 26 October, 2.

Weiss, Linda, John Mathews and Elizabeth Thurbon (2004), *How to Kill a Country: Australia's Devastating Trade Deal with the US*, Crows Nest, NSW: Allen & Unwin.

Wesley, Michael (2009), 'Asia, America and Australia', *American Review*, **1**(1), 52–62.

Woolcott, Richard (2009), 'Towards an Asia Pacific Community', *Asialink Essays*, November, 1–4.

Zakaria, Fareed (2008), *The Post-American World*, New York: W.W. Norton & Co.

Zhao, Quansheng and Guoli Liu (eds) (2008), *Managing the China Challenge: Global Perspectives*, Abingdon: Routledge.

15. The utility and limits of the 'European Model' for the regional institutionalization of East Asia

Richard Higgott

15.1 INTRODUCTION

There is a large literature on regionalism (the creation of formalized regions with agreed membership) and regionalization (the process by which regional economies and societies become more integrated).[1] There is also a large and growing body of literature on regionalism and regionalization in East Asia and the Pacific; notably on the Association of Southeast Asian Nations (ASEAN) and the Asia-Pacific Economic Cooperation (APEC), and of late on the emergence of differing 'East Asian' voices of the region as the major Northeast Asian powers vie with each other to make their presence felt. There is a growing body of literature comparing regionalism and regionalization in Europe with East Asia in particular.[2] There are large bodies of scholarly literature in economics and political science on the theory and practice of institutionalism and international organization.[3] This body of literature is evolving and on many issues it is not settled. Finally, there is a vast range of speculative literature emanating from think-tanks and blogs that revolves around the alphabet soup of meetings and events that take place in the region in any 12-month period (see www.eastasiaforum.org). Indeed, if the volume of literature written on a region was an indicator of the strength of regional institutional development, then the Asia-Pacific would be a highly institutionalized region.

But, we are not close to a settled theory of regionalism. There are lessons to be drawn from different regions but this does not amount to what we might call a comparative theory of regionalism. Specifically, there is as yet little or no substantial analysis of the importance of the theory and practice of institutionalism as a significant predictor of enhanced regionalism in an East Asian context. Theories of institutionalism in Europe might offer insights (see Rosamond, 2005) but they do not offer hard, replicable theory. There is a range of reasons for this. From the perspective of scholars of institutionalism and international organization, East Asia until recently has simply not been a region where they could ply their craft in a meaningful way. The laboratories were to be found either in the multilateral organizations, or in the study of the European project – for many, the one exercise in regionalization worthy of theoretical study. For the analyst-cum-practitioner involved in the various regional discourses taking place in the Asia-Pacific, and East Asia in particular, from the closing decade of the 20th century, the very idea of 'institutionalizing' this dialogue in a meaningful way, or certainly on the basis of some European model, was unthinkable. Indeed, senior members of the Asian regional policy community, especially within ASEAN, were often heard to rail against what they saw as the dangerous excesses of European legal formalism and the prospect of creating 'Brussels in Asia'.

Since the turn of the century there has been a change of mood in East Asia. Driven by a number of factors in the wake of the financial crises, observers have focused on the enhanced dialogue on regional monetary cooperation, especially following the Chiang Mai agreement, and the development of ASEAN+3 (APT) through ASEAN+6 to ASEAN+8 as a sign of new interest in enhanced cooperation in the region. Explanations of this trend are mixed. Most explanations point to economic drivers, notwithstanding the absence of substantive evidence in the economic data (see Ravenhill, 2010). Indeed, as I will suggest in this chapter, political drivers hold stronger explanatory power. But I do not seek to provide just another review of the evolution of East Asian regionalism.[4] Rather, I propose to take the theory and practice of institutions and institutionalization seriously and ask exactly what the prospects for such institutionalism are in East Asia in the early 21st century. This is done in a comparative context with the theoretical literature on institutionalism embedded in the empirical context in which it has found strongest expression to date – the European project. At this time in the history of the European Union (EU), the comparison with East Asia warrants further interrogation, especially since the normative advocacy of institutionalism in East Asia would appear to be strengthening at the very time when the limits of this process in Europe are being questioned more strongly than at any time in the last 25 years. The difficult birth of the Lisbon Treaty and the strains put on the political solidarity and governmental efficacy of Brussels in the wake of the global financial crisis represent an unprecedented level of systemic strain on the EU.

But the question is worth asking. Does the history of the European project tell us anything about the utility and limits of regional institutionalism in East Asia? If so, does it do so in a way that takes us beyond the early 1990s dichotomous analytical impasse that gave us the 'No Brussels in Asia' school of thought on the one hand, and the 'No serious regional cooperation in Asia until it adopts the European model' on the other (for discussions see Maull et al., 1998 and Breslin, 2005)? Does a comparative reading of the European and East Asian institutional projects in the contemporary era allow us to offer a more dynamic explanation for regionalization in East Asia that sees a process of adaptation, or what Acharya (2004) calls 'norm localization', rather than one of either mere mimicry or rejection? My answer is 'Yes'. The often Eurocentrically smug analyses of the 1990s – that saw European regionalism overcoming the negative constraints of state sovereignty on the one hand, while Asia hovered on the edge of perilous security and regional disorder on the other (Friedberg, 1993–4; Buzan and Segal, 1994) – were crudely overdrawn. As time progresses they become even starker as the European project seems to have hit a wall and East Asia charts a course unimagined a decade ago.

The body of this chapter is in five parts. Following the introduction, the chapter first discusses the current state of the theory and practice of regionalism in comparative perspective. Second, it locates the theory and practice of institutionalism in a regional setting. Third, it asks how relevant contemporary European institutional cooperation might be for understanding the way forward in East Asia. In so doing, it recognizes not only the significance of the European project, but also the limits of that project as a vehicle for transcending sovereignty, advancing supranationalism and enhancing the potential for regional transformation in East Asia. Fourth, it outlines important lessons from and for East Asia within the framework of 'the new regionalism'. Fifth, it outlines the importance of leadership to the East Asian institutionalization process. Europe, since the Lisbon Treaty, would appear to have gone about as far as it can down the institutional path. East Asia is only at the first step on that path. The interesting policy question is not whether East Asia will become more institutionalized rather than what form that institutionalization might take. The interesting scholarly question is: what are the key drivers that might assist or impede that process of regional institutionalization?

Europe is questioning the status of the institutions and practices that characterized the European project in the closing decades of the 20th century; but so too has Asia begun to question the underdeveloped nature of its institutional practices, especially since the financial crises of 1996–97. The 'Asia-Pacific way', characterized by weak informal norms of consensus-based decision-making and non-interference, is giving way to calls to establish substantive institutional practices of decision-making, especially in the domains of trade and monetary relations at both regional and bilateral levels, even though the practical direction and application of initiatives such as ASEAN+3/6/8 remain to be determined. In this context, the issue of regional 'leadership' and institution building is identified as the key issue for early 21st century East Asian regionalism. At its core, the degree and the nature of regional leadership in the emerging Asian integration process that is provided by China and/or Japan will prove crucial to the success of the current endeavours to secure enhanced regional economic (and political) institutional cooperation in the region. The presence of, or absence of, some kind of collective leadership, or at least consensual cooperation amongst the regional great powers, is the major instrument for, or obstacle to, any advancement of regionalism in Asia. Without a 'historic compromise' between China and Japan, not dissimilar that that which occurred between France and Germany after the Second World War, economic integration will remain a distant prospect.

15.2 THEORIZING REGIONALISM: EUROPE AND ASIA COMPARED

Regionalism is invariably conceptualized with comparative reference to Europe, even though it is clear that policy learning and the politics of emulation (or in many cases the politics of avoidance) are major features of current deliberations about regionalism in other parts of the world, and especially East Asia. This is especially the case as regionalism is increasingly seen as a response to the growing liberalization of trade and internationalization of technology, finance and communication that characterize what we now commonly call globalization. The time lag between European developments and the construction of regional orders elsewhere has meant that region-building elites have had the opportunity to learn from the European experience. As often as not this has led to a desire for avoidance of, rather than the emulation of, the 'Brussels model'. The less institutionalized approach that emerged in Asia in the early 1990s was in part a deliberate choice to avoid the 'legal formalism' of the EU (see Higgott, 1998b).

So, whether viewed negatively or positively, the European experience looms large. This search for 'European correspondence' is an obstacle to the development of analytical and theoretical studies of regional integration elsewhere (Breslin, 2005). The oft-repeated characterization of Asian regionalism as 'loose' or 'informal' reflects a teleological prejudice informed by the assumption that 'progress' in regional organization is defined in terms of EU-style institutionalization. An assumption prevailed that the EU was, and indeed remains, *the* paradigmatic case of regionalism against which all other regional projects are judged. Indeed, for some, the Union's longevity, institutional complexity and policy reach means

BOX 15.1 BALASSA'S FOUR STAGES OF REGIONAL ECONOMIC INTEGRATION

- Free trade area (with the removal of trade restrictions).
- Customs union (with a common external trade policy towards non-members).
- Common market (with free movement of factors of production between member states).
- Economic union (harmonization of economic policies under supranational control).

that it is more than just an international organization. Hix (1994, 1999) argues that the EU is a political system rather than an integration project. This is an extreme position (see Rosamond, 2000), but it raises the issue of whether the EU is in fact an instance of integration, and thus of regionalism, at all and thus of any comparative use for trying to explain the direction of regionalism in Asia in the 21st century.

This dominance of the EU on our mental maps imposes an understanding of regionalism as bound up with 'formal institutionalization'. But to equate mature regionalism with the creation of supranational politico-institutional bodies equivalent to the European Commission, the European Parliament and the European Court of Justice prejudices any conclusions we might want to make about the emergence of a world order based on alternative forms of regional organization and cooperation. To use Europe as the direct comparison in East Asia mitigates our ability to recognize what is a unique exercise in regional cooperation emerging in East Asia. This approach also assumes that key political economy questions pertaining to economic cooperation can only be addressed in this context. This emphasis on institutional regionalism proceeding through a mixture of intergovernmental dialogue and continual progressive treaty revision is at the heart of the now classic model of economic integration (see Box 15.1) developed over 40 years ago by Bela Balassa (1962). Balassa used the term 'economic integration' to refer to the creation of formal cooperation between states and the forward movement from a free trade area to a customs union, a common market, a monetary union and finally total economic integration.

This view of regionalism, with its teleological reasoning, also informed the early neo-functionalist versions of integration theory emanating from American political science (Webb, 1983). In these explanations of regional cooperation neo-functionalists saw 'spillovers' leading to economic and (ultimately) political integration. They theorized the transcendence of the state system rather than its survival. Economic and political integration was driven by rational actors. For a while neo-functionalists used Europe to generalize about the prospects for regional integration elsewhere (Haas, 1958, 1964; Lindberg, 1966; Schmitter, 1971; Nye, 1968, 1971). But this was short-lived. The publication of Haas's auto-critique, *The Obsolescence of Regional Integration Theory* (1975), suggested that the very idea of producing replicable models of regionalism was misconceived. Two problems with integration theory had emerged:

- The European experience from the creation of the European Coal and Steel Community through to the achievement of the Common Market was not replicated. Analogous projects such as the Latin American Free Trade Area and the East African Common Market failed.
- Integration theory in Europe had underestimated the pervasiveness of nationalist sentiment and the intergovernmental direction community policy making had taken (Wallace, 1996; Moravcsik, 1994, 1998). Explanations of European integration remained, as common sense should have told us it would, complicated by the domestic politics of the member states.

But the dissolution of 'integration theory' was not just a consequence of the discrepancies between theoretical predictions and empirical 'reality'. It was also marginalized by a growing distaste for grand predictive social theory and a growing interest in explanations that privileged international 'interdependence' as the forerunner to globalization (see Katzenstein et al., 1998). It was only with the emergence of the single market programme in the mid-1980s that we saw a partial revival of neo-functionalist integration theorizing. An activist Commission, under Jacques Delors, offered an empirical reinstatement of the neo-functionalist idea of supranationalism and the single market was suggestive of a number of spillovers into social policy, economic and monetary union and political integration more generally (Tranholm-Mikkelsen, 1991). More traditional state-centric accounts of integration, clinging to outdated realist state theory, failed to capture the 'everyday' regulatory complexity of the European policy process (see Rosamond, 2000).

Interestingly, this reawakening of European integration occurred more or less simultaneously with the appearance of regional free trade areas elsewhere. The appearance of schemes in North and South America, the Asia-Pacific and Southern Africa were suggestive of a new regionalized world order, which would be triadic, with Europe, the US and East Asia as the nodal points. The drivers of this process were twofold:

- The revised, essentially looser, geopolitical security structure that followed the end of the Cold War enhanced transborder activity and interstate exchange.
- The growth of globalization: especially, but not only, the liberalization of global trade and the deregulation of global financial markets which challenged economic relations founded on the premise of national territory (Held and McGrew, 2000; Scholte, 2005).

Both drivers stressed the fuzziness of the distinction between the 'domestic' and the 'international'. Regional cooperation was thought to enhance global competitiveness. This general assumption is crucial to comparative analysis of the European and emerging Asian experience. Nowhere did regionalism appear to be getting stronger throughout the first half of the 1990s than in East Asia and the Pacific. For many, the growth of ASEAN and the so-called 'Asian way' of regional cooperation was a new form of regionalism explained by the need to respond to globalization (see Acharya, 1997, 2001). The development of APEC in the early 1990s strengthened this view (see Higgott et al., 1993) while the financial crises of the late 1990s challenged this view.

15.3 BEYOND EUROPE: REGIONALISM IN ASIA AFTER THE FINANCIAL CRISES

The financial crises of the late 1990s proved to be a watershed for both the analysis and the practice of regionalism in East Asia. They provided clarity of observation and represented a political reality check on a number of issues of regional and global economic management that had been obscured during the heady 'Asian miracle' era of the early 1990s. Despite the hype that accompanied its development throughout the 1990s, the much-vaunted APEC initiative seemed incapable of even delivering short-term palliative responses to the regional financial crises, posing serious questions about APEC as an emergent mode of regional organization in the Asia-Pacific (see Ravenhill, 2001). This reading was further justified by the abortive Japanese initiative to establish an Asian Monetary Fund (AMF) in the wake of the crises. The collapse of this plan in the face of US opposition highlighted the fragility of a Pacific-wide regional project that seemed dependent on US blessing.

It can, of course, be argued that APEC was only ever a trade-led initiative, neither intended nor equipped to deal with financial crises (Harris, 2002) in the closing years of the 20th century or a war on terrorism in the early years of the 21st century. On the other hand, an argument can be made that the financial crises opened the way for a less idealistic, more pragmatic thinking about regionalism in Asia (see Higgott, 1998a). In the longer term the crises pushed states to think again about how best to build a regional order capable of preventing financial crises (or at least competent to deal with those crises when they arise). The creation of a network of currency swaps and other financial arrangements arising from, and subsequent to, the Asian Development Bank meetings in May 2000 reflect this approach to regional cooperation.

The discussions that have taken place since then, and especially against the backdrop of China's growing global economic importance over the last decade, suggest a sense of urgency to identify growing regional self-definition of 'East Asia' as a valid economic space with a discernible political voice. Analytically, this suggests that such policy initiatives do not simply arise just as 'rational spillovers' from financial integration. Rather, they depend also on a range of political factors such as an emergent sense of collective identity on the one hand, or political struggles between large regional players on the other, that frames the way in which policy elites respond to exogenous shocks. This highlights the centrality of three important variables in the study of regionalism which are often overlooked in the economic literature on regional integration:

- The importance of identities in region building.
- The catalytic impact on regionalization of exogenous political as well as economic challenges emanating from the rapid growth of globalization.
- The similar catalytic impact of interstate politics and rivalry endogenous to the region, of the kind exhibited by Germany and France in Europe and now China and Japan in Asia.

Events in Asia since 1996 allow us to identify roles that nascent regional organizations play as mediating layers of governance between the nation-state and global institutions. In the Asian case this has involved the increasingly less passive acceptance of dominant Western ideologies and preferences, and the economic models bound up with the philosophies and actions of the international financial institutions. We saw this after the Asian financial crisis, and now in its second iteration in the wake of the global financial crisis and its aftermath since 2008 where the 'Asian voice' is a key factor in the fate and future of the G20. This is not dissimilar to the situation in Europe, where one purpose of such a mediating layer, certainly in the late 20th century, involved the protection of the 'European social model' against the assimilating tendencies of deregulated Anglo-American capitalism (Hay and Rosamond, 2002).

We thus need to treat institutions (such as regular forums for regional dialogue) as socio-political venues or sites rather than just capsules in which rational economic action takes place. Observers of regional cooperation in Asia need to recognize the salience of the relationship between institutionalized interaction on the one hand, and the emergence of regional identities and interests on the other. Rationalists need not just follow well-worn state-centric paths. Strategic action by state actors may still be, indeed certainly is, important but such action must continue to be placed within a wider complex of actors (both state and non-state) and institutional venues that conspire to influence the development of regionalism (Hurrell, 1995b). It is in this context that the role of institutions, and indeed the theory that underpins institutional growth and activity, is more important than has traditionally been thought to be the case in the dialogue on regionalism that prevailed in Asia prior to the Asian financial crises. If, with the benefit of analytical hindsight, we can now see its importance in the past it behoves not to repeat the mistake and underestimate its importance in the contemporary era.

15.4 WHY INSTITUTIONS MATTER AND WHY EUROPE IS DIFFERENT

> Institutions are the rules of the game in a society or, more formally, the humanly devised constraints that shape human interaction. . . . Institutions reduce uncertainty by providing structure to everyday life . . . institutions define and limit the set of choices of individuals (North, 1990: 3–4)

> Institutions are '. . . persistent and connected sets of ruled (formal and informal) that prescribe behavioural roles, constrain activity and shape expectations'. (Keohane, 1989: 3)

As processes of economic globalization deepen, they need to be institutionalized if they are to avoid increased hostile and negative responses. The continued liberalization of trade, the deregulation of finance and a limited role for the state in the process of market globalization require trusted and legitimated structures (institutions) if the excesses of globalization are not to be the source of its own downfall. Nothing better illustrates this point than the occurrence of the global financial crisis, the painfully manifest consequences of the absence of an institutional structure capable of mitigating financial excess. The level at which these institutions will flourish is yet to be fully determined. What is clear is that this cannot be either/or global or regional; it has to be both. It is a multilevel enterprise in which the failure of institutionalism at the global level is likely to enhance

BOX 15.2 INSTITUTIONAL PRINCIPLES DEVELOPED IN THE 20th CENTURY

- Institutions lower transactions costs by the provision and sharing of information.
- Institutions reduce uncertainty.
- Institutions help make promises and commitments credible.
- Institutions facilitate deal-making.
- Institutions enhance compliance.
- Institutions are vehicles for learning and socialization.
- Institutions help shape collective identities.[a]

Note: [a] For discussion of institutions and institutional theory see Keohane, 1984, 1989, 2002; Simmons and Martin 2002; Higgott, 2006.

institutional thinking at the regional level. As problem-solving at the global level becomes more difficult, enhanced collective-action problem-solving at the regional level becomes more attractive.

But much that we have learned about institutions is seemingly in danger of being unlearned. We are correct to point to deficiencies in the United Nations (UN). We are correct to want to reform it and the international economic institutions such as the International Monetary Fund (IMF), World Bank and World Trade Organization (WTO). What is alarming however is a growing willingness to question the very utility of institutions – or more precisely, institutionalism as a way of organizing international behaviour – in key quarters of the global policy community. Social science has demonstrated the theoretical and practical importance of institutions as the reducers of uncertainty and transaction costs, and the importance of their role in making promises credible (see Box 15.2). We may be cynical about institutions and distrust them, but if they did not exist we would most certainly be reinventing them in one way or another. Institutions facilitate deal-making between actors that may be in adversarial situations. But, institutionalism as a trust-enhancing commitment to principled behaviour lacks support at the global level. It is difficult for societal actors to give loyalty to transaction cost reducers.

These principles do not give us a clear-cut definition of what constitutes an institution. It is not, for example, always easy to distinguish in practice between an institution and a norm of behaviour. Moreover, for some analysts the concepts of 'organization' and 'institution' are interchangeable, while for others not all institutions are organizations. What constitutes an institution is also amorphous. For economists, for example, 'property rights' are an institution, and an important one in explaining the stability and predictability of market behaviour under conditions of globalization. For political scientists, a key institution for global problem-solving is multilateralism.

It is therefore worth recalling the standard definition of multilateralism as the management of transnational problems with three or more parties making policy on the basis of a series of acceptable 'generalized principles of conduct' (Ruggie, 1993: 11). The key principles identified by Ruggie are indivisibility, non-discrimination and diffuse reciprocity. It was expected that over time, decision-making underwritten by these principles would lead to collective trust amongst players within an institution. A key element in the development of trust would come from the willingness of the institutional hegemon – that is, the strongest member of the institution – to agree to be bound by these principles. That is, to accept the principle of 'self-binding' (Martin, 2003).

But it is not sufficient simply to identify the principles inherent in multilateralism. We must also understand the degree to which these processes do, or do not, deliver outcomes; the prominence of an international organization (*pace* APEC) does not always correlate with a high rate of success in problem-solving in a given area of international relations. Ambitious organizations might try to structure rules and behaviour in some of the key policy areas of contemporary global politics, but often to little avail. Thus, the decreasing salience of the principal international institutions has been a growing factor in the search for regional solutions to collective-action problem-solving.

Recently, insight has moved beyond the 'institutionalist' literature on institutions to take more account of history, culture and identity. Powerful insights into the intersubjective socio-legal context for interstate behaviour have also emerged (see Kratochwil and Ruggie, 1986). These approaches found fullest expression in the constructivist theorizing of the late 20th century (see Wendt, 1992, 2000), which focused less on the role of international institutions as actors and more on their role as norm brokers (see Finnemore, 1996). States not only use international institutions to reduce uncertainty and transaction costs; they also use them 'to create information, ideas, norms and expectations . . . [and] . . . to legitimate or delegitimate particular ideas and practices' (Abbott and Snidal, 1998: 8). Institutions are thus more than arbiters and trustees; they are also norm producers, brokers and 'enforcers'. This is an important theoretical insight that has only partially found its way into the analysis of East Asian regionalism (see Acharya, 2004).

This discussion of institutionalism has clear implications for the prospects of enhanced instiutionalization taking place in East Asia in the contemporary era in other ways too. In the language of institutional theory, we should ask to what extent are the processes that are in train in East Asia maximizing information-sharing, generating transparency in decision-making, and advancing the institutional ability to generate credible collective action problem-solving in a given issue area and eventually, in some if not all instances, leading to the development of enforcement and compliance mechanisms and dispute resolution procedures? In short institutional design and institutional effectiveness matter. To be blunt, ASEAN's achievements have never matched its lofty rhetoric, and its institutional ineffectiveness must be at the heart of any explanation of the disjuncture between theory and practice. The question for the future is whether the broadened scope of regional dialogue via the ASEAN processes and the debate around an East Asian or Asia-Pacific Community (APC) will overcome these well-understood procedural limitations (see Aggarwal and Koo, 2008).

We should of course note that this is not only a question for East Asia. There is a general issue at stake in both the global political and global economic orders. Are we in danger of unlearning these principles in the early 21st century? Specifically, is the United States (US) unlearning the message about the role of institutions at the very time when other parts of the world (including Europe, and notwithstanding the current economic and political situation) are learning of their importance? But the need for institutions is particularly important in those regions of the world in which the market economy is less embedded, and where these questions will continue to cast massive policy shadows. East Asia needs to learn the principles of institutionalism that flourished in the 20th century. This is not to suggest that their implementation will follow the same paths in the 21st century. Indeed, what makes East Asia so interesting is precisely the fact that it is a vehicle for adaptation of some of the key principles of governance behaviour that developed countries took on board during the 20th century. The approach of the EU to institutionalization is unlikely to be replicated in Asia.

If we look at the EU, then a major purpose of it as an institution has been to create 'credible commitments' amongst its member states in areas where the need for collective-action problem-solving has been accepted (Moravcsik, 1998). It has done so via a pooling and delegation of sovereignty in key areas. This is the main difference between the EU and other regional integration schemes in the modern era. Pooling and delegating sovereign decision-making is what has given the EU institutional capacity. Relevant key elements of the development of the EU that make it different from other systems can be noted:

1. Europe has substantial elements of an integrated governance system, linking institutional structures, policies, legal instruments that bring together the national and supranational level of decision-making and policy-implementation necessary for the success of any governance system.
2. In individual policy areas (for example, trade and competition policy) Europe has a sophisticated regulatory framework unequalled at the global level. Only Europe has developed a competition framework based upon the adoption by each state of common standards, procedures and laws. This is a framework that will not pass easily to the global trade community embodied in the WTO.
3. The EU governance model relies heavily on the rule of law (see Stone Sweet, 2004). The role of the European Court of Justice (ECJ) is crucial in ensuring a system that is both effective and fair. The ECJ has a key role to play in ensuring that the legal provisions of the Treaty of Rome (and subsequent amending treaties such as Lisbon) are upheld by the member state governments, the supranational institutions, and by organizations and individuals.
4. Access to the ECJ for private individuals as well as member states and the supranational institutions makes it distinctive from other international governance models. Contrast it with the WTO, where only states can make a complaint to the Dispute Settlement Body. If these legal principles of direct effect and supremacy were to be fully incorporated into other international agreements, there would be a radical change in the effectiveness, the capacity and the fairness of international and global governance.
5. The EU, for all its shortcomings, has managed to instil a spirit of cooperation amongst a diverse group of member states, succeeding in proving that cooperation need not be zero-sum and can be learned. In essence, cooperation within the context of an international governance system produces results where the participants can perceive cooperative action as a public good. This is not to suggest, of course, that cooperation among sovereign states or between states and non-state actors is automatic or anything other than a highly charged political process. Successful cooperation depends on a public sector push as well as an emerging supranational structure.
6. The EU has evolved towards a model of governance with a degree of democratic legitimacy. Despite real criticisms and a literature on the democratic deficit (for a discussion see Bellamy, 2005 and Moravcsik, 2004) the EU consciously strives to address the imbalance between the supranational and the national democratic structures.

7. While the European Union has emerged as a major actor in the world economy, with a reasonably developed and coherent set of trade policies, it is not so successful as a global political actor. Notwithstanding the creation of the External Action Services, a vehicle for the development of a common foreign policy, for the EU to be taken seriously in the international arena and to exert influence appropriate to its economic weight in the international institutions that currently form the global governance system, it needs a political identity as an effective and legitimate actor able to represent the interests of all member states. This, of course, is proving easier in theory than in practice. Finding legitimacy among its citizens and in public discourse within the EU on the one hand, and among the actors and institutions of global governance on the other, has proved difficult and events can and do derail these processes.
8. The European Union has built a dense web of cooperative relations with countries and regions in other parts of the world. These form a set of bilateral and multilateral relations linked to trade, aid, investment and other forms of development cooperation. Determined by historical, political and geographical factors, these links demonstrate distinctive priorities, value systems and normative considerations in the negotiation processes and decision-making frameworks, all of which shape the European approach to reform of the global governance system. Inter-regional cooperation has increased in both the scope and density of the agreements. Although often misunderstood, the Asia–Europe (ASEM) process, EU–Mexico, EU–Mercosur and the Cotonou Agreements constitute examples of the increased aspirations of a regional group to build a density of relations and foster trust and understanding fundamental to a global governance framework.

These developments, and the networking and bargaining surrounding them, provide many lessons for regional and global governance in general and for the prospects of institutionalization at the regional level in particular. European experience (and European scholarship; see Higgott, 2005b) can make a serious theoretical and practical contribution to our changing understanding of sovereignty. European approaches to governance have developed flexible and multidimensional concepts of sovereignty in the international system which contrast with the often bounded, state-based or intergovernmental characterizations of sovereignty and international relations as understood by most US practice and scholarship, and reflected in many other parts of the world where state consolidation rather than sovereignty pooling remains a principal preoccupation of a governing regime. Institutions, especially regional ones, are the essential conduits between the state and the global economic and political orders. Enhanced global economic integration requires innovation in thinking about governance at both regional and global levels.

If we are thinking normatively, it remains important to make an intellectual leap to overcome these more bounded notions of sovereignty that beset decision-makers in all East Asian states. The repressive potential of the state remains considerable, especially given the changing dynamics of international security in the post-9/11 era. We need to escape from a bounded notion of sovereignty and narrow definitions of security and state interest if the global and regional integration process is to deliver better governance at both regional and global levels. Central to overcoming these limitations must be the recognition that sovereignty can be disaggregated and redistributed across institutional levels from the local to the global, with the regional level, if the EU experience is anything to go by, capable of playing an important intermediary role. Thus the importance of institutionalism is no mere theoretical indulgence. How seriously we take it, and in what domains, will determine the nature of regional cooperation in the early years of the 21st century. Institutions will be important interlocutors in the relationship between globalization and regionalization, especially as the recourse to regionalism becomes an increasingly common response to globalization.

Some early depictions of globalization missed the complex interplay in the relationship between the 'global' and the 'regional' in the foreign economic policies of states. These analyses made judgements on technical and economic change and then extrapolated from them into the socio-political sphere in a manner for which the evidence was, at best, flimsy. Nowhere was this better illustrated than in what is often called the 'hyper-globalist' literature, which saw the declining salience of state actors and state borders in the rise of what Kenichi Ohmae (1995), with the breathless cartography of the 1990s business consultant, labelled 'region states'. In so doing he prematurely reduced the state to the role of a passive actor in cross-border processes. The 'hyperglobalization' thesis misconstrued how economic space is politically and socially constructed, and indeed reconstructed, over time. At the very least, economic regionalization requires governments to sanction the relaxation of barriers to trade and investment or, more proactively, to facilitate the provision of incentives to investment and trade sponsorship.

As Linda Weiss (2002) noted a decade ago, states are reasserting themselves. This proposition is reinforced in the wake of the global financial crisis (GFC) where the response of the major players, notwithstanding the collective endeavours of the G20, has been primarily state-driven. But states do not reassert themselves in the same way in all parts of the world. In some parts of the world, regionalization, seen here as a meso-level process of state-led governance and regulation, continues to grow in influence in the early stages of the 21st century. But this regionalism will not necessarily follow the European model, leading to some 'sovereignty pooling'. Europe's regional present is not Asia's regional future. Rather, in East Asia we are seeing the rise of 'regulatory regionalism' (Jayasuriya, 2004) as state actors develop selective, issue-specific strategies to manage regional stability and enhance competitiveness in the face of recognized limitations in the contemporary institutional structures of global economic and political management.

15.5 THE NEW REGIONALISM: SOME IMPORTANT LESSONS FROM AND FOR EAST ASIA[5]

It may help if we embed our discussion of East Asia in the wider context of what has come to be known as the 'new regionalism' that, as Breslin (2005: 6) rightly notes, is 'a framework, not a theory'.[6] At its core, new regionalism was a response to globalization, and especially the recognition of the inseparability of what Wallace (1990) called 'informal' and 'formal' integration and Higgott (1997) identified as de facto and de jure integration. The former refers to integration via the emergence of transnational space among private market actors. The latter sees integration led by the authority of governmental actors through agreement or treaty. 'New regionalism', as a framework, captures the importance of the ideology of regionalism; that is, region-building as a political project rather than one driven simply by gravity models of economic integration. The new regionalism also has structural consequences beyond the region in which it has taken place; witness the growth of institutions and organizations, or at least discourses, attempting to mediate between regions (such as the ASEM process). If this occurs in a formalized way, we speak of inter-regionalism.

It is increasingly accepted that regionalization refers to those processes of integration that arise from markets, private trade and investment flows, and from the policies and decisions of companies rather the predetermined plans of national or local governments. Regionalism refers to those state-led projects of cooperation that emerge as a result of intergovernmental dialogues and treaties. But, as in the relationship between regionalization and globalization, these are not mutually exclusive processes. Failure to recognize the dialectic between globalization and regionalization can mean that we impose a regional level of analysis on something that is actually global, or vice versa. We must also consider the salience of extra-regional relations when considering regionalization.

The growth in intra-regional trade in East Asia is the consequence of the dissagregation of production across national boundaries. With components produced across a region, the traded component in the production of a commodity increases dramatically. But the final goods produced as a result of intra-regional trade still have to be sold somewhere, be it inside or outside the region. Is this regionalization or globalization? The dichotomy does not help. The answer is that it is both: the processes of developing regional production networks are themselves driven by global processes and are contingent on global markets.

How we map economic and political space is also a concern. Strict national or sovereign parameters should be avoided when identifying regionalization. In addition to looking for a correlation between the national state and regional membership, we should also examine the wider groups and classes of actors that are involved in processes of integration. The growth of transnational networks and alliances that integrate elites, but not usually the wider populations, of a given country is the key here. Nowhere is this better illustrated than in the context of the development of APEC, where throughout the 1990s and early 21st century there has been a clear disjuncture between the enthusiasm for the process amongst intellectual, corporate and bureaucratic elites (if not all political ones), and the lack of knowledge and disinterest – and in some instances, hostility – towards the project in the wider communities of the member states.

New regionalisms are invariably defined by the rejection of the old; 'old' in terms of both theory and practice. At the level of practice, the first key feature of the 'new' is the sheer number of formal regional arrangements. There are few countries that are not members of at least one regional organization, and most are members of more than one. This upsurge in regional activity can be explained in several ways:

- The promotion of export growth strategies has advanced the reality of increased economic regionalization. In this regard, the increased adoption of varieties of domestic neoliberal policies is one explanatory variable for regional initiatives.
- An understanding that state actors are but one set of agents among many is at the heart of newer approaches. Moving away from this old 'statist' approach is a defining characteristic of 'new regionalisms'. Newer perspectives recognize the complex cocktail of state actors, interstate and global institutions, and non-state actors (especially multinational corporations, emerging civil society organizations and non-governmental organizations – NGOs) that all have an effect upon regional outcomes.
- The need to respond to globalization or participate in the global economy is a driving factor for governments, both weak and strong.

BOX 15.3 FOUR CONTRASTING APPROACHES TO REGIONALISM

1. ***De facto Regionalism:*** Informal, market-led and leading to enhanced economic integration. This is principally rationalist-economic in analytical orientation.
2. ***De jure Regionalism:*** Formal, rule-governed, state-led enhanced institutionalized cooperation. This approach is principally legal-political in analytical orientation.
3. ***Instrumental Regionalism:*** Initially informal and interest-led. Built on the identification of the interest to be gained by the development of a common policy towards third parties in a given issue area. This is principally a power politics realist analytical orientation.
4. ***Cognitive Regionalism:*** Initially informal. Built on shared cultural, historical and emotional affiliations which distinguish 'insiders' from 'outsiders'. This is principally socio-cultural or constructivist in analytical orientation.

Hence it is at the meso level, between globalization and the nation-state, that effort is applied to the management of multi-territorial collective-action problem-solving. While moves toward regional problem-solving have been more active in Europe than in other parts of the world, this is not only a European phenomenon. Elsewhere, the growing linkages between different schemes, such as the free trade agreement (FTA) between the EU and Mercosur, or the development of the ASEAN FTA, are evident (see Sampson and Woolcock, 2003). There is also a tendency to devolve competencies from state to local levels in countries participating in integration processes. Political authority becomes dispersed, while economic activities become globalized. In addition, non-state actors become involved in governance. This process is replete with policy implications. We should stop thinking in terms of hierarchical layers of competence separated by the subsidiarity principle. We cannot ignore the strong tendency towards networking arrangements at all levels of governance shaping, proposing, implementing and monitoring policy together. In this context, we can identify at least four different ways of trying to explain contemporary regionalism, as shown in Box 15.3.

The salience of these approaches varies over time. Trying to find a 'one size fits all' explanation is pointless, and rather than building (or joining) regional arrangements to enhance independence from the global economy (as in the immediate post-colonial era), many developing states now see regionalism as a measure to ensure continued participation in the global economy. Thus, and by extension, the distinction between de facto and de jure regional activity becomes less salient in the contemporary era. While markets remain the key drivers of economic regionalization, state-led initiatives to enhance integration into the global economy lead to the pursuit of more strongly politico-strategic regional policies (regionalism).

But for a range of reasons that we are only just coming to understand, East Asia, notwithstanding a growing keenness for enhanced regional cooperation, is unlikely to repeat the four-stage sequential process of integration outlined by Balassa in a European context. Globalization has had the effect of enhancing transborder activities and interstate exchange. Moreover, the security-driven disciplines of the Cold War era that ensured tight bipolarity have disappeared, and the growth of a neoliberal ideology (and practice) of freer trade and financial deregulation amongst global economic actors have combined to challenge traditional economic relations once founded on the premises of 'national economies'. In their place we had a growing recognition from the last quarter of the 20th century of regional projects as a response (both defensive and offensive) to the power of global markets and the need to ensure the flow of foreign direct investment (FDI) into a region in the search for competitiveness.

The difference with the Asian regional experiment in the 21st century is that it is less trade-led than the European project of the 20th century. Of course, de facto market-led integration is strong. Intra-regional trade at 26.5 per cent of regional gross domestic product (GDP) in 2002 is larger than that for any developing region (Evian Group, 2005: 5). But Asian regional trade intensity is declining (see Ravenhill, 2010: 183) and such has been the success in liberalizing trade in goods under the General Agreement on Tariffs and Trade (GATT) that the need to free up trade in goods on a regional basis has become less pressing. This is not to suggest that trade is not the motor of growth in East Asia – it remains so. Rather, it is to suggest that it is not the only motor of the regional economic discourse.

Much of the hyperbole surrounding the evolution of APEC in the first half of the 1990s saw only the benefits of free trade. But the export-oriented countries of East Asia needed little convincing of these benefits, and discussions in APEC in the first half of the 1990s missed the major changes taking place in the global economy and the potentially adverse effects they could have. What was not understood until the financial crises of 1997–98 was the manner in which dramatic increases in deregulated, unrestricted capital mobility could lead to the kind of catastrophic volatility seen in these crises and subsequently in the GFC. Since that time we have seen two seemingly opposing, but nevertheless compatible trends. These trends are the gradual movement towards enhanced monetary cooperation in East Asia on the one hand, and the growing interest in bilateral trading arrangements on the other. What makes them compatible is that both are wrapped up in the wider recognition of the importance of 'East Asia', as opposed to the 'Asia-Pacific', as the 'voice' of the region. The ASEAN FTA was the only preferential trade arrangement (PTA) in Asia at the turn of the century (see Nesadurai, 2003). By 2006 there were 45 regional PTAs in existence and nearly as many under negotiation; most of which, it should be noted, were with third parties external to the region (see Dent, 2006).

Of course, the US remains the dominant presence in the region defined as the Asia-Pacific (in both economic and military terms), but it is also an unwitting exogenous catalyst in the 'East Asianization' of the Western Pacific seaboard. APEC, rather than being a potential instrument for trade liberalization at the Asia-Pacific level, has come to be seen in large sectors of the policy communities of East Asia as but an additional means by which the US might advance its own agendas, such as for further capital market liberalization and, since 9/11, as a vehicle for advancing the US security agenda (see Higgott, 2004). The US suggestion for an Asia-Pacific Free Trade area was resisted by East Asian leaders at the November 2006 APEC Summit in Vietnam.

As is well known, since the late 1990s, regular ASEAN summits were initially expanded by the participation of Japan, China and South Korea in ASEAN+3 (APT) meetings. The first East Asian summit took place in Kuala Lumpur in December 2005. Asian policy elites, seeming no longer to want their policies controlled from Washington when economic crises occur, began the search for 'purpose-designed' East Asian responses to economic policy uncertainty. In this regard, 'instrumentalism regionalism' drove the growing regional interest in monetary cooperation and the perceived need to cooperate in the face of the shared common problem of financial volatility. In many ways, as evinced by the rapid growth of bilateral PTAs, this reflected a stronger urge than the desire to liberalize trade on a regional level. Initiatives emanating from this mode of thinking, especially those in the monetary domain, include not only the 2001 Chiang Mai Initiative (CMI) to create a regional liquidity (swap) fund, but also the Asian Bond Fund Initiative (ABF) proposed in June 2003, and the suggestion of a regional stock exchange, both of which have the aim of reducing the distances between the individual national markets and exchanges. One clear benefit of this process is the raising of standards and regulatory norms and practices in the region. The CMI and the ABF collectively enhance, although they do not guarantee, the regional capability of resisting financial volatility.

In terms of 'cognitive' influences in East Asia, the changing leadership role of the United States is important. It represents a growing 'other' in the Asian regional foreign policy context as regional players move to secure greater autonomy vis-à-vis the erstwhile regional hegemon. The nascent nature of regional cooperation, when accompanied by the fear of being on the receiving end of asymmetrical agreements in times of low trust in the multilateral trading system, has also seen governments in Asia developing bilateral strategies. This can be seen in the proliferation of preferential trading agreements in the region (see Dent, 2006).

What the Asian crisis told us, and the GFC confirmed, was that there was no consensus on how to manage the international economic order in the closing stages of the 20th century and the early stages of the 21st century. The major financial institutions were caught between competing nationalist and liberal views of how the world should work. The international financial institutions (IFIs) were found wanting in both theory and practice by the events in East Asia and in the GFC. Both crises provided a learning experience at the multilateral level: globalization requires institutional capability for prudential regulation, and it does so at a range of different levels. While most regional analysts recognize that regulation is best pursued at the global level, regional-level initiatives of the type outlined in the Manila framework and discussion of an Asian Monetary Fund will continue to evolve. The GFC may not be as catalytic for Asia as was the directly regional financial crisis of 1997–8, but casting its eye to Europe, Asia is likely to become less, rather than more, enthusiastic about initiatives for a regional common currency.

Where early regionalism might have been identified as a defensive mechanism to reduce dependence on the international economy, the 'new regionalism' sees it as more proactive. It is a means of greater access to global markets, not securing regional autarchy. Regionalism is also now more multifaceted and multidimensional than in the past. States engage in any number of overlapping endeavours without sensing contradictions in such a process. Where the defensive legacies of the earlier phase remain – among political elites sceptical of the unregulated nature of contemporary global capitalism – this does not imply a regional resistance to all elements of the globalization process. Indeed, the extent to which regional organizations act as a spur to global economic liberalization is an important question. APEC was designed to facilitate wider global processes and could be read as a (seemingly failing) attempt on the part of its Caucasian members to prevent the emergence of a specific 'East Asian' regionalism.

We should also consider the impact of joining (or forming) regional organizations for many developing states. On one level, the formal criteria established for membership by organizations – such as EU requirements in 2004 – force policy change on aspirant members. In the process of liberalizing to meet EU standards, these economies have become more open to the global economy. Thus regionalism can be seen as a pathway to globalization. This is a key distinction between current and old explanations for regional projects. Rather than building (or joining) regional arrangements to enhance independence from the global economy, many developing states now see regionalism as a measure to ensure continued participation in it, but with emerging regionalism as a meso-level comfort zone.

Thus regionalism can be simultaneously a response to, and a dynamic behind, globalization. We are dealing, in short, with mutually reinforcing and co-constitutive rather than contending processes. Regional regimes are not per se barriers to globalization. Rather, the regional project is both part of and a facilitator of globalization and a regional countergovernance layer in the world political economy. This relationship between regions and neoliberal paradigms and economic policies stands at the heart of the new assessments of regionalism and regionalization in the 21st century.

15.5.1 Trends in East Asian Regionalism

Since the turn of the century several broad trends have emerged:

- The growing malaise of APEC, notwithstanding the trappings of multilateral diplomacy, as the foremost regional construct has continued.
- The growth of bilateral PTAs and FTAs in the region continues to strengthen.
- The development of two pan-East Asian understandings of regionalism (embodied initially in the development of the ASEAN+3 and the first East Asian Summit).
- Closely linked to the above point, the development of an East Asian interest in mitigating the prospects of further financial volatility at a regional level via the gradual development of policies promoting monetary regionalism.

The defining issue in the development of these regional trends is not 9/11; rather, it is the Asian financial crises of 1997–98. For most Asian states these crises, their aftermath and Asian responses to US policy and the rise of China in the period since then provide the most salient components of an explanation of current trends and policies.

15.5.2 Bilateral Trade Policy and Regional Theory

While the rhetorical support for markets remains strong, the impact of politics on markets is never far away. And the growing interest in bilateral trade arrangements is determined by a number of factors. In the economic domain, the WTO had not fared well since its inception and the ability to secure a satisfactory conclusion to the Doha Multinational Trade Negotiations (MTN) Round has proved particularly indigestible in many parts of the world, giving rise to the growth of interest in bilateral preferential trading relationships (PTAs). This interest was (is) not simply a US phenomenon. But if the Europeans started it, and other, smaller and weaker states also began to explore it, it has been the role of the US, as the strongest partner in any bilateral relationship, which has been disproportionately influential. In the politico-security domain, the offer of preferential bilateral trading relationships in return for support in Iraq in particular and the war on terror in general has been a major instrument of US foreign policy.

The Asian interest in bilateral agreements reflects a general appreciation of the success of the GATT in reducing tariffs and, albeit to a lesser extent, non-tariff barriers in the second half of the 20th century on the one hand, but a concern about the direction of the WTO in the 21st century on the other. But the benefits of regional, multilateral free trade agreements are much less significant in economic terms than they were thought to be. Industry leaders in the region (de facto agents of market-led economic integration) are acutely aware of the degree to which manufacturing is now more global than regional. Building large, multi-member, regional trade blocs in an era of globalization is deemed less relevant. Rather, bilateral trade arrangements – in many ways a defining feature of the regional political economy in the early 21st century – are felt to give regional policy elites greater control over national trade policies. Whilst the important East Asian countries – Japan, South Korea and China – had long refrained from negotiating preferential agreements, these countries have been extremely active in the push for PTAs since the turn of the century.

This reflects Asian fears that their influence over deliberations at the WTO is not always as great as they would wish. As such, bilateral free trade agreements are statements of sovereignty. PTAs allow governments to secure easy wins in trade negotiations while excluding or protecting sensitive areas of the domestic economy from the liberalization demands present in multilateral trade negotiations. East Asian leaders also see them as a useful policy tool with both interregional and indeed extra-regional pay-offs given that the majority of PTAs under negotiation are with states external to East Asia. The effects of this trend can be, at one and the same time, to both enhance regional convergence in one area of activity yet also exacerbate regional divergence in another area of economic activity.

If bilateral economic cooperation in the trade domain is a fact of life in East Asia in the early years of the 21st century, the key issue for this chapter is the degree to which it might enhance the regional project overall or detract from greater regional economic policy coordination and integration. This is clearly not an either/or situation. Elements of both enhanced cooperation and increased competition are present in the contemporary regional policy process. In a 'structural argument', bilateralism can bolster the economic foundations of the region with the prospect of enhanced cooperation at the regional level. It can provide a regional 'lattice' of technical and institutional arrangements to reinforce the regional project (Dent, 2004).

By contrast, a 'process-led argument' in favour of bilateralism suggests that it has the effect of enhancing the broader discourse on regional economic cooperation and integration. No state, it is argued, pursues just a bilateral or multilateral trade policy. Bilateral activity should be seen as a complement to other initiatives such as the development of an ASEAN Economic Community and the APT, both of which have different but complementary agendas and functions. This is a position advanced by Singapore and Thailand as part of their trade strategies (see Desker, 2004).

In sum, support for enhanced economic cooperation and integration at the regional level is a possible outcome of the trend towards bilateralism in East Asia, but it is not inevitable and strong countervailing tendencies and outcomes are equally possible. We have little or nothing in the historical or scholarly armoury to make a strong prediction one way or the other at this stage. The risks may outweigh the opportunities. The degree to which the positive outcome might prevail will in part be determined by the success or failure of activities in other areas of the policy domain and with other putative economic initiatives, such as monetary cooperation, where the collective regional urge in East Asia in the early 21st century appears stronger than a regional urge in the trade context. But the jury is out on the strength of these arguments for the foreseeable future.

Opponents argue that the increasing recourse to bilateral initiatives has the effect of undermining the wider regional project in East Asia. Intellectual and technical capability and political will (key components of institution-building) are finite resources that cannot be indefinitely subdivided without diminishing their utility and effectiveness. At the ASEAN level, bilateral activities must inevitably be in competition for attention with attempts to upgrade the ASEAN FTA (AFTA) to the ASEAN Economic Community (AEC) by 2020 (Hew and Soesastro, 2003). A longer-term outcome of this competition in the trade domain could be the consolidation of existing asymmetries, enhanced interstate rivalry amongst regional neighbours and a diminution of the region's ability to present a united front to other global actors in other policy domains.

15.5.3 Monetary Regionalism and Cooperation

Narratives of the development of cooperation in this area abound (Deiter and Higgott, 2003; Hamilton-Hart, 2005; Pempel, 2005b) but several points about regional monetary policy as an example of cooperation can be drawn out. Nascent regional cooperation, when accompanied by the fear of asymmetrical agreements in times of low trust in the multilateral trading system, has seen governments developing bilateral strategies. But the search for a new voice of Asian regionalism remains problematic. Dialogue at the Asia-Pacific level has faltered. APEC's identity crisis persists. However, the regional dialogue moved on dramatically between the regional financial crises of 1997–98 and the GFC of 2007–08. It is the crises of the late 1990s that have contributed to the evolution of a new type of regionalism in Asia. Before the crises, trade-led regionalism in the Asia-Pacific had been driven by the Caucasian members of APEC. But even prior to 9/11, Asian observers had increasingly evaluated APEC as a tool of American foreign policy. The resistance of Asian policymakers to a strengthened APEC was caused by their fear of American dominance (Kahler, 2000: 568). They became increasingly critical of the lack of tangible benefits that APEC provided (Ravenhill, 2001). The manner in which the US has treated APEC in the wake of 9/11 has confirmed these initial Asian perceptions.

The debate about cooperation at the level of East Asia, writ small to mean ASEAN, continues with discussions about the creation of an AEC to integrate the activities of AFTA, the ASEAN Framework Agreement on Services, and the ASEAN Investment Agreement. But it is at the level of East Asia – writ large to include ASEAN, China, Japan and South Korea – that a dialogue on how best to mitigate the kind of volatility experienced during the financial crises of 1997–98 has developed most rapidly. Notwithstanding the failed attempt to establish an AMF in 1998, the principle behind the proposal did not die. By the end of 1999, the worst of the Asian crisis was over and East Asian policy circles once again addressed the topic of regional cooperation. The regular ASEAN summits were expanded by the participation of Japan, China and South Korea, the new body being called ASEAN+3 (APT), with the first East Asian Summit taking place in Kuala Lumpur in December 2005. Since then, steps in the search for a new monetary regionalism have been frequent and numerous. They represent a contribution to the debate over a regional institutional economic architecture that departs from previous cooperation models in Asia.

Efforts to secure monetary cooperation are very much part of the wider exercise of soul-searching that has been taking place both within ASEAN, and between ASEAN and its other East Asian partners, since the turn of the century. The crucial point of these exploratory exercises is not their immediate significance. Nor is the point to underestimate the difficulties of such policy coordination in the region. To see ASEAN+3 as but an exercise in extended conference diplomacy, reflecting weakness rather than strength, would be misleading. True, in the opening years of the 21st century it is too early to see what kinds of institutional structures will eventually be embedded in the region, but the range of interactions developing is unprecedented.

ASEAN+3 has moved rapidly, if not always coherently, from initial leadership meetings. Considerable deepening has taken place with regular ministerial meetings across most policy domains (economics and finance, agriculture, forestry, tourism and so on) (see Stubbs, 2002; Suzuki, 2004; Thomas, 2004). In T.J. Pempel's perceptive view:

> a strikingly contradictory view of the East Asian region emerges . . . [D]espite the overwhelming structural impediments to integration, East Asia has in recent years become considerably more interdependent, connected and cohesive. [It is] . . . a region that has developed an increasingly dense network of cross border cooperation, collaboration, interdependence and even formalized institutional integration. (Pempel, 2005a: 2)

In keeping with earlier analysis of the importance of a concept of 'East Asia' (Higgott and Stubbs, 1995), what we are seeing is a trend later picked up by others (Bergsten, 2000; Webber, 2001; Rapkin, 2001); namely, the emergence of a voice of the region beyond that of the subregions – Southeast and Northeast Asia – but more restricted than that of the Pacific as a mega region. The voice of the region that is emerging in the global political economy is an 'East Asian' one. The whole will be greater than the sum of its parts if momentum is maintained. The degree to which this is likely to be the case will be conditioned by the structure of regional leadership that emerges in the early 21st century and this is clearly contested if not beyond resolution.

15.6 INSTITUTIONALIZING EAST ASIA: THE LEADERSHIP ISSUE

In essence, and in addition to APEC, two essential pan-East Asian cooperative dialogues have developed. It is the tussle for leadership in this context that may well determine the future institutional structure of East

Asia as we move deeper into the 21st century. Leadership is one of the most difficult analytical concepts in the lexicon of the modern-day policy sciences. It is a little-understood popular and populist concept. The key distinction drawn in this section is between what we might call structural or institutional leadership, and agency-oriented or political leadership. The two are of course not distinct but they do provide a useful way of identifying the problems and prospects for leadership in the enhancement of Asian regional cooperation over the short to medium term. Specifically, a twofold classification allows us to distinguish between leadership and hegemony.

Leadership is not the same as hegemony (read: economic and military preponderance). Leadership can be intellectual and inspirational. If we look at the development of the EU, for example, then we can see both kinds of leadership over the life of the organization, in the intellectual leadership of figures such as Schuman and Monnet in the crucial agenda-setting period of the 1950s, and the cooperative hegemony of France and Germany at the economic core of Europe in the following era. From such a judgement it is easy to suggest that part of the problem that Europe faces at the moment is the absence of either kind of leadership. From this position we can also ask a series of similar questions about leadership in Asia in the early 21st century. Several specific questions come to the fore in this context:

- From where will the leadership come to take the cooperative dialogue in East Asia forward at this time? Where are the necessary actors to be found? Where are the Schumans and Monnets?
- What structural constraints on actor-based leadership are emerging, and can they be overcome? The leadership and political resolve required to advance regional institutional cooperation of the kind seen in Europe in the second half of the 20th century has yet to emerge in East Asia.
- What are the roles for the principal actors in the region over the short (five years) to medium (20 years) period? Will the USA play a supportive role in building East Asian cooperation in the 21st century, as it did in the building of the European Union in the second half of the 20th century? Can China and/or Japan play the kind of role that Germany and France played in the EU?

15.6.1 The US and the Question of Hegemony

To talk of regionalism in East Asia without addressing the specific question of the role of the US is not possible. To do so is to miss the context of the US in East Asia since the Second World War, especially when compared with its role in the reconstruction of Western Europe. This is especially, but not solely, the case since the advent of the Bush administration and the policy changes emanating from the events of 9 September 2001. US policy towards the region is shaped by its own agenda. Between 9/11 and the GFC this was increasingly a security-driven agenda, at the expense of what we might call the neoliberal economic agenda that underwrote its policies towards the region prior to then. Since the GFC the pendulum has swung back towards an economic agenda, and especially in a regional context the relationship with China over questions of trade imbalances and currency relations.

In historical terms the US role as an exogenous actor in the development of a European community was pivotal (see Latham, 1997). Within a Cold War context US foreign policy proactively supported the European project. Regional cooperation in Europe may have taken place without US support in any circumstances, but we will never know what form it would have taken. But we do know that the US via a range of initiatives, especially the Marshall Plan, gave considerable impetus and assistance to the early collaborative efforts of the European project. This is not the contemporary case in East Asia. Indeed, Mark Beeson (2005: 978–81) would argue that one of the key reasons for the slowness of enhanced economic cooperation in East Asia has been precisely because of the constraining role played by the US in the Cold War context. Moreover, US hegemony and the geopolitical setting in the contemporary era remain, as Beeson notes:

> still crucial influences on regional processes, they are having an inadvertent rather than intentional impact. Whereas the EU sprang from a highly successful attempt to reconstruct Western Europe on a new integrated basis, in East Asia American foreign policy is having a more ambivalent impact on the region that is gradually moving to assume greater autonomy despite, rather than because of, American policy. (Beeson, 2005: 970. For more discussion of the effects of US foreign policy see also Beeson and Higgott, 2005)

If the Cold War in Europe was centripetal, in East Asia it has been centrifugal. For 50 years, US policy split the region along ideological lines and built a structure of bilateral 'hub and spoke' relationships between it and its East Asian partners on the one hand, and propagated Cold War divisions on the other, that rendered impossible any leadership pretensions of the region's two major powers. Japan for the second half of the 20th century subordinated any leadership ambitions to its asymmetrical bilateral relationship with the US. Indeed, Japan's rise to become the world's second-largest economic power in the 1980s and 1990s was achieved at the expense of its own regional leadership ambitions. Similarly, China (for Cold War reasons) was not in a position to contribute to East Asia-wide regional cooperation. For most of the second half of the 20th century, both states – China for ideological reasons, Japan for its own particular debilitating historical reasons – were effectively denied regional leadership ambitions.

The historical balance sheet on US economic leadership in the post-Second World War era is mixed, or perhaps more precisely divided into two eras. In the first era it provided massive reconstruction funding, especially for Korea and Taiwan (see Stubbs, 2005). It also provided relatively open market access for the rapidly growing Japanese economy and other newly industrialized countries (NICS) in the first three decades after the Second World War without receiving reciprocal openness from these trading partners. This is traditionally explained as part of a wider grand strategy in the Cold War context. From the early 1970s, however, this benign (Kindleberger-esque) reading of US hegemony needs to be revised. From that time we have seen a well-documented recourse to an increasingly aggressive US economic policy aimed to manage access to the US economy for East Asian exports, and to open East Asian markets to US exporters. This has taken place through a range of strategies variously described as 'aggressive unilateralism' (Bhagwati and Patrick, 1990), strategic trade policy (Krugman, 1986) and the recourse to sectoral protectionist activities with euphemistic names such as Voluntary Export Restraints, Orderly Marketing Arrangements, Structural Impediments Initiatives and the like and, since the 1980s, a more or less permanent pressure on the major countries of the region progressively to deregulate their financial markets.

In contemporary terms, it is perhaps inevitable in the wake of 9/11 that we should see the robust reassertion by the US of the geosecurity agenda over the geo-economic agenda that prevailed in the 1990s. US attitudes towards regional projects are now ambiguous, to say the least. This is the case not only as regards to Europe in the wake of the war in Iraq, but also in its attitude towards enhanced regional cooperation in an East Asian context. While keeping a sense of perspective, we should note that the principal contemporary trends are not substantially different to those that were developing prior to 9/11. The US, since the time of the Asian financial crises and the attempts to establish an AMF, has opposed (or at best feigned indifference to) regional initiatives that run counter to its perceived regional interests.

But economic relationships between the US and East Asia are becoming less economically asymmetrical and, as a consequence, the ability of the US to set the regional agenda is becoming less convincing than at any time in the last two decades. As such, the likelihood that it will actively support greater institutional cooperation in the region should not be taken for granted. Indeed, there are obvious signs of concern in the US foreign economic policy community that events in East Asia, especially closer regional economic cooperation, have the capacity to 'develop in a way that excludes the US' (Marcus Noland, *Financial Times*, 14 September, 2005: 6; but see also Munakata, 2003: 10). As a consequence, some would argue that the task at hand is 'keeping the United States engaged in Asia' (Tanaka, 2007).

Resulting from a persistent trend over the last 30 years, US GDP is now only 80 per cent of that of East Asia. East Asia's share of total world trade is, at approximately 25 per cent, almost double that of the US at 13 per cent. As of 2003, East Asian exports were double those of the US; inter-regional trade in East Asia was strengthening rapidly and the US share of East Asian export trade had declined to 25 per cent. Holdings of foreign currency reserves in East Asia are now more than 20 times those of the United States. US technological superiority notwithstanding, when judged by the increase in its share of patent registrations, East Asia is making some inroads into US preponderance. The wars in Afghanistan and Iraq, the GFC, and above all the declining economic asymmetry in its relationship with China, have called into question the limitations of US power.

Of course, quantitative indicators alone are not definitive, especially when dealing with a concept as elusive as hegemony. Individual Chinese or East Asian aggregate performance does not axiomatically find its way into enhanced political leverage over the US, given that the region does not formulate policy towards the US on the basis of an 'East Asian' interest or via regional institutional policymaking machinery capable of reflecting any such aggregate interest. Decision-making resides firmly at the level of the constituent states, not at the level of the wider regional collective. In this context the agenda-setting abilities of the US still far outweigh those of any single East Asian state individually or, even given the probability of some enhanced cooperative decision-making emerging in the region from a successful pan-East Asian initiative, collectively for years to come. For East Asia to minimize the asymmetry in decision-making with the US to accompany the declining gap in material capability, it needs to enhance its collective decision-making capabilities. For this to occur, leadership endogenous to the region needs to strengthen. How this might be achieved is, of course, the single most important regional policy issue for the future.

15.6.2 Geopolitics, Leadership and East Asian Cooperation

East Asian responses to US economic policy are not insignificant. Major strides have been made by East Asian states in using existing institutional opportunities to defend sectoral interests, for example via the WTO Dispute Settlement Mechanism (see Pekkanen, 2004), although notwithstanding the growth of influence of Asia in the G20 the region remains basically under-represented in the Bretton Woods institutions that still reflect the configuration of global power at the end of the Second World War. However, Japanese and Chinese leadership aspirations continue to grow and the discursive practices of regionalization continue to evolve in a non-trivial, albeit contested manner.

Whether the Asians will be successful or not in their endeavours, there can be little doubt that the continued exploration of cooperation as a way to combat vulnerability is an established item on the regional policy agenda in the early 21st century, and it demonstrates a marked contrast with the late 20th century. Take three examples.

Firstly, if we consider APEC as the dominant regional initiative of the closing decade of the last century, then during this period we saw the US as strongly proactive; Japan as a passive or reactive actor in the organization; and China giving its support to the East Asia Economic Caucus (EAEC) initiative of the Malaysians rather than APEC. But the Asian financial crises exposed the limitations of the progressively excessive expectations that were heaped on APEC from the time of the first summit in 1993 until the crises of 1996–97.

Secondly, the AMF initiative of the late 1990s, initiated by the Japanese, met with resistance (albeit low key) from the Chinese and outright hostility from the US. From that time on, soft rhetoric has been replaced by harder realist lenses as APEC lost its appeal for Asian policymakers in particular. No significant economic initiatives have emerged from APEC since that time. Other factors diminished its attraction as an 'institution' for Asian leaders; especially the 'securitization' of APEC following 9/11 (Higgott, 2004). APEC's potential to be anything more than a vehicle for general dialogue, notwithstanding detailed technical work in its subgroups and committees by some of its members, has always been overhyped. East Asian regional support for APEC has always been constrained by national interest concerns that eschew any serious commitment to APEC's core analytical and policy concepts of 'open regionalism' and 'concerted unilateral liberalization'.

Thirdly, and most significantly, in the early 21st century the major regional agenda item has been the successful attempt to develop enhanced monetary cooperation, to prevent a reoccurrence of the Asian Financial Crisis. The Chiang Mai Initiative, begun in 2000, has been the major exercise in regional cooperation in the 21st century. In this initiative we see, for the first time, a position where both the Japanese and the Chinese are strongly supportive of this regional project. While the US is opposed, it is not minded to develop strong countermeasures. China and Japan are not, it should be stressed, engaged in a concerted coordination of their foreign policies. Rather, what we have seen is a coincidence where both powers recognize that the regional agenda for enhanced monetary policy coordination can be supported and advanced comfortably in the knowledge that it is a positive-sum, not a zero-sum game. This cooperation reflects the primacy of instrumental regionalism. At the risk of labouring the point, in contexts where Japanese and Chinese instrumental interests cohere, this will be a powerful force for regional cooperation in East Asia. In contexts where they are at odds, it will be very counterproductive. The jury is out on which of these two tendencies will prevail.

15.6.3 China and Regional Cooperation

How the relationship between China and the rest of the region plays out in the long run is the key to security, cooperation and institution-building in East Asia in the 21st century. This issue is best approached by posing a question rather than by offering unsustainable assertions regarding future behaviour: 'Does increased wealth and power lead to greater cooperation or greater competition?' This is a perennial question of international relations. It is central to the relationship between China and Japan. The evolution of their respective economies, over the last two decades at least, has been complementary rather than competitive in terms of what they produce for the global market and what they take bilaterally from each other. China is Japan's second-largest trade partner after the US. Japan is both the largest trade partner and the largest source of official development assistance (ODA) to China and, since 2001, Japanese FDI to China is third only to that of Hong Kong and the US (Taniguchi, 2003).

Longer-term, however, it is likely that the relationship will become increasingly competitive as they compete (both bilaterally and with the US) in their search for inputs into their respective economies – especially in their search for sources of energy and other resources. In 2004 China overtook Japan as the world's second-largest oil importer. It is also now, depending on statistical interpretation, the world's second-largest economic power in purchasing power parity (PPP) terms, and the world's third-largest trading power. It has also been argued that US policy fuels rather than cools the competition between the two Asian superpowers as it grapples to adjust to changes in the global power structure brought about by China's rising role (see Johnson, 2005).

And of course there are also still strong, residual nationalistic antagonisms between the two countries that cannot be assigned to the historical past. Aaron Friedberg's (1993–94) suggestion that the region is 'ripe for rivalry' could be countered by T.J. Pempel's (2005a) recent assertion that the region could just as easily be 'ripe for cooperation'. But how it turns out will depend on how the regional conversation is managed in the coming decades. In essence, there are thus two scenarios for consideration.

In the worst-case scenario, contemporary strains in the relationships between the regional great powers are seen as fundamentally irresolvable. There are several factors that we might anticipate in this scenario:

1. The unwillingness of Japanese policymakers to distance themselves and their country sufficiently from the atrocities of the Second World War continues, and remains unacceptable to the rest of the region. The historical roots are deep and continue to cast ominous policy shadows over its relationships with the key players in East Asia in a way that has long ceased to be the case in Germany's relationships with the rest of Europe.
2. Japan sides with the US in attempting to block China's greater participation in the regional economic order and political orders, and this is seen as a fundamental act of hostility by the Chinese government.
3. A conflictual rather than a peaceful outcome to the increasing contest for energy supplies between the US, China (and Japan) must remain a possibility if not necessarily a probability. Demand in both countries and the Asian region in general (not to mention India) will grow rapidly. But provided the increased pressure is exerted fairly evenly rather than skewed in favour of one country, and brings on gradual structural reform of the system rather than provoking direct confrontation between these rising great powers, then there is hope for a non-conflictual outcome.
4. A conflictual, rather than consensual, battle between China and Japan to design the institutional architecture of East Asia for the 21st century.

The worst-case scenario also assumes certain resistant courses of action by the US towards greater regional economic cooperation in East Asia. In grand strategic terms, Asian economic cooperation is not nearly as useful to the US in the 21st century as European integration was in the second half of the 20th century. There is no longer any need to demonstrate the superiority of the market economy. Again, notwithstanding the negative impact on the Anglo-Saxon model of capitalism identified in the excesses of the GFC, the supremacy of the market remains undiminished. But successful economic integration in Asia today by China (more so than Japan, notwithstanding parallels with the 1980s) is a challenge to

US competitiveness (and for some analysts, its security). Indeed, Asian regionalism is seen by much of the current US policy community as but a vehicle for China's ambitions. If Asia were to emancipate itself from American 'guidance', Washington's hold on the region would deteriorate sharply. Most importantly, US–China competition for scarce energy supplies could impact adversely on the US's wider geopolitical objectives in, say, the Middle East or Latin America. As Shambaugh persuasively argues (2005: 90–91), the Sino–US relationship, notwithstanding China's strengthening position in the region, does not have to be zero-sum. How the US takes it forward is yet to be determined. But the omens in the early 21st century have not been promising. Washington's desire to establish China as the source of many of its own economic problems, with all the attendant demands for retaliation that such an approach calls forth, is not encouraging.

Thinking more positively, there is an alternative, more favourable scenario that can be developed around the rise of a less ideological, more instrumental and 'regulatory regionalism'. The key elements of this are enhanced regional economic dialogue and interaction both amongst the states of Northeast Asia (China, Japan and South Korea) and between these states and the states of Southeast Asia through the development of the ASEAN+3 process leading to an East Asian Community. Here, the roles and attitudes of China and Japan towards regional governance will prove pivotal to the development of the regional architecture in the 21st century. In part their views are a reflection of the manner in which their polities are unfolding. While there are overlaps, two broad positions might be identified. In truncated form, Japan is a regional postmodern and post-industrial power concerned with non-traditional elements of security, human security and environmental issues, with a rapidly evolving civil society. It does, of course, retain some modern hangovers concerning territorial and historical issues with China, and managing its poor relations with the US. China, by contrast, is essentially a modern society with traditional concerns about power politics, territorial integrity, military modernization, nationalism and rivalry – especially with the US. Contemporary Chinese–Japanese rivalry is manifest in their competing visions of regional governance.

These differences lead to an inevitable tension. Japan is anxious to avoid a China-focused approach towards regional community-building in East Asia – hence its commitment to broadening via the inclusions of Australia and New Zealand (with their close links to the United States) and the universal values that they bring in the regional understanding of a community in East Asia. The 2000 East Asian Vision Group (EAVG) suggested the establishment of an East Asian Community (EAC) combining

ASEAN plus, China, Japan and South Korea. In effect a de jure state-led institutional activity, this proposal was outpaced by de facto market activity. Instead of an institutional regional FTA, states have opted for a series of FTAs. The three major Northeast Asian states have each arranged individual FTAs with ASEAN. The three Northeast Asian states (China, Japan and South Korea) have also introduced (since 2008) their own trilateral summits.

The inaugural 2005 East Asian Summit and the Japanese call for a Comprehensive Economic Partnership in East Asia represented a key stage in the development of wider regional functional economic partnership. ASEAN+3 was the core unit, but ASEAN+6 reflected the Japanese desire (along with that of others) to embed China in a wider unit with other major players. This was seen as an instrument for advancing both economic governance and security governance. By embedding China in a community with India and Australia it enhances Japanese (and US) interests in the areas of democratic governance, intellectual property and human rights. For its part, China's regional economic diplomacy is advanced through actions such as the creation of the China–ASEAN FTA and its forward-leaning policies to share a key role in the CMI initiative alongside Japan. Its input into the CMI has grown progressively, especially since the time of the first Northeast Asian summit in 2008 at which it increased its bilateral swap offers.

Japan's proposals for an ASEAN+6 based on a similar membership to that of the East Asia Summit (EAS) was clearly a strategy to outflank China's growing influence in East Asia. It is a response to China's enhanced challenge to Japan's leadership role in ASEAN+3 as the fiction of ASEAN leadership is stripped away. But from a specifically East Asian regional perspective, ASEAN+3 is the strongest agreed definition of East Asia – Northeast Asia (NEA) + Southeast Asia (SEA). It has a far better chance of evolving as an East Asian Community than the EAS or the APC. China knows this. It can lead East Asia through the APT. It is unlikely to block US or Russian membership of the EAS, which is the acronym of choice for all those that are not part of SEA or NEA (Australia, India, New Zealand, US). Japan is the only major player in both the APT and EAS that stands to benefit from the development of the EAS as opposed to the APT. But the more diverse the EAS becomes, the more likely that the APT will consolidate as the voice of Asia in the long run. Even with the extension of the EAS to Russia and US, specifically intra-Asian frameworks are unlikely to be undermined. A configuration based on ASEAN+6 by a process of institutional Darwinism is likely to triumph.

The question thrown up by the debates over the emerging shape and voice of the region for this chapter is: 'Are the economic and security benefits that accrue from the development of an East Asian community strong enough to overcome the historical legacies, territorial disputes and political obstacles emanating from the heterogeneity of the regional political systems?' The answer may lie externally to the region in the context of the contemporary debates over global governance. Notwithstanding its greater representation in the G20, and notwithstanding its deep integration into the global economy, Asia does not have a unified voice in either the global political or the global economic contexts – and this at a time when its salience to global decision-making is increasing dramatically. Indeed, its responsibilities in the global economy are not reflected in its representation and influence over the structures of the emerging global polity. This search for greater representation and a global voice may well be a stronger impetus to the development of an East Asian community than any internal economic cooperation which is developing under different routes and dynamics.

There is, of course, no agreed body of principles or values that is common to all countries of the East Asian region. This is the starting point which realist scholars of international relations (such as White, 2010) would require prior to conceding the prospect of the development of a serious institutional architecture. We will be waiting a long time for that. Rather, the way to go is to recognize the pluralism inherent in the region, across the politico-economic and socio-cultural spectrums, and see to what extent the region can develop and consolidate a set of processes and rules of engagement. I stress here 'processes and rules of engagement' rather than 'norms and values'. The development of a regional rules-based system which relies on instrumentally driven functional collective-action problem-solving is of course difficult, but is not impossible – the emerging regional history of East Asia suggests this. If the instrumental incentives are strong enough, then the presence of a strong sense of community is not essential for cooperation.

15.6.4 Regulatory Regionalism

This is not the kind of regional cooperation that has its antecedents in a European intellectual context. Rather, it links national and global understandings of regulation via the region as a 'meso' level. Effectively, regionalism is a transmission belt for global disciplines to the national level via the depoliticizing and softening process of the region in which regional policy coordination – as opposed to regional governance – becomes a link between the national and the global. Its emergence reflects several trends in East Asia where:

1. Regional policy coordination to mitigate risk is delegated to the state. It is sovereignty-enhancing. Indeed, there is a strong relationship between state form, the global economic and political orders, and the nature of regional governance emerging. This compromise is inevitable if the continuing tension between highly charged political nationalism and a cooler instrumental regionalism in East Asia is not to jeopardize the cooperative endeavour.
2. The meshing of a multilevel process of regulation reinforces the connections between the international institutions (especially the IMF and World Bank) and, since the GFC, recommendations coming out of the G20 and regional institutions such as the Asian Development Bank (ADB) and the emerging instruments of regulation developing in the context of monetary regionalism at the level of ASEAN+3, such as the ASEAN regional surveillance process (ASP) and the Executives' Meeting of East Asia Pacific Central Banks (EMEAP).
3. The transmission of internationally agreed codes, emanating from the perceived best practice of international institutions such as the IMF, that help enforce market standards, and do so much more than sceptics concede (see Manupipatpong, 2002).

It is in the area of monetary regionalism, not regional trade liberalization, that concrete cooperation is advancing. It is not de facto trade-led regionalism driving the agenda – this is now taken care of much more at the global multilateral and bilateral levels. The key to monetary regionalism is closer integration through the development of common national 'regulation' rather than regional institution-building. Nor is it simply de jure state-led cooperation driving the agenda. The discourse of regulatory regionalism carries fewer negative connotations for sovereignty and regime autonomy than 'regional institution-building'. Similarly, and perhaps surprisingly, the developments in defence policy cooperation with the institutionalization of the ASEAN Defence Ministers Meetings (ADMM) fits this model.

Institution-building throughout the pre-crisis days in East Asia carried with it the implications of sovereignty pooling of the European Cartesian legal formalist variety that alarmed Asian regional elites. Regulatory regionalism in the 21st century does not have the same echoes. It is instrumental regionalism built on transregional networks of regulators. While it reflects a different understanding of regionalism from that which prevails in Europe, it nevertheless demonstrates perhaps a greater interest in the development of regional institutions and inter-regional relationships to enhance collective-action problem-solving under conditions of globalization (and a greater similarity with Europe) than is to be found, for example, in contemporary US foreign economic policy.

Americans and Europeans project sharp differences in their approaches towards world politics in general, and global and regional institutional cooperation in particular. The US and the EU, for example, differ on questions of 'partnership', 'burden sharing' and 'exceptionalism' as approaches to global management. For the US administrations (and this means Obama and Clinton as much as Bush) what secures contemporary world order is primacy, realpolitik and freedom to manoeuvre. For Europeans it is globalization and interdependence. The EU disposition for multilevel governance and 'sovereignty pooling' is incomprehensible to US policymakers. The *acquis communautaire* (the body of common standards and regulations that have developed over the life of the European project), notwithstanding perpetual complaints about excessive bureaucracy and the rejection of the constitution, are generally accepted in Europe. Europe, in theory if not always in practice, exhibits a stronger normative attitude towards multilateral governance structures and constitutional and regulatory frameworks that transcend the nation-state than is to be found in the US. With the benefit of the longer-term historical perspective, what looks like weakness through traditional state-centric, realist, power politics lenses actually looks like strength through the newer lenses of the increasingly diffused and networked nature of power in the contemporary global era (see Hall and Biersteker, 2002; Slaughter, 2004).

Similar differences towards regionalism and multilateralism in East Asia may also be found with the US in the early 21st century. Without overstating the case, East Asia too places a greater stress on multilateral and regional cooperation than the US although there may be a marked disconnect between theory and rhetoric on the one hand and application and practice on the other. But we live in an era of the 'new regionalism' in East Asia that has progressed apace since the financial crises of the latter part of the 1990s. The key elements of this new regionalism are enhanced regional economic dialogue and interaction both amongst the states of Northeast Asia (China, Japan and South Korea) and between these states and the states of Southeast Asia. This tendency is not, of course, unproblematic and the behaviour of China in East Asia over the medium to longer term is crucial. How it adapts to and uses its new-found status and power will be crucial. The continual war of words between China and Japan over the past decade has not stopped China replacing the US as Japan's major trading partner. On the other hand, its at times excessively forward-leaning postures on contested politico-strategic issues in the region in the current period is undermining some of the confidence that smaller regional players had gained in China in the first decade of the 21st century.

The US is still a major presence in the region defined as the Asia-Pacific (in both economic and military terms). It is more of a passive actor, but is also, ironically, an exogenous catalyst in the 'East Asianization' of the Western Pacific. The US has become the 'other' enhancing the growth of a cognitive understanding of East Asian regionalism. Similarly, while the growth of bilateral initiatives may be suboptimal in terms of pure economic theory, they should not cause alarm if they lead to competitive liberalization, domestic reform and enhanced regional knowledge and transparency. In contrast to the view from Geneva (see Warwick Commission, 2007) this is the positive gloss that might be put on what one scholar calls the 'Sino-Japanese FTA Race' (Munakata, 2003: 6).

When looked at collectively, the processes in train in East Asia may actually represent a more systematic package of regional governance activities than would at first sight appear to be the case. The APT process is being institutionalized through the evolution of an overlapping multi-dimensional process of regional conference diplomacy which is strengthening, and indeed creating, links between the states of Northeast Asia and Southeast Asia (Suzuki, 2004). Whether Asians will be successful or not in their endeavours, there can be little doubt that the continued exploration of cooperation as a way to combat vulnerability is an established item on the regional policy agenda in the early 21st century, as even the normally sceptical *Economist* in a recent editorial was prepared to acknowledge (26–27 March 2005).

Of course, the future of successful regional discourse seems dependent not only on Japanese economic reform, but also on a willingness of the People's Republic of China (PRC) to continue its new-found regional cooperative economic role that has developed since 1997 (see Shambaugh, 2005). If this continues in a positive way and trust can be built in the region between the major actors, then regionalism will grow into an important activity as a meso-level instrumental expression of the desire to optimize sovereign decision-making by states confronting the rigours of global competition. If Japanese and Chinese instrumental regional interests can be privileged over cognitive regional differences, this could be a powerful force for regional cooperation in East Asia. Without their input and indeed eventual leadership, long-term ASEAN-driven attempts to secure East Asian regionalism will amount to little. The extent to which either major player is committed remains problematic and for both, but especially Japan, it is in many ways a function of their relationship with the United States. Both Japan and China remain reluctant regional institutionalists and the US, in contrast to its role in Europe in the post-Second

World War era, does nothing to dissuade either of them from that position.

These alternative scenarios are not merely determined regionally. They need to be located in the overall discussion about globalization and regionalization in the early 21st century. There is a general principle that we can draw about power and regionalism from a comparative discussion of Europe and Asia. Again, it is better put as a question than offered as an assertion: 'Is it likely that we are entering an era where large sections of the global community look less to the major multilateral institutions – so much the playthings of the major powers – as vehicles for collective action problem-solving, and more towards the development of regional activities and communities?' If so, then the growing salience of the regional dialogue is a positive trend in international relations in general, and in East Asia in particular.

Regionalism is an effort to transcend a unipolar world in which the hegemonic power shows an increasing reluctance, in contrast to times past, to engage as an 'altruistic' hegemon, as opposed to what Jagdish Bhagwati (1994) calls a 'selfish' hegemon. To this extent, although this is not the intended outcome, contemporary US foreign policy can act as a catalyst to regional consolidation in Asia. Growing discontent with US policy in, and towards, the East Asian region – especially since the Asian financial crises, and even more so since the GFC for which Asia blames the US directly – has been a significant factor in the enhanced regional dialogue of the 21st century. Taken to extremes, it is not impossible to envisage a situation in which the world does become more multipolar. Not necessarily multipolar in the traditional realist sense of other regions combining to 'balance' against the US, but multipolar in the sense that the US becomes less salient as an actor in the development and activities of other regions. Indeed, regional observer Amitav Acharya (2009) asks whether we might be entering an era of 'regio-polarity'. That we can even pose such an hypothesis is testament to the magnitude of change that has taken place in thinking about the strength of the glue holding contemporary global order together in the early 21st century.

The US, having won the Cold War through a combination of hard power and soft power, now seems to hope that raw material power will be sufficient to intimidate other great powers. This assumes that China, Japan (and East Asia) as well as Europe, Russia, India, Brazil and Latin America are not capable of developing policies and strategies to mitigate the influence of US economic and military power. US hegemony, or primacy in the military sphere, is not preventing the development of multipolar initiatives in geopolitical and economic domains, as the nature of regional institution-building without US participation attests.

None of this should allow us to underestimate the continuing power and influence of the US in East Asia. A growing Asian rhetorical resistance to US policy in the region (agency-driven sources of power and leadership) should not cause us to neglect the residual and continuingly strong structural influences from the US, what Nye (2002) would call 'soft power', especially strong support for the broad neoliberal economic agenda. Moreover, for most states of the region, notwithstanding the increasingly influential role of China, the US remains their major bilateral relationship; although the Bush administration has been the most self-regarding US administration any Asian post-colonial leaders have known.

15.7 CONCLUSION

Both the practice and the theory of regionalism are undergoing a period of significant change. The key element is a shift from a Cold War to a post-Cold War, globalization era. During the Cold War, regional theory was statist, European-influenced and stressed intergovernmental bargains. In the era of globalization it is more complex, multidimensional and, notwithstanding the increased salience of security issues post-9/11, still primarily economically focussed. In the first era, the 'economic' and the 'political' were largely treated as separate issue areas for investigation and action. In the second era, politics and economics are more clearly linked and the state is joined by a series of other significant, non-state actors in the practice of regionalism as the relationship between state authority and market power becomes fuzzier, especially after the GFC of 2008.

In addition, the early Balassian model of regional integration, based on a reading of the evolution of the EU, no longer stands scrutiny in the context of globalization, where guarding against the volatility and erratic mobility of capital is in many ways now as great, if not greater, a regional concern than guaranteeing the openness of the trade regime. Balassian-style theory pays insufficient attention to the possibility of different routes to, or different agendas for, regional cooperation. The Balassian approach is also silent on the significance of socio-cultural factors – especially the role of identity in region-building – in an era of globalization. In this sense, the contemporary discussion in East Asia illustrates the differences between the two eras and the two approaches to theorizing regional integration, and offers us an alternative reading of regionalism in a wider global context.

East Asia is a region of economic experimentation. The glue of regionalism at the level of the Asia-Pacific – embodied in APEC – has come unstuck since the time of the Asian financial crisis. Events post-9/11 have exacerbated this trend. Moreover, Asian policy communities have learned that globalization and regionalization are not mutually exclusive activities, but rather exist in a dialectical relationship. Regionalism is not an alternative to globalization. Following this logic allows us to explain the emergence of a multiplicity of policy responses to recent economic issues in the Asia-Pacific. These responses reflect, in part at least, Asian resistance to Western-driven models. Specifically, the financial crises of the late 1990s forced regional scholars and policymakers alike to examine not only their national economic policies, but also their very understanding of regionalism.

The regionalism we see emerging in East Asia in the 21st century is not the kind of regional cooperation with a European intellectual pedigree. It is clearly unrealistic to imagine the development of institutions involving the transfer of elements of state sovereignty to regional institutions, as has happened in Europe. Rather it is a 'regulatory regionalism' that links national and global understandings of regulation via the intermediary regional level. This regulatory urge is not simply restricted to trade or the area of monetary regionalism in which it is advancing most rapidly. The key to monetary regionalism is closer integration through common national 'regulation' rather than regional institution-building. In discursive terms, 'regional regulation' carries fewer negative connotations for sovereignty and regime autonomy than 'regional institution-building'. Institution-building throughout the pre-crisis days in East Asia carried with it the unwanted implication of European-style 'sovereignty pooling'.

In the absence of global structures of economic governance we must expect policymakers to explore more manageable alternatives. State-centric, power politics approaches to the management of the world order under conditions of globalization are becoming less salient. More diffuse networked understandings of power, with loosely institutionalized regulatory actions providing a modus operandi for cooperation, are becoming increasingly attractive. The role of institutional capacity – especially institutions as transaction cost reducers and vehicles for the enhancement of norm compliance – casts increasingly long policy shadows over current regional activities in East Asia. It is here that the current discourse on regionalism (and multilevel governance, for all its faults and all its detractors) offers the bones of an alternative model. The European experience, or that of the multilateral international organizations, is not simply an 'off the shelf' export model. Some key elements, especially those of a sovereignty pooling nature, will be resisted. But other elements, especially best institutional procedural practices, will be adjusted and/or localized in a specifically East Asian fashion. The degree to which East Asia can develop institutional capacity in the absence of some sovereignty pooling is the key research and policy question for the future. Meso-level, regulatory regionalism can enhance cooperation only so far. The process of institutionalism in East Asia will not mirror that in Europe in the second half of the 20th century, but neither will it be trivial. For both the scholar and the practitioner of regionalism and institutionalism, these are indeed interesting times in East Asia.

NOTES

1. See, *inter alia*, Coleman and Underhill, 1998; Fawcett and Hurrell, 1995; Gamble and Payne, 1996; Grugel and Hoult, 1999; Mansfield and Milner, 1997; Mattli, 1999.
2. For reviews of this literature see Beeson, 2005; Higgott, 1998b, 2005a; and Acharya, 2005.
3. Katzenstein et al., 1998; Simmons and Martin, 2002; Kratochwil et al., 2005; Higgott, 2006.
4. The literature on the state of the contemporary regional project in East Asia is large. For a flavour see Beeson, 2005; Higgott, 2005a; Pempel, 2005a; Ravenhill, 2005, 2010; Stubbs, 2002.
5. There is a plethora of activity in East Asia in the current era. It is difficult to keep up with the panoply of bilateral initiatives to secure FTAs in the region. For reviews see Dent, 2004; Soesastro, 2005; Defraigne et al., 2005.
6. A term first used, according to Breslin (2005), by Andrew Hurrell (1995a). The growing body of literature that we can gather under the rubric of the 'new regionalism' cannot be reviewed here. But see, *inter alia*, Gamble and Payne, 1996; Hettne et al., 1999, 2000, 2001; Breslin et al., 2002; Soderbaum and Shaw, 2003; Breslin, 2005.

REFERENCES

Abbott, Kenneth W. and Duncan Snidal (1998), 'Why States Act through Formal International Organizations', *The Journal of Conflict Resolution*, **42**(1), 3–32.

Acharya, Amitav (1997), 'Ideas, Identity and Institution Building: From ASEAN Way to the Asia Pacific Way', *Pacific Review*, **10**(2), 319–46.

Acharya, Amitav (2001), *Constructing a Security Community in Southeast Asia: ASEAN and the Problem of Regional Order*, London: Routledge.

Acharya, Amitav (2004), 'How Ideas Spread: Whose Norms Matter? Norm Localization and Institutional Change in Asian Regionalism', *International Organization*, **58**(2), 239–75.

Acharya, Amitav (2005), 'Europe and Asia: Reflections on a Tale of Two Regionalisms', in Douglas Webber and Bertrand Fort (eds), *Regional Integration in Europe and East Asia: Convergence or Divergence*, London: Routledge, pp. 312–21.

Acharya, A. (2009), 'Regional Worlds in a Post-Hegemonic Era', Cahiers de SPIRIT, available at http://www.spirit.sciencespobordeaux.fr/Cahiers%20de%20SPIRIT/Cahiers%20de%20SPIRIT_1_Acharya.pdf.

Aggarwal, Vinod K. and Min Gyo Koo (2008), 'Asia's New Institutional

Architecture: Evolving Structures for Managing Trade, Financial, and Security Relations', in Vinod K. Aggarwal and Min Gyo Koo (eds), *Asia's New Institutional Architecture: Evolving Structures for Managing Trade, Financial, and Security Relations*, London: Springer, pp. 1–34.

Balassa, Bela (1962), *The Theory of Economic Integration*, Homewood, IL: Richard Irwin.

Beeson, Mark (2005), 'Rethinking Regionalism: Europe and East Asia in Comparative Historical Perspective', *European Journal of Public Policy*, **12**(6), 969–85.

Beeson, Mark and Richard Higgott (2005), 'Hegemony, Institutionalism and US Foreign Policy: Theory and Practice in Comparative Historical Perspective', *Third World Quarterly*, **26**(7), 1173–88.

Bellamy, Richard (2005), 'Still in Deficit: Rights, Regulation and Democracy in the EU', for the Democracy Task Force of the EU 6th Framework Integrated Project on *New Modes of Governance*, 1–31, available at: http://www.eu-newgov.org/database/DELIV/DDTFD02a_Rights_Regulation_and_Democracy_in_the_EU.pdf.

Bergsten, C. Fred (2000), 'East Asian Regionalism: Towards a Tripartite World', *The Economist*, 15 July.

Bhagwati, Jagdish (1994), 'The World Trading System', *Journal of International Affairs*, **48**(1), 279–85.

Bhagwati, Jagdish (2002), *Free Trade Today*, Princeton, NJ: Princeton University Press.

Bhagwati, Jagdish and Hugh Patrick (eds) (1990), *Aggressive Unilateralism: America's 301 Trade Policy and the World Trading System*, Ann Arbor, MI: University of Michigan Press.

Breslin, Shaun (2005), 'Studying Regions: Comparativism and Eurocentrism', *Conference on China and Asian Regionalism*, Shanghai: Fudan University, January, pp. 1–39.

Breslin, Shaun, Chris Hughes, Nicola Phillips and Ben Rosamond (eds) (2002), *New Regionalisms in the Global Political Economy: Theories and Cases*, London: Routledge.

Buzan, Barry and Gerald Segal (1994),'Rethinking East Asian Security', *Survival*, **36**(2), 3–21.

Coleman, William and Geoffrey Underhill (eds) (1998), *Regionalism and Global Economic Integration: Asia, Europe and the Americas*, London: Routledge.

Defraigne, Jean Christophe, Heribert Dieter, Richard Higgott and Pascal Lamy (2005), *East Asian Integration: Opportunities and Obstacles for Enhanced Economic Cooperation, Report for JETRO*, Paris: Notre Europe.

Deiter, Heribert and Richard Higgott (2003), 'Exploring Alternative Theories of Economic Regionalism: From Trade to Finance in Asian Co-operation', *Review of International Political Economy*, **10**(3), 430–54.

Dent, Christopher (2004), 'The New Economic Bilateralism and Southeast Asia: Region Convergent or Region Divergent', British International Studies Association, IPEG Papers in Global Political Economy, No. 7, April.

Dent, Christopher (2006), *New Free Trade Agreements in the Asia Pacific*, Basingstoke: Palgrave.

Desker, Barry (2004), 'In Defence of FTAs: From Purity to Pragmatism in East Asia', *Pacific Review*, **17**(1), 3–26.

Evian Group (2005), 'East Asian Regionalism: Integrative versus

Disintegrative Forces', *2005 Evian Hong Kong Initiative*, Hong Kong, 17–18 May, pp. 1–12.
Fawcett, Louise and Andrew Hurrell (eds) (1995), *Regionalism in World Politics: Regional Organisation and International Order*, Oxford: Oxford University Press.
Finnemore, Martha (1996), 'Norms, Culture and World Politics: Insights from Sociology's Institutionalism', *International Organization*, **50**(2), 887–918.
Friedberg, Aaron (1993–94), 'Ripe for Rivalry: Prospects for Peace in Multi-Polar Asia', *International Security*, **18**(3), 5–33.
Gamble, Andrew and A.J. Payne (eds) (1996), *Regionalism and World Order*, Basingstoke: Macmillan.
Grugel, Jean and Wil Hoult (eds) (1999), *Regionalism across the North–South Divide: State Strategies and Globalisation*, London: Routledge.
Haas, Ernst B. (1958), *The Uniting of Europe: Political, Social and Economic Forces, 1950–1957*, Stanford, CA: Stanford University Press.
Haas, Ernst B. (1964), *Beyond the Nation-State: Functionalism and International Organization*, Stanford, CA: Stanford University Press.
Haas, Ernst B. (1975), *The Obsolescence of Regional Integration Theory*, Berkeley, CA: Institute for International Studies.
Hall, Rodney Bruce and Thomas J. Biersteker (eds) (2002), *The Emergence of Private Authority in Global Governance*, Cambridge: Cambridge University Press.
Hamilton-Hart, Natasha (2005), 'The Chiang Mai Initiative and the Prospects for Closer Monetary Cooperation in East Asia', in Douglas Webber and Bertrand Fort (eds), *Regional Integration in Europe and East Asia: Convergence or Divergence*, London: Routledge, pp. 109–28.
Harris, Stuart (2002), 'Asian Multilateral Institutions and their Response to the Asian Economic Crisis: Regional and Global Implications', in S. Breslin, C. Hughes, N. Phillips and B. Rosamond (eds), *New Regionalisms in the Global Political Economy: Theories and Cases*, London: Routledge, pp. 119–36.
Hay, C. and B. Rosamond (2002), 'Globalisation, European Integration and the Discursive Construction of Economic Imperatives', *European Journal of Public Policy*, **9**(2), 147–67.
Held, David and Anthony McGrew (eds) (2000), *The Global Transformations Reader: An Introduction to the Globalization Debate*, London: Polity.
Hettne, Bjorn, Andres Inotai and Osvaldo Sunkel (eds) (1999), *National Perspectives on the New Regionalism in the Third World*, London: Palgrave.
Hettne, Bjorn, Andres Inotai and Osvaldo Sunkel (eds) (2000), *National Perspectives on the New Regionalism in the North*, London: Palgrave.
Hettne, Bjorn, Andres Inotai and Osvaldo Sunkel (eds) (2001), *Comparing Regionalisms: Implications for Global Development*, London: Palgrave.
Hew, Denis and Hadi Soesastro (2003), 'Realising the ASEAN Economic Community by 2020: ISEAS and ASEAN ISIS Approaches', *ASEAN Economic Bulletin*, **20**(3), 292–6.
Higgott, Richard (1997), '*De facto* or *De Jure* Regionalism: The Double Discourse of Regionalisation in the Asia Pacific', *Global Society: Journal of Interdisciplinary International Relations*, **11**(2), 165–83.
Higgott, Richard (1998a), 'The Asian Financial Crisis: A Study in the Politics of Resentment', *New Political Economy*, **3**(3), 33–56.
Higgott, Richard (1998b), 'The International Political Economy of Regionalism: The Asia-Pacific and Europe Compared', in William Coleman and Geoffrey

Underhill (eds), *Regionalism and Global Economic Integration: Asia, Europe and the Americas*, London: Routledge, pp. 42–67.
Higgott, Richard (2004), 'The "Securitisation" of US Foreign Economic Policy in East Asia', *Critical Asian Studies*, **36**(3), 425–44.
Higgott, Richard (2005a), 'Economic Regionalism in East Asia: Consolidation with Centrifugal Tendencies', in Richard Stubbs and Geoffrey Underhill (eds), *Political Economy and the Changing Global Order*, Oxford: Oxford University Press, p. 344.
Higgott, Richard (2005b), 'The Theory and Practice of Global Governance: Accommodating American Exceptionalism and European Pluralism', *European Foreign Affairs Review*, **10**(4), 1–10.
Higgott, Richard (2006), 'International (Political) Institutions', in R.A.W. Rhodes, Sarah A. Binder and Bert A. Rockman (eds), *The Oxford Handbook of Political Institutions*, Oxford: Oxford University Press, pp. 611–33.
Higgott, Richard and Richard Stubbs (1995), 'Competing Conceptions of Economic Regionalism: APEC versus EAEC', *Review of International Political Economy*, **2**(3), 516–35.
Higgott, Richard, Richard Leaver and John Ravenhill (eds) (1993), *Pacific Economic Relation in the 1990s: Cooperation and Conflict*, Boulder, CO: Lynne Reinner.
Hix, Simon (1994), 'The Study of the European Community: The Challenge for Comparative Politics', *West European Politics*, **17**(1), 1–30.
Hix, Simon (1999), *The Political System of the European Union*, Basingstoke: Macmillan.
Hurrell, Andrew (1995a), 'Explaining the Resurgence of Regionalism in World Politics', *Review of International Studies*, **21**(4), 331–58.
Hurrell, Andrew (1995b), 'Regionalism in Theoretical Perspective', in Louise Fawcett and Andrew Hurrell (eds), *Regionalism in World Politics: Regional Organisation and International Order*, Oxford: Oxford University Press, pp. 37–74.
Jayasuriya, Kanishka (ed.) (2004), *Asian Regional Governance: Crisis and Change*, London: Routledge.
Johnson, Chalmers (2005), 'No Longer the "Lone" Superpower: Coming to Terms with China', Japan Policy Research Institute, Working Paper 105, San Francisco, CA, March, available at www.jpri.org/publications/wp105.html.
Kahler, Miles (2000), 'Legalization as a Strategy: The Asia Pacific Case', *International Organization*, **54**(3), 549–71.
Katzenstein, Peter, Robert O. Keohane and Stephen Krasner (1998), 'International Organisation and the Study of World Politics', *International Organisation*, **52**(4), 645–85.
Keohane, Robert (1984), *After Hegemony: Cooperation and Discord in the World Political Economy*, Princeton, NJ: Princeton University Press.
Keohane, Robert (1989), *International Institutions and State Power: Essay in International Relations Theory*, Boulder, CO: Westview Press.
Keohane, Robert (2002), *Power and Governance in a Partially Globalized World*, London: Routledge.
Kooiman, Jan (2003), *Governing as Governance*, London: Sage.
Kratochwil, Freidrich and John Ruggie (1986), 'The State of the Art on an Art of the State', *International Organization*, **40**(4), 753–75.
Kratochwil, Freidrich, John Ruggie and Edward Mansfield (eds) (2005), *International Organisation: A Reader*, New York: Longman Publishers.

Krugman, Paul (ed.) (1986), *Strategic Trade Policy and the 'New' International Economics*, Cambridge, MA: MIT Press.
Latham, Andrew (1997), *The Liberal Moment: Modernity, Security, and the Making of Postwar International Order*, New York: Columbia University Press.
Lindberg, Leon (1966), *The Political Dynamics of European Economic Integration*, Stanford, CA: Stanford University Press.
Mansfield, E.D. and Helen Milner (eds) (1997), *The Political Economy of Regionalism*, New York: Columbia University Press.
Manupipatpong, W. (2002), 'The ASEAN Surveillance Process and the East Asian Monetary Fund', *ASEAN Economic Bulletin*, **19**(1), 114–15.
Martin, Lisa (2003), 'Multilateral Organisations after the US–Iraq War of 2003', *The Iraq War and its Consequences: Thoughts of Nobel Peace Laureates and Eminent Scholars*, London: World Scientific Publishing, pp. 359–74.
Mattli, W. (1999), *The Logic of Regional Integration*, Cambridge: Cambridge University Press.
Maull, Hans, Gerry Segal and Jusuf Wanandi (eds) (1998), *Europe and the Asia Pacific*, London: Routledge.
Moravcsik, Andrew (1994), 'Preferences and Power in the European Community: A Liberal Intergovernmental Approach', in Simon Bulmer and Andrew Scott (eds), *Economic and Political Integration in Europe*, Oxford: Blackwells.
Moravcsik, Andrew (1998), *The Choice for Europe: Social Purpose and State Power: From Messina to Maastricht*, Ithaca, NY: Cornell University Press.
Moravcsik, Andrew (2004), 'Is there a "Democratic Deficit" in World Politics? A Framework for Analysis', *Government and Opposition*, **39**(3), 344–46.
Munakata, Nana (2003), 'The Impact of the Rise of China and Regional Economic Integration in Asia: A Japanese Perspective', *Statement to US–China Economic and Security Review Commission Hearings on China's Growth as a Regional Economic Power*, Washington, DC – 13 December.
Nesadurai, Helen (2003), *Globalisation, Domestic Politics and Regionalism: The ASEAN Free Trade Area*, London: Routledge.
North, Douglass (1990), *Institutions, Institutional Change and Economic Performance*, Cambridge: Cambridge University Press.
Nye, Joseph (1968), 'Comparative Regional Integration: Concepts and Measurement', *International Organisation*, **22**(4), 855–80.
Nye, Joseph (1971), *Peace in Parts: Integration and Conflict in International Organisations*, Boston, MA: Little Brown.
Nye, Joseph (2002), *The Paradox of American Power: Why the World's Only Superpower Cannot Go it Alone*, New York: Oxford University Press.
Ohmae, Kenichi (1995), *The End of the Nation State: The Rise of Regional Economies*, New York: Harper Collins.
Pekkanen, Saadia (2004), 'At Play in the Legal Realm: The WTO and the Changing Nature of US–Japan Anti-Dumping Disputes', in Ellis Krauss and T.J. Pempel (eds), *Beyond Bilateralism: US–Japan Relations in the New Asia Pacific*, Stanford, CA: Stanford University Press.
Pempel, T.J. (2005a), Introduction: 'Emerging Webs of Regional Connectedness', in T.J. Pempel (ed.), *Remapping East Asia: The Construction of a Region*, Ithaca, NY: Cornell University Press, pp. 1–30.
Pempel, T.J. (2005b), 'Firebreak: East Asia Institutionalizes its Finances', *Institutionalizing North East Asia: Making the Impossible Possible?* Tokyo, UNU and Aoyama-Gakuin University, 20–22 September.

Rapkin, David P. (2001), 'The United States, Japan, and the Power to Block. The APEC and AMF Cases', *Pacific Review*, **14**(3), 373–410.
Ravenhill, John (2001), *APEC and the Construction of Pacific Rim Regionalism*, Cambridge: Cambridge University Press.
Ravenhill, John (2005), 'US Economic Relations with East Asia: From Hegemony to Complex Interdependence', in M. Beeson (ed.), *Bush and Asia: America's Evolving Relations with East Asia*, London: Routledge, pp. 42–63.
Ravenhill, John (2010), 'The "New East Asian Regionalism": A Political Domino Effect', *Review of International Political Economy*, **17**(2), 178–208.
Rosamond, B.J. (2000), *Theories of European Integration*, Basingstoke: Palgrave.
Rosamond, Ben (2005), 'The Uniting of Europe and the Foundation of EU Studies: Revisiting the Neofunctionalism of Ernst B. Haas', *Journal of European Public Policy*, **12**(2), 237–54.
Ruggie, John G. (1993), 'Multilateralism: The Anatomy of an Institution', in John G. Ruggie (ed.), *Multilateralism Matters: The Theory and Praxis of an Institutional Form*, New York: Columbia University Press.
Sampson, Gary and Stephen Woolcock (eds) (2003), *Regionalism, Multilateralism and Economic Integration: The Recent Experience*, Tokyo: UNU Press.
Schmitter, Phillipe (1971), 'A Revised Theory of European Integration', in Leon Lindberg and Stuart Scheingold (eds), *Regional Integration: Theory and Research*, Cambridge, MA: Harvard University Press.
Scholte, Jan Aart (2005), *Globalisation: A Critical Introduction*, 2nd edn, London: Palgrave.
Shambaugh, David (2005), 'China Engages Asia', *International Security*, **29**(3), 64–99.
Simmons, Beth and Lisa Martin (2002), 'International Organisations and Institutions', in Walter Carlsnaes, Thomas Risse and Beth Simmons (eds), *Handbook of International Relations*, London: Sage, pp. 192–211.
Slaughter, Anne Marie (2004), *A New World Order*, Princeton, NJ: Princeton University Press.
Soderbaum, Frederick and Timothy J. Shaw (eds) (2003), *Theories of New Regionalism: A Palgrave Reader*, Basingstoke: Palgrave Macmillan.
Soesastro, Hadi (2005), 'Realizing the East Asian Vision', CSIS Economics Working Paper Series, Jakarta, www.csis.or.id/papers/wpe090.
Stone Sweet, Alex (2004), *The Judicial Construction of Europe*, Oxford: Oxford University Press.
Stubbs, Richard (2002), 'ASEAN Plus Three: Emerging East Asian Regionalism', *Asian Survey*, **42**(3), 440–55.
Stubbs, Richard (2005), *Rethinking Asia's Economic Miracle: War, Prosperity and Crisis*, Basingstoke: Palgrave.
Suzuki, Sanae (2004), 'East Asian Cooperation through Conference Diplomacy: Institutional Aspects of the ASEAN Plus Three (APT) Framework'. Working Paper 03-04, Tokyo: Institute for Developing Economies, APEC Study Centre, JETRO.
Tanaka, Hitoshi (2007), 'Japan's Policy for East Asia', *Asia-Pacific Review*, **14**(2), 30–44.
Taniguchi, Makoto (2003), 'Towards the Establishment of an East Asian Economic Zone: How can Japan, China and Korea Cooperate to Attain This Aim?' Working Paper 171, Tokyo, Research Institute of Economy, Trade and Industry, 1–11 June.

Thomas, Nick (2004), 'An East Asian Economic Community: Multilateralism Beyond APEC', Conference on Asia Pacific Economies: Multilateral versus Bilateral Relationships, Hong Kong: City University, 19–21 May.

Tranholm-Mikkelsen, Jeppe (1991), 'Neo-functionalism: Obstinate or Obsolete? A Reappraisal in the Light of the New Dynamism of the EC', *Millennium: A Journal of International Studies*, **20**(1), 1–22.

Wallace, Helen (1996), 'The Institutions of the EU: Experience and Experiments', in Helen Wallace and William Wallace (eds), *Policy-Making in the European Union*, Oxford: Oxford University Press.

Wallace, William (1990), 'Introduction: The Dynamics of European Integration', in William Wallace (ed.), *The Dynamics of European Integration*, London: Pinter/Chatham House.

Warwick Commission (2007), 'The Multilateral Trade Regime: Which Way Forward?' Geneva: University of Warwick with the Centre for International Governance Innovation and the GARNET Network of Excellence, available online at http://www2.warwick.ac.uk/research/warwickcommission/worldtrade.

Webb, Carole (1983), 'Theoretical Approaches and Problems', in Helen Wallace and William Wallace (eds), *Policy-Making in the European Union*, 2nd edn, Chichester, John Wiley.

Webber, Douglas (2001), 'Two Funerals and a Wedding? The Ups and Downs of Regionalism in East Asia and the Asia Pacific after the Asian Financial Crisis', *Pacific Review*, **14**(3), 339–72.

Weiss, Linda (ed.) (2002), *States in the Global Economy: Bringing Domestic Institutions Back In*, Cambridge and New York: Cambridge University Press.

Wendt, Alexander (1992), 'Anarchy is What States Make of it: The Social Construction of Power Politics', *International Organization*, **46**(3), 391–425.

Wendt, Alexander (2000), *Social Theory of International Politics*, Cambridge: Cambridge University Press.

White, Hugh (2010), 'Power Shift: Australia's Future between Washington and Beijing', *Quarterly Essay*, 39.

16. Conclusion: from the Asian community to the world economy government

Jehoon Park

Since the global financial crisis originating in the US in 2008, the global economy has been suffering from recession and a worldwide slump. More recently the European fiscal crisis has emerged as the most dangerous factor driving the global economy towards a double-dip crisis. This book deals with various issues related to Asian responses to the global financial crisis. It focuses on two aspects. One is regionalism in Asia. The other is the G20. Many Asian countries actively participate in the G20 as member countries, so the G20 is becoming a global institution reflecting the increasing powers and roles of Asian countries in global issues. The book starts by dealing with the so-called multipolar world-system. Wallerstein (Chapter 1) argues that we are now living in a world-system in which there are emerging eight to ten centres of relative geopolitical autonomy. Among them, the four strongest such centres are located in what is sometimes called the global North. They are the United States, Western Europe and Russia. The fourth such centre is Northeast Asia, by which he means China, Korea and Japan. He concludes by emphasizing why he does not think that our existing historical system will be able to persist for much longer. He argues that the chaotic fluctuations we see today will grow stronger, not weaker, in the 21st century. He believes that our historical system has entered into a bifurcation that will culminate in a new world-system (or perhaps multiple world-systems) that will be different from that in which we are presently living. His final statement continues the pessimistic theme, saying again that we cannot know, in this bifurcation, which of two possible alternative paths the world will in the end take, and we cannot be sure that what will emerge will be morally and politically better or worse. Likewise, by 2020, the political leadership of the Northeast Asian countries – and indeed of the rest of the world – will almost certainly be different. We do not know if they will be wiser, but they will be different. So we are living amidst the greatest possible global uncertainty.

From the more orthodox perspective, Chapter 2 points out the absence of global coordination and the prevalence of economic distortions throughout the world due to outdated growth models as challenges to policymakers, business leaders and ordinary citizens around the world. It dissects these underlying economic forces, highlighting particularly how the developing countries will be driving the worldwide price and productivity convergence. It argues that there exist potentially massive gains for all if we can manage the risks and loss allocations associated with the deepening and continuation of centuries of globalized industrialization and urbanization. On the other hand, Gerard Roland (2010) argues that the Washington Consensus definitely died in the aftermath of the Great Recession, and a new consensus is needed based on an institutional approach recognizing the key role of institutions and their diverse evolutions.

In Chapter 3, Edward K.Y. Chen talks about Asian capitalism from the perspective of the Beijing Consensus as an economic development model for the 21st century. According to him, there are varieties of capitalism: American (US), European and Asian. While American capitalism was cherished as the gold standard for economic success for many decades, recent development experience indicates that Asian capitalism characterized by an open market economy with significant government intervention explains the rapid growth of many Asian economies in the 1960s and 1970s. Although some Asian economies suffered from the Asian financial crisis, their better performances relative to Europe and America during the recent global financial crisis were notable. In particular, the emergence of China as a global economic power has generated interesting debates on the Washington Consensus versus the Beijing Consensus (which can better be described by Chen's Chinese Economic Model, CEM). According to him, the essence of the Chinese model is not only appropriate reforms, but also and more importantly the sequencing of reforms.

Yoonbai Kim and Gil Kim (Chapter 4) deal with the Chinese economy from a different perspective. According to them, many argue that the renminbi (RMB) is undervalued and causes huge imbalances in current account balances with the United States. China has been resisting pressure to appreciate its currency and move to a floating exchange rate regime on the grounds that RMB appreciation will handicap its crucial export sector and create a host of other economic problems. The Japanese experience of prolonged appreciation and decades-long recession has often been invoked as a reason for the resistance. The authors briefly review the ongoing debates and then present empirical evidence that shows some important differences between the experiences of Japan and China. Currency appreciation in Japan reduces current account surpluses and boosts real income, albeit insignificantly, while generating deflationary pressure on the economy. On the other hand, RMB appreciation is not likely to have any significant effects on the current account balance while (insignificantly) raising real income instead of reducing it. Their results imply that pressuring China to undertake RMB appreciation for the purpose of current account adjustment is ill guided. At the same time, rejecting the external pressure on the grounds of avoiding a Japan-like experience is not supported by the data.

Following a similar logic to the above, Jing Ma and Lihui Tian (Chapter 5) argue that the Chinese government significantly contributes to dealing with external shocks from world financial markets, particularly with the stabilization of domestic stock markets, real estate policies and the promotion of producer and consumer confidence. The evidence from China during market failures supports the theories of developmentalists or the Keynesian prescription on the active role of governments in economic development.

Chapter 6 reviews the effects of the global financial crisis on the East Asian economies. Pilhyun Kim argues that overdependence on overseas markets and weak financial markets were the main reasons why the global financial crisis affected East Asian economies disproportionately. He suggests that to avoid future crises East Asia needs to step up efforts to integrate its real and financial sectors. He concludes with some practical policy recommendations including the establishment of a 'neo-AMF' (Asian Monetary Fund) to oversee the regional financial markets and maintain stability of the region's foreign exchange markets.

With respect to the roles of the G20, Deok Ryong Yoon (Chapter 7) argues that the G20 was called in as a firefighter to respond to the global financial crisis. Today, the G20 is at a critical juncture in many respects as the global economy recovers. He stresses the role of Asian countries in the G20, saying that Asian countries stand at the centre of the G20 in terms of prestige and their burden of responsibility. He also mentions the necessity of cooperation among them because Asian countries have faced macroeconomic instability repeatedly, but an effective mechanism other than the accumulation of reserves has yet to be put forward. A more active macroeconomic cooperation in Asia might be cited as a possible way to stabilize the Asian economies. He says that the Asian countries faced two problems concerning the global imbalance: one is their high external dependency, and the other is increasing criticism from outside of the region due to their reserve hoarding. The new challenge to the Asian economy is the high global expectations. However, Asian member countries lack a cooperation scheme. As a useful instrument for effective cooperation, he suggests a regional caucus where China, Japan and Korea may initiate an Asian regional caucus, making use of their institutionalized summit.

Chapter 8 deals with the G20 and Asian monetary cooperation from the perspective of South Korea. The prevention and containment of financial crises for a country like Korea necessitates a solution at national, regional and global levels. Firstly, Korea should strengthen its bilateral cooperation, particularly with the United States (US) and the European Union (EU). Given that the dollar and the euro are the two most important international currencies, closer cooperation with these countries is essential, and in this regard, Korea should take full advantage of the newly concluded Korea–US and Korea–EU free trade agreements (FTAs). Secondly, Korea should strengthen its monetary and financial cooperation with its neighbouring Asian countries. In particular, it should strengthen the trilateral cooperation between Korea, Japan and China. Thirdly, as a global-level strategy, Korea should continue to emphasize the importance of a global financial safety net as it has already done for the G20 Seoul Summit.

Tomoyoshi Nakajima (Chapter 9) stresses the role of the Asia-Pacific Economic Cooperation (APEC). Today, many of APEC's members have concluded bilateral or regional FTAs with countries and territories within and outside the region, and have realized the liberalization of trade and investment by means of exclusive frameworks. Moreover, in East Asia, which is an important part of APEC, regional economic integration is being sought by means of frameworks such as the Association of Southeast Asian Nations Plus Three (ASEAN+3) and ASEAN+6. Such moves have an impact on the United States, which faces the possibility of being excluded from them, and has induced major changes in its East Asian trade policy. Today, as a specific response thereto, the United States is proposing an FTA or Free Trade Area of the Asia Pacific (FTAAP), with its area being APEC in its entirety. The author concludes by mentioning the subsequent path for Japan's trade policy, which can be said to be at a major crossroads. Aiming towards the long-term objective of the realization of an FTAAP, should Japan prioritize ASEAN+3 (East Asia FTA – EAFTA) and ASEAN+6 (Comprehensive Economic Partnership for East Asia – CEPEA) which have been moved forward to date with East Asian nations, or should it prioritize integration into the Trans-Pacific Partnership (TPP) for which actual negotiations have started?

On the other hand, Taeyoon Kim (Chapter 10) emphasizes the role of ASEAN, which is a driving force to facilitate East Asia economic integration; ASEAN+3, which can be a main vehicle for East Asia economic integration; and the East Asia Summit (EAS) which would provide great momentum in strengthening a regional economic cooperation as well as a security cooperation because of two new members, the US and Russia, which joined in 2011.

Gerard Roland suggests a kind of emerging market bloc within the G20: 'The international order must better reflect this bottom-up order. Emerging market economies should form a joint front within the G20 (a sub-G11) to better unify their positions and take initiatives in new multipolar world' (Roland, 2010).

Yoon (Chapter 7) suggests that the formation of the Asian caucus may have various possibilities. The first option will be to form a caucus among just the Asian G20 members. They could have a meeting before the G20 Summit to discuss possible cooperation and collective action. Even if they cannot always find a consensus for collective action, the countries could at least communicate each other's position, hopefully to reach a better understanding of these different positions. The second possibility would be to form a partial regional caucus. For instance, China, Japan and Korea could form one caucus and India, Indonesia and Saudi Arabia another partial caucus. Australia could join one of these partial caucuses, should it choose. The third possibility would be an expansion of the caucus by inviting non-member countries. To raise efficiency, Asian countries may try a partial caucus at first, and then establish a full caucus. They could expand the caucus to non-member countries according to the agendas (Chapter 7).

The Asia Economic Community Forum 2010 adopted a Proposal for the Incheon Consensus. As a global consensus it emphasized that the G20 is also changing the status of the G8 into a preliminary body for closing the gaps in the policies among Western countries before the G20. It made a suggestion that Asian countries should establish a subgroup, the GA8 (the Group of Asia 8, Korea, China, Japan, India, Indonesia, Australia, Saudi Arabia, Russia) and share consensus in advance.

In Chapter 11, 'Global financial regulation: G2 or G20?' T.J. Pempel argues that from the most recent perspective, the G20 appears to be doing extremely well in its coordination efforts. And because the body's collective economic muscle is so great, its actions are likely to have a considerable impact on global finance. At the same time, over the longer haul it remains to be seen whether the G20 can deal with two serious problems. Firstly, will it be able to reach and implement coordinated agreements once the immediate sense of crisis has passed? Secondly, will the now most powerful members, most particularly the US but also China, be prepared to surrender elements of their national autonomy to such a global body? Such questions are of course unanswerable at present. Pempel concludes that the outcome at Seoul suggests that the G20 may well have a significant future as the key coordinating body for global finance.

Chapter 12 deals with a Chinese perspective toward East Asian community building. Wei Pan addresses three related issues: (1) showing obstacles to the progress of our community building; (2) explaining the obstacles through presenting the new logic of international relations (IR) in the 21st century; (3) following the new logic, suggesting solutions to overcome the obstacles. He emphasizes that the old IR logic is becoming obsolete, and military means are no longer as effective as they once were. The radical differences in socio-political settings may not prevent community building, as is shown in the ASEAN case. Despite major disputes, the economic cooperation between China and Japan, China and the US, and China and the EU has been rapidly expanding. In the 19th and 20th centuries, people's welfare used to depend on military solutions and racial or ideological bias. In the 21st century those are no longer viable solutions. Pan concludes by emphasizing the importance of trust building: 'Because of China's size and rapid growth, material conflicts are less of a problem for East Asian community building. The problem mainly lies in distrust among one another, doubt and suspicion about China's military intentions, and prevailing bias against China's socio-political setting. Therefore, the problem is less economic than socio-cultural' (p. 174).

From another Chinese perspective, Liu Yongtao (Chapter 13) argues that one possible way to predict the direction of the relationship between China and the US in security politics is to observe the relationship by putting the two states into a given systemic and analytic level and examining their physical and ideational interactions. Taking a mixed material–normative approach, he imagines five possible scenarios that may emerge in the 21st century international system of East Asia in which Sino–US relations are unfolding. He concludes that the possible scenario of an international system in East Asia is very likely to be one similar to a hegemonic arrangement by a predominant power, as one sees it now. However, if the US and China can expand their shared values, ideas and knowledge in other aspects (say, dealing with common global problems, and reaching consensus on global strategic goals of security), then it will be conducive to reducing the disputes and conflicts derived from their political and social differences, making their competitive relationship move to a friendly relationship.

Chapter 14 compares Australia and Korea from the perspective of the middle powers and the building of regional order. It analyses how two alliance partners of the United States, Australia and the Republic of Korea, are adjusting to the transition from the Cold War order in the Asia-Pacific to a new, as yet undefined regional order. As states occupying positions of privilege in the US-led Cold War order, these two middle powers have engaged with the ASEAN grouping, the main driver of the coming order, while maintaining traditional alliance commitments to the United States. That chapter focuses on conscious efforts at institution-building, and also other policies which can influence regional order. In selecting an Asian and a non-Asian state, it also considers how identity shapes states' attitudes to the concepts of region and order.

Richard Higgott (Chapter 15) talks about the utility and limits of the 'European model' for regional institutionalization in East Asia. The role of institutional capacity – especially institutions as transaction cost reducers and vehicles for the enhancement of norm compliance – casts increasingly long policy shadows over current regional activities in East Asia. It is here that the current discourse on regionalism (and multi-level governance, for all its faults and detractors) offers the bones of an alternative model. The European experience, or that of the multilateral international organizations, is not simply an 'off the shelf' export model. Some key elements, especially those of a sovereignty pooling nature, will be resisted. But other elements, especially best institutional procedural practices, will be adjusted and/or localized in a specifically East Asian fashion. The degree to which East Asia can develop institutional capacity in the absence of some sovereignty pooling is the key research and policy question for the future. Meso-level, regulatory regionalism can enhance cooperation only so far. East Asia will not mirror what we understand by the term 'institutionalism' in Europe in the second half of the 20th century, but neither will it be trivial. For both the scholar and the practitioner of regionalism and institutionalism, these are indeed interesting times in East Asia.

THE ASIAN MODEL OF REGIONAL INTEGRATION

Jehoon Park (2008, pp. 160–63) introduced 'a comprehensive model for Northeast Asian regional integration'. Here I want to expand and revise it beyond Northeast Asia to Asia in general. This means that the number of member countries and their diversity will increase to a great extent. Three kinds of 'Asian model' for regional integration could be suggested. They are the 'Weberian model', the 'multi-core model' and the 'community model' (Park, 2011b).

Firstly, as the Northeast Asian model is based on the Weberian model, which is a kind of top-down model or state-led integration model, we may argue that the Asian model could be based on the Weberian model. The regional integration index study confirms that Northeast Asia is retarded compared to ASEAN, ASEAN+3 and ASEAN+6 in terms of degree of regional integration (Kim et al., 2011). Also, South Asia has

SAARC (South Asian Association for Regional Cooperation), Central Asia has the SCO (Shanghai Cooperation Organization) and ECO (Economic Cooperation Organization) and Middle East oil-producing countries have the GCC (Gulf Cooperation Council) as their own regional cooperation bodies. Therefore it seems that other subregions of Asia including Southeast Asia are in advance of Northeast Asia, at least in terms of formality of integration. Nonetheless, the roles of state and political leadership are still strongly required in order to unite Asia in general into a community or a regional integration body. In this respect we may argue that the Weberian model emphasizing the top-down integration model by state could be a base for the Asia model, rather than the Marxian model which explains long-term and spontaneous bottom-up integration by market or private sector. Even though one can counter that the Marxian model is still applicable to Asia by pointing out the fact that spontaneous and long-term exchange or functional integration should be mature before full-scale integration starts, we want to suppose that the Asian model should be based on the Weberian model considering the relative importance of the role of the state sector in Asia.

In order to formulate the Asian model, we should consider the fact that there exist big gaps in the development level among Asian countries. In East Asia, notably in ASEAN, the level of functional integration is relatively high compared to other subregions in Asia. In this case the role of the state is important in establishing the framework for institutional integration. Central Asia and West Asia are the regions where the level of economic development is low, and the aspects of development or cooperation are needed more than integration. Here the role of the state is important in enhancing the level of functional integration. Therefore there could be two types of Weberian model in Asian regional integration. One is the 'market integration' type. This is the type where the economy is the main axis for integration, and foreign trade or finance play important roles. This type is related to the Weberian model in terms of the fact that the role of the state in upgrading functional integration to institutional integration is emphasized. This could also be called the 'advanced' type, focusing on the stage of institutional integration among relatively developed countries. The other is the 'development cooperation' type, where security cooperation is the main axis for integration, and development cooperation and industrial cooperation play important roles. This type is related to the Weberian model in terms of the fact that the role of the state for enhancing the relatively low level of functional integration is emphasized. This could also be called the 'backward' type focusing on the stage of functional integration among developing countries. Summarizing the above arguments, we could say that the Weberian model focuses on the state initiatives and the developmental gaps in Asia. Evaluating the current situation of Asian regional integration, it seems that the market integration type dominating in the ASEAN+ system is emerging as the main type for the Asian model.

The second model is the 'multi-core model', focusing on the characteristic of Asia's vast size. While the Weberian model is a 'present model' explaining the current states of Asia's regional integration, the multi-core model is a 'process model' explaining the process of regional integration in Asia. The model says that there should be several cores leading regional integration, considering the fact that Asia is a vast region and there are many subregions in Asia: Northeast Asia, Southeast Asia, Central Asia, South Asia and the Middle East. Currently, the fastest-advancing core in terms of regional integration is ASEAN. In addition to that, China–Japan–Korea (CJK), South Asia (India and Pakistan) and the Middle East are potential candidates for integration cores. This model leads to the strategy of differentiation according to subregion and phase.

The third model is the 'community model'. The model considers the feature of Asia's diversity, that is, the fact that Asia is a very diverse region in terms of politics, economy, culture, and so on. It is a 'result model', stipulating the goals or the vision of Asian regional integration. According to the model, firstly, regional integration should start from a low level of loose integration without institutional mechanisms such as sovereignty delegation[1] and be a democratic and equal community respecting small countries' voices. Secondly, the model emphasizes the importance of socio-cultural approaches based on cultural mutual understanding and trust-building, rather than politics and economics. Thirdly, the Asian community should be a community of new concepts, that is, an open community welcoming every country that wants to attend and considers itself an Asian country. Fourthly, the community pursues a new economy model differentiated from the existing US or European market capitalist models. The 'communitarian market economy' or the 'communitarian capitalist economy' is trying to pursue harmony and balance between the individual and the community or the market and the community. This economy could be based on: the New Economic Thinking for Asia which stresses the golden mean, namely the search for a balanced, harmonious and optimal point; the desirability of sensitivity to the relationship between market and government (or) 'invisible hand' and 'Leviathan'; the links between theory and reality; and the importance of not sticking blindly to a certain ideology of a school of thought (Park, 2011a).

THE ASIAN WAY OR STRATEGIES OF INTEGRATION BY APPLICATION OF THE MODEL

As the leading country for regional integration in Asia, the candidates are China, Japan and India. Yet, none of the three has all the qualities and qualification to take the initiative. Japan is not totally free from its past, of invasions and colonization. China is a source of intimidation for its neighbours, who fear the giant may have an eye on hegemony. India lacks firm leadership. The power struggle between China and Japan, and China and India, also discourages any of the three from standing at the front line of regional integration. This is where the middle-power countries such as ASEAN, Korea or other Asian countries come into play. At present, ASEAN is the central axis in the regional collaboration, such as ASEAN+3. Korea should enhance its role as a mediator among Northeast Asian regional cooperation mechanisms including the China, Japan and Korea (CJK) framework. This can be facilitated by building a new regional system that designates Korea and ASEAN as two mediators, and the US, Russia and the EU as external advocates. The US should be involved as a stakeholder by expanding APEC's function on the economic side, and holding a presence in Northeast Asia via the Northeast Asia Security Cooperation System, an organization evolved from the Six-Party Talks, and in Southeast Asia via the ASEAN Regional Forum (ARF). Its participation in ASEAN+6 should be directed towards promoting regional integration.

Asia is divided into five main subregions of Northeast Asia, Southeast Asia, Central Asia, South Asia and the Middle East. Since regional integration of all countries covering such a vast area is neither realistic nor desirable, ASEAN+3 or other new frameworks should be tapped into in seeking phased-in integration. Given the strong presence of Korea, China and Japan in Asia, progress in Northeast Asian integration is the condition for making integration across Asia a reality. In that sense, the decision by Korea, China and Japan regularly to hold summit talks separately from ASEAN+, and the opening of a permanent trilateral cooperation secretariat, are significant. A driving mechanism is needed for Asian or East Asian regional integration with two subsystems, where one is the Northeast Asian system with Korea as the mediator, and the other is the ASEAN+ system with ASEAN as the mediator. The ASEAN+ system could be linked to the so-called 'Southern Track' where regional integration would be expanded into Australia, New Zealand, India (ASEAN+6) and South Asian countries or the US through the Pacific and Indian oceans based on the 'market integration model'. In parallel with this, we may suppose the so-called 'Northern Track' where the Northeast

Asian system centred on China–Japan–Korea (CJK) could be linked to North Asian countries like Mongolia, Central Asia and Russia through the Eurasian road based on the 'development cooperation model'. Even though the Northern Track is yet less activated than the Southern Track, we should watch the former, considering the member countries' willingness to participate and the potential of energy and natural resources. We should utilize the already established subregional systems in South Asia, Central Asia and the Middle East such as SAARC, the SCO, ECO and the GCC. Based on the 'multi-core model', this could lead to the strategy where the multi-cores are established first, and then they are linked together later. Another strategy is that integration of advanced subregions like ASEAN or CJK establishes the core first and then expands the integration into other subregions.[2] Currently it seems that the latter, which is close to the European way, is emerging as dominant (Park, 2011b).

TOWARD THE CONSTRUCTION OF THE 'WORLD ECONOMY GOVERNMENT'

The existing theories of regional integration explain the European cases, which are cases of matured integration. On the other hand, the current degree of Asian integration is lower than that of European integration when the European Coal and Steel Community (ECSC) was launched in 1952. Therefore, the existing theories can only explain why Asia has not been integrated, but cannot explain how Asia should be integrated. The Asian model of regional integration should be the model which explains how the integration can occur in the future, and which form of integration is preferable. As the European fiscal crisis has deepened since the global financial crisis, scepticism about the European model is increasing. It is true that the European model has been working as a benchmarking model for Asia, even though Asia cannot directly copy Europe. Now the crisis of the European model is pushing Asia into establishing its own new and creative model, learning lessons from the European integration. At the same time the decline of global capitalist market economies centred on the US and the EU makes Asia more interested in the issue of what form of Asian integration the Asian community may end up with. This is not simply an issue of regional integration. This could be an issue of civilization implying that we should search for even the alternative to the current civilization.

The key to resolving the current global economic crisis lies in how fast to construct a global governance system. A more urgent task is the construction of a regulation and monitoring system for global financial transactions. One of the causes of the current crisis can be found in the attempts to simply apply the liberalization of trade to financial transactions. There are many roles Asian countries could play in the construction of a global governance system. They may suggest a vision for the establishment of a 'World Economy Government' which will lead globally to the comprehensive management of overall economic policy. This could be a kind of economic United Nations (UN). This initiative, however, could be realized only if the efforts for the construction of an Asian Union are accompanied. The G20 could play a role of an intermediate institution toward designing the global economic governance system.

NOTES

1. Kanishka Jayasuriya points out that much of the debate about regional integration in Asia has focused on institutional frameworks that promote trade liberalization and the creation of an Asian community. She argues that this approach misses altogether the emergence of a new force for regionalism: the evolution of a complex web of private and public regulatory regimes that is slowly tying the region together. According to her, regulatory regionalism, in this context, is the development of regional regulatory frameworks within the political and policymaking institutions of 'national governments'. It creates new mechanisms of regulatory governance, enrols new public and private actors in regulatory governance, and frames social and economic issues in regional terms (Jayasuriya, 2009).
2. Currently ASEAN is a stronger candidate for the single core for Asian regional integration than CJK. But in order to accelerate integration in Asia, it is necessary to have at least dual cores, of ASEAN and CJK.

REFERENCES

In English

Asia Economic Community Forum (2010), 'A Proposal for the Incheon Consensus'.

Jayasuriya, Kanishka (2009), 'In the Asia-Pacific: Drivers, Instruments and Actors', *Australian Journal of International Affairs*, **63**(3), 335–47.

Kim, Won-Ho, Heungchong Kim and Jehoon Park (2011), 'A Comparative Analysis on Regional Integration Communities and Implications for East Asia: A Regional Integration Index Approach', in Jehoon Park, T.J. Pempel and Heungchong Kim (eds), *Regionalism, Economic Integration and Security in Asia: A Political Economy Approach*, Cheltenham, UK and Northampton, MA, USA: Edward Elgar, pp. 26–56.

Park, Jehoon (2008), 'Conclusion: Searching for Models of Regional Integration in Northeast Asia', Jehoon Park, T.J. Pempel and Gerard Roland (eds), *Political Economy of Northeast Asian Regionalism: Political Conflict and Economic Integration*, Cheltenham, UK and Northampton, MA, USA: Edward Elgar, pp. 150–67.

Park, Jehoon (2011a), 'Conclusion: Expanding the Perspective Beyond Political Economy', in Jehoon Park, T.J. Pempel and Heungchong Kim (eds), *Regionalism, Economic Integration and Security in Asia: A Political Economy Approach*, Cheltenham, UK and Northampton, MA, USA: Edward Elgar, pp. 150–69.

Roland, Gerard (2010), 'The Washington Consensus: An Institutionalist Perspective', paper presented for the Asia Economic Community Forum 2010, Incheon, Korea, 7–9 November.

In Korean

Park, Jehoon (2011b), 'Northeast Asian Regionalism: Model's Expansion and Application', *Comparative Economic Review*, **18**(1), 51–91.

Index